Rated M for Mature

Rated M for Mature

Sex and Sexuality in Video Games

**EDITED BY
MATTHEW WYSOCKI
AND
EVAN W. LAUTERIA**

Bloomsbury Academic
An imprint of Bloomsbury Publishing Plc

B L O O M S B U R Y
NEW YORK · LONDON · OXFORD · NEW DELHI · SYDNEY

Bloomsbury Academic

An imprint of Bloomsbury Publishing Inc

1385 Broadway	50 Bedford Square
New York	London
NY 10018	WC1B 3DP
USA	UK

www.bloomsbury.com

BLOOMSBURY and the Diana logo are trademarks of Bloomsbury Publishing Plc

First published 2015

© Matthew Wysocki, Evan W. Lauteria, and Contributors, 2015

Library of Congress Cataloging-in-Publication Data
Rated M for mature : sex and sexuality in video games /
edited by Matthew Wysocki and Evan W. Lauteria.
pages cm
Includes bibliographical references and index.
ISBN 978-1-62892-576-0 (hardback : alk. paper) – ISBN 978-1-62892-577-7
(pbk. : alk. paper) 1. Video games–Social aspects. 2. Sex. I. Wysocki, Matthew.
GV1469.34.S52R37 2015
794.8–dc23
2015013074

ISBN: HB: 978-1-6289-2576-0
PB: 978-1-6289-2577-7
ePub: 978-1-6289-2575-3
ePDF: 978-1-6289-2574-6

Typeset by Deanta Global Publishing Services, Chennai, India
Printed and bound in the United States of America

Contents

Acknowledgments

Matthew Wysocki and Evan Lauteria would like to recognize several individuals. Courtney Peters for her editorial assistant work on copyediting our references was invaluable. Katie Gallof and the staff at Bloomsbury provided tremendous support. Diana Pozo improved upon the cover art. And all our authors crafted such stimulating work without which there could be no collection.

An earlier version of Tanya Krzywinska's chapter "The Strange Case of the Misappearance of Sex in Videogames" appeared in *Computer Games and New Media Cultures: A Handbook of Digital Games Studies* (2012), edited by Johannes Fromme and Alexander Unger. It has been updated and reprinted here with permission.

Notes on the Contributors

Rob Gallagher is a postdoctoral researcher at King's College London, UK, where he is investigating the impact of new media on practices of self-representation and conceptions of identity. Rob's research interests include video gaming, digital aesthetics and gendered embodiment, and his work has appeared in journals such as *Games and Culture*, *Media-N*, and *G|A|M|E*.

Shaila García-Catalán (Castellón, 1983) is a researcher in communication at the Universitat Jaume I of Castellón, Spain. Her PhD dissertation deals with science fiction, neuroscience, and hypertexts. She teaches visual culture and mass media in a game design degree and is interested in complex contemporary narratives.

Summer Glassie is a doctoral candidate in the Department of English at Old Dominion University, USA, with a track in technology and media. She received her MA at Florida Gulf Coast University, USA, in 2012. Her research focuses on video games as literature and as educational tools for students at all levels.

Casey Hart teaches broadcasting and writing for multimedia at Stephen F. Austin State University in Nacogdoches, Texas, USA. He received his PhD from the University of Southern Mississippi, USA, in mass media and society. His major research interest has been in representation of race and gender roles within television, film, and advertising.

Brent Kice is an assistant professor of communication at the University of Houston-Clear Lake, USA. His work has appeared in *POROI: An Interdisciplinary Journal of Rhetorical Analysis and Invention*, the *Texas Speech Communication Journal Online*, the *Communication and Theatre Association of Minnesota Journal*, the *Memphis Theological Seminary Journal*, and the edited collection *CTRL-ALT-PLAY: Essays on Control in Video Gaming*. He enjoys teaching an interdisciplinary course on communicating with video games.

Bridget Kies is a PhD student in media, cinema, and digital studies at the University of Wisconsin-Milwaukee, USA. Her research examines gender and sexuality in popular media. She has previously published in the *Journal of Transformative Works and Cultures* and several edited collections on various television series.

Tanya Krzywinska is a professor with the Academy of Innovation and Research at Falmouth University, Cornwall, UK, where she leads a research and PhD program in digital games. She is editor of the journal *Games and Culture* and the author of many books and articles on games design, cinema, and transmedial culture, including *Sex and the Cinema* (2006). She is currently writing a book that investigates uses of the Gothic in digital games and has recently published work on games and weird fiction.

Evan W. Lauteria is a PhD student in sociology at the University of California, Davis, USA. His research interests include the production of culture, Japanese video game translation, and queer game studies. Evan has published in the UK Literary Magazine *Berfrois* on the topic of queer game mechanics in *Reconstruction* on the resistant politics of queer game mods.

Dan Mills has a PhD in English from Georgia State University, USA, where he wrote his dissertation on early modern utopian literature. He has published articles in the journals *Pedagogy*, *Cahiers Elisabethans*, and *In-Between: Essays and Studies in Literary Criticism* and has forthcoming articles in edited collections on critical theory and early modern literature and Western encounters with the East.

Víctor Navarro-Remesal is a researcher in video game design theory. His PhD dissertation presents the idea of "directed freedom" as the basis of the relationship between player and discourse. He teaches videogames at Centro de Enseñanaza Superior Alberta Giménez (CESAG), in Palma de Mallorca, Spain, and his interests are freedom, ludonarrative, player representation and ethics design.

Jérémie Pelletier-Gagnon is a PhD student at the University of Alberta, Canada, in the departments of Digital Humanities and Comparative Literature and is a former recipient of the 2012 Research Student Monbukagakusho Fellowship awarded by the Japanese Ministry of Education, Culture, Sports, Sciences, and Technologies. His main research topics include the Japanese arcade gaming aesthetic and culture as well as the translational circulation of video games. He received his master's degree in East Asian studies at McGill University in 2011. He gave papers in international conferences in Japan such as the International Conference on Japan Game Studies at Ritsumeikan

University in Kyoto and the East Asian Studies Conference Japan at J. F. Oberlin University in Tokyo.

Martin Picard is a postdoctoral scholar and lecturer at the University of Montreal, Canada. He recently completed a Japan Foundation Research Fellowship on Japanese video game culture at Wako University in Tokyo. Previously, he was a postdoctoral fellow at McGill University and received his PhD in literature and film studies from the University of Montreal. His teaching and research interests cover Japanese popular culture, video game culture and history, film, and digital media. His publications consist of articles and chapters in anthologies such as *The Routledge Companion to Video Game Studies* (2014), *Encyclopaedia of Video Games: The Culture, Technology, and Art of Gaming* (2012), *Horror Video Games: Essays on the Fusion of Fear and Play* (2009), *The Video Game Theory Reader 2* (2009), and *The Video Game Explosion: A History From PONG to PlayStation and Beyond* (2008).

Diana Pozo is a PhD candidate in film and media studies at the University of California at Santa Barbara, USA. Her research on "haptic media" combines approaches from feminist film theory, video game studies, queer theory, new media, and porn studies to argue for the centrality of touch and affect in media production and reception. Pozo's work appears in journals and collections including *New Review of Film and Television Studies*, *Media Fields Journal*, *Mediascape*, and *The Routledge Encyclopedia of Film Theory*.

Zach Saltz is a PhD student in the Department of Film and Media Studies at the University of Kansas, USA. He has published articles for *Reconstruction* and the Scarecrow Press and is a frequent presenter at the Society for Cinema and Media Studies Conference and the Popular Culture Association/American Culture Association Conference. His areas of interest are media and the law, censorship, and political economy of film and TV.

Aaron Trammell is a doctoral candidate at the Rutgers University School of Communication and Information, USA. He is also a blogger, board game designer, and musician. Aaron is coeditor-in-chief of the journal *Analog Game Studies*, serves on the editorial board of *Games and Culture*, and is the multimedia editor of the sound studies journal, *Sounding Out!* His dissertation investigates the historical relationship between game theory and role-playing, from their inception in Cold War think tanks, like The RAND Corporation, to their appropriation by fan subcultures in the game *Dungeons & Dragons*. Aaron has edited a special issue of *Games and Culture* (with Anne Gilbert) entitled *Extending Play to Critical Media Studies*, which is based on the proceedings of the Extending Play conference he chaired in 2013.

Emma Leigh Waldron is a doctoral student in the Performance Studies Graduate Group at the University of California, Davis, USA, and received her MA in performance research from the University of Bristol, UK. Emma is coeditor-in-chief of the journal *Analog Game Studies*. Her work on larp (live-action role-playing games) is informed by her interest in performance practice-as-research, embodied knowledge and phenomenology, feminist studies, and critical sexuality studies.

Nicholas Ware is a PhD candidate in texts and technology at the University of Central Florida, USA. He has written and presented on several topics, including the adopting of video game logic into film, immersive design techniques, an online ethnography of fighting game players, and popular depictions of Japanese yokai. His main areas of interest are games studies and gaming culture with additional interest in Japanese folk culture and dystopian/postapocalyptic narratives. His current efforts are devoted to creating an original, surrealist model for games research and design. He performs improv comedy in his spare time.

Matthew Wysocki is an associate professor of media studies at Flagler College, USA. He is the cochair for the Game Studies area of the National Popular Culture Association and the American Culture Association. His research interests focus on "deviance" and technology, including computer hacker subculture, professional wrestling, and pornography. His research in the area of video games studies looks at issues of control and agency in games and the roles that players create as producers of their own vehicles of consumption. He is the editor of *CTRL-ALT-PLAY: Essays on Control in Video Gaming*, and his work has appeared in *CTRL-ALT-PLAY*, *NMEDIAC: The Journal of New Media and Culture*, and *The Play Versus Story Divide in Game Studies: Critical Essays* (forthcoming).

Jordan Youngblood is an associate professor of English and new media studies at Eastern Connecticut State University, USA. His work focuses on the intersections between queer theory and video game theory, particularly relating to aspects of embodied performance and action. His work has appeared in *ADA: A Journal of Gender, New Media, and Technology*, along with multiple conference presentations; an additional essay is forthcoming in a collection on queerness in gaming.

Introduction

Evan W. Lauteria (University of California, Davis, USA) and Matthew Wysocki (Flagler College, USA)

Sex and play are intricately tied together. When looking to engage in safer sex practices exclusively, one might state that he or she "plays safe only." Recreational drug use during sexual intercourse is colloquially known as PnP or "party and play." Folks solely interested in romantic relationships with long-term goals might be against "playing games." Baseball metaphors are used to describe varying levels of sexual intimacy such as "bases," and among queer folks "pitching," "catching," "switch-hitting," and "playing for the other team" denote sexual positions and romantic partner choice. Masturbation and autoerotic arousal are most often referred to as "playing with oneself," and when couples are interested in exploring options of including a third partner, they offer to "play together only."

But what about sex and video games more explicitly? According to Brenda Brathwaite (2007), the connection between sex and video games has "always been here, right from the beginning of the computer game industry, and even earlier if one counts the emergent sexual behavior of players in MUDs or the alleged phallic controls on the arcade games of the 1970s" (2007, 40). For Mia Consalvo, "sex and sexuality have been integral (if subtextual) parts of many games" (2003, 171). Even the media logics of video games can be linked to sex. By Eric Zimmerman's (2012) account, "mainstream AAA videogames operate on principles akin to porn: highly repetitive activities premised on visceral pleasure and spectacle." In their design, representative features, and play affordances, contemporary video games are influenced by and directly linked to sex, sexuality, pornography, romance, and desire.

These connections—between sex, sexuality, and video games—have become more visible in recent decades. The "Hot Coffee" mod (modification) controversy in 2005 for *Grand Theft Auto: San Andreas* brought public attention to the limits of permissible sexual content in commercial games, despite the inclusion of and access to murder, robbery, and sex work in the unmodded version of the game. Games like *God of War* and *Bayonetta* position sex and sexuality as central representative and play features of their playful power fantasies, and *Heavy Rain* allows players to play through, step-by-step, a romantic love scene between two of the game's protagonists. As Consalvo suggested in 2003, however, the expression of sexuality in games "generally reifies conservative beliefs about heterosexuality and 'proper' romance" (171). This, too, has changed in recent years, with games like *The Sims*, *Fable*, *Mass Effect*, *Shin Megami Tensei: Persona 4*, *Dragon Age: Origins*, *Fallout: New Vegas*, and *The Elder Scrolls V: Skyrim* pushing back against the heteronormative standard with the inclusion of lesbian, gay, bisexual, transgender, and queer (LGBTQ) representation and same-sex romance and gender-variant play mechanics. Alongside these developments in mainstream, industry-led game design, numerous independent game designers have grappled with ideas of sex, queer identity, BDSM, coming out, and sexual consent through games as diverse as *Queer Power*, *Mighty Jill Off*, *A Closed World*, and *Hurt Me Plenty*. Sex and sexuality are increasingly more visible, more complex, and more nuanced in video games.

These changes in the landscape of video games, coupled with a growing scholarly interest in evaluating and analyzing such changes, are precisely why we proposed such a collection. We are witnessing both the video game industry and game studies as a discipline "maturing" in relation to the topics of sex and sexuality. Indeed, many of the aforementioned games received an "M for Mature" rating from the Electronic Software Rating Board (ESRB) upon release in the United States, and scholars have invested great energy in theorizing and researching sex and sexuality in these games (see Alexander 2007; Brathwaite 2007; Consalvo 2003; Ouellette 2013; Pulos 2013; Shaw 2009). And this change in the evaluation of games, allowing games and their study to "mature," is precisely why our book is titled as such. The ESRB rating system, first established in 1994, marked a major shift for the video game industry. For the first time, it was made publicly clear that not all games were for children, that some games dealt with more "adult" themes and imagery, and that such content could and perhaps even should be sold to consuming audiences. That is, "Rated M for Mature" conjures up three distinct images: (1) a specific moment in the history of video games that informs our understanding of gaming's past, present, and future; (2) a rethinking of the player body as one with a sexuality, desiring of sexual content and play; and (3) an openness to admitting that video games may represent and simulate complex, "mature" ideas like sex and sexuality. The organization of this book into three sections, addressing history, content and play, and design possibilities, respectively, reflects these images. Despite approaching the topic from varied perspectives and disciplinary training, each author in this collection grapples with sex and sexuality with the scholarly "maturity" we are witnessing in the larger field of game production and game studies. It is our hope that this collection contributes to game studies' continued maturation with innovative, nuanced approaches to the topic of sex and sexuality.

The (r)evolution of video games and sex

Part 1 of this book addresses the complex, multilayered history of video games and the politics of sex, sexuality, and sexually explicit content. Each chapter concentrates on different dimensions of the history of game production and design, with substantive foci ranging from discourses of console and game production to the historical emergence of regulatory market structures and institutions.

In Chapter 1, Rob Gallagher provides a look at the generations of PlayStation home consoles and of the *Metal Gear Solid* and *Siren* series. Adopting feminist and queer theory's interest in the normativity of linear time, fraught with concerns of reproductive futurity and the pressures of patrilineal descent, Gallagher illustrates how heteronormative discourses infiltrate and frame design and marketing logic. He suggests that the PlayStation "family" of home consoles and these two series "manifest an unusual preoccupation with reproduction, mutation, inheritance, and infection." In this analysis, Gallagher encourages us as scholars of sex and sexuality in video games to rethink our approach to such topics, arguing that the way in which design and release patterns are narrativized illustrates the deep connections between heteronormativity and reproductive imperative and the video game industry.

Martin Picard and Jérémie Pelletier-Gagnon, in Chapter 2, explore the history and political and social conditions under which *eroge*, or erotic games, emerged as a video game genre in Japan. Opening with a discussion of the negative reactions of Westerners to the Japanese game *Rapelay*, the authors offer insights into a nuanced, self-regulating world of erotic game production in Japan otherwise unfamiliar to Western consumers. In their analysis, Picard and Pelletier-Gagnon illustrate the complex ecological connections between social discomfort with teen culture and truant behavior, emergent and sometimes indirect policing of pornographic content, and cultural trauma and memory that influenced the contemporary landscape of *eroge* design and dissemination.

For Chapter 3, Evan Lauteria continues this section's interest in Japanese video game production history by examining the sociocultural conditions that influenced queer representation in Super Nintendo games. Taking *Final*

Fight and *Chrono Trigger* as cases, Lauteria walks through the cultural politics of Japanese queer and trans* identities and the obstacles of video game translation and localization to suggest that queer representations in games are directly tied to their circumstances of production. He contemplates linguistic incommensurability, Nintendo censorship policy, and business organizational structure as influential factors in determining what and how Japanese queer content is made available to American consumers.

Chapter 4 moves across the Pacific, as Zach Saltz reviews the history of contemporary censorship policy and First Amendment protections for video games in the United States. Comparing the *Brown v. EMA* video game content case in 2011 to the 1952 *Burstyn v. Wilson* case for sexual content in film, Saltz argues that turning to the history of censorship and sexual content in film will inform us of how sexual content in video games will evolve and grow in the twenty-first century. He walks through the legal history of sexual content in film as a gateway to understanding legal framing of video games, and through such framing is able to illuminate the complicated legal and cultural logics of censorship, obscenity, free speech, and content ratings running throughout the *Brown v. EMA* Supreme Court case, particularly the rhetoric surrounding the effectiveness and limits of the ESRB as a regulatory institution.

Next, Dan Mills visits the collapse of the Atari-led American video game market in the early 1980s, providing an overview of sexually explicit, unlicensed video games for the Atari 2600, such as *Custer's Revenge*, for Chapter 5. Applying Baudrillard and Deleuze to repetitive sexual play in video games, Mills highlights how desensitization to sex and violence in postmodernity, coupled with the repetitive actions mandated by video game systems, dangerously break down the boundary between the real and the virtual. And by Mills' account, the connection between unlicensed Atari sex games containing explicit coercion, rape, and objectification of women and contemporary video games is quite strong. Despite increasing institutional support for content regulation and control over third-party game development since the early 1980s, sexual content in video games continues to reflect and reify the degradation of society in the postmodern era.

Video games and sexual (dis)embodiment

The chapters in Part 2 analyze sex and sexuality as video game content, both theoretically and empirically. United by interest in the sexual body—what sort of bodily activities are represented or simulated, what bodies can do during play, and what happens to bodies under certain video game design choices—these chapters illustrate the value of merging various media critiques, chiefly feminist and queer studies, with game studies.

Tanya Krzywinska opens this section with an updated version of her 2012 piece, "The Strange Case of the Misappearance of Sex in Videogames." Responding to public media attention to the supposed rampant sexual content in video games, Krzywinska reviews the sociocultural and commercial constraints that limit the degree and kind of sexual explicitness permitted within mainstream video games. She typologizes sexual video game content into representative and mechanical sex in an effort to highlight the similarities and limits of sexual expression across time and hardware. She argues, ultimately, for a rethinking of the potential of sex in video games, calling on designers to work against the dominant rhetorics that confine and constrain sexual possibility in games.

Victor Navarro-Remesal and Shaila García-Catalán, in Chapter 7, review BDSM mechanics in video games as a case study in their concept of "directed freedom," a theoretical attempt to solve the "player/game problem" by bridging the issues of gamic structures versus player agency. By examining AAA industry, independent, and kink website games, this chapter illustrates how the relationship between control and freedom is not unidirectional or always clear; players consent to control as a means of enacting their agentic freedom in diverse ways. Navarro-Remesal and García-Catalán argue that through an examination of the intersections of sex, BDSM, and game design, all of which grapple with issues of control and freedom, we can better come to understand the role of the player in video games.

In Chapter 8, Diana Pozo provides an overview of sex-based video game peripherals and designs that she dubs part of the "2000s countergaming movement." Providing close readings of the fan-made Joydick peripheral for Atari and the work of Heather Kelley, Pozo suggests that these new hacking and design practices around sex and games challenge Alexander Galloway's belief that the countergaming project is yet unrealized. Invoking Anna Anthropy's language of "the rise of the videogame zinesters," the chapter illustrates that pornographic alterations and modifications of video games and their hardware, despite some feminist discomfort regarding the potential of video games and pornographic content for liberatory purpose, offer a promising avenue for feminist and queer resistance.

Casey Hart examines how sex is employed in the design of *Mass Effect*, *Fable*, and *Grand Theft Auto* for Chapter 9. Illustrating the extent to which sex in contemporary video games is divorced of intimacy, monogamy, and social consequence, Hart argues that designers today employ sex as a "commodified game dynamic." Players are either encouraged to engage in sex and sexual activity through some reward other than the sex itself or presented with false-choice mechanics and dynamics that ultimately undermine video games' capacity to represent or simulate possibilities beyond the dominant social order. Further, Hart argues, each game studied vastly limited the degree of agency afforded to sexual partners in-game. Dangers of objectifying content abound, and Hart encourages fellow scholars and media-literate consumers to critically engage with these shortcomings in hopes of changing the terrain of sex in video games.

Continuing the examination of limits in sex and representation, Chapter 10 analyzes the Asari, a monogendered species in the *Mass Effect* universe. Summer Glassie compares the codex-based *Mass Effect* lore and the spoken experiences of character Liara T'Soni to explore the shortcomings, obstacles, and triumphs of representing nonhuman, nonheteronormative sexuality and gender in a contemporary video game. Glassie articulates the vast limits of such design practices, illustrating that the confines of English language and Western gender-sexual constructs inhibit designer and player ability to grasp Asari gender and culture. Conversely, however, Glassie also suggests that such an attempt to push forward nonnormative sexuality and gender via science fiction gameplay affords players an opportunity to engage in sexual and gender possibilities that might otherwise feel unsafe or be met with hostility. She ultimately applauds *Mass Effect* for its effort to represent nonnormative sexuality and gender in a safe yet Othered manner and views such effort as a positive, progressive step in video game content.

Systems/spaces of sexual (im)possibilities

Part 3 of this collected edition addresses design practice and player consumption activities as a look toward the future of sex and sexuality in video games. While each author approaches these issues differently, all offer compelling cases for envisioning progressive futures and encouraging continued sex-positive, feminist, and queer behaviors around video game design and play.

Chapter 11 begins this final section with a turn to analog, live-action games. Aaron Trammell and Emma Waldron explore the inclusion of sex, romance, and intimacy in Nordic larp, a more avant-garde school of live-action role-playing (larp) design, to offer suggestions for meaningful adaptation of such mechanics in video game design. They offer a powerful critique of rampant violence in video games, linking such imagery to video games' history as military simulation technologies, and respond to such violence with advocacy for care and intimacy through sex mechanics. They argue that support for intimacy in games opens the possibility of thinking of games as a vehicle for self-betterment, as tools for exploring self-care and care for others, and as spaces of dialogue and transformative potential.

Matthew Wysocki, in Chapter 12, explores the video game modding scene in the context of sex mods, the application of software- and/or hardware-altering patches or design changes to video games to afford new sex-based play experiences. Theorizing the work of modders as "playbour"—a hybrid act of simultaneous playful consumption and production—he begins his exploration of mods with a brief history of the most famous sex mod, the Hot Coffee mod for *Grand Theft Auto: San Andreas*. From there, Wysocki typologizes sex-related mods into nude skin mods and sexual encounter mods, highlighting how mods can affect games' representative or mechanical play features. The amount of "playbour" invested in these mods illustrates the desire for sexually explicit content, and mod communities continue to offer rebellious spaces for the production of such content where mainstream game companies are unwilling, or unable, to offer such content to consumers.

Bridget Kies takes a different approach to sexual content in Chapter 13, examining a game that employs content on queer sexuality "that isn't sexual." Looking at *Gay Fighter Supreme*, a fighting game featuring combatants that are all based on LGBTQ stereotypes, Kies explores how sexuality can be included in video games without the incorporation of explicit sex. She begins with a comparative exploration of queer content in *Mass Effect*, *Left Behind*, *Gone Home*, and *The Last of Us*, ultimately arguing that, despite positive trends resisting heteronormativity in the video game industry, such games conflate sexual identity with sexual behavior. In her analysis, *Gay Fighter Supreme* offers a meaningful space for rethinking the representation of sexual identity and the LGBTQ community beyond romance or sex.

In Chapter 14, Nicholas Ware takes sexism and heternormativity in game design to task by critiquing iterative play practices in connection to "Nice Guy Syndrome." He argues that, given the ability to reload saves and constantly retry dialogue trees and behaviors in video games, iterative play practices functionally reflect and support "Nice Guy Syndrome," the sexist belief that when men engage in positive, kind behaviors they will be rewarded with romance and sex. Ware makes a strong case for the unfortunate similarities between play and real life, with examples like social links in *Shin Megami Tensei: Persona 4* and romance dialogue in *Mass Effect* providing particularly compelling examples of iterative play regarding sex. Ware concludes his critique of iterative play by offering suggestions for better video games to resist the Nice Guy Syndrome tendency in contemporary game design.

Jordan Youngblood explores *Catherine*, a Japanese puzzle game and life simulator, in Chapter 15 of our collection. Drawing upon Sara Ahmed's *Queer Phenomenology* and her theorization of the "orientation" in "sexual orientation,"

Youngblood links queer theory with attention to spatiality in game studies, offering an analysis of *Catherine* that takes seriously the spatial dimensions of sexuality and queerness in video games. Reading the imperatives of the game's goals—a demand to continue climbing upward—in relation to its anxieties over infidelity and reproductive futurity, Youngblood illustrates the importance of thinking about queerness as a spatial feature of games and play. In doing so, Youngblood complicates an otherwise heterosexual narrative in *Catherine*, illustrating how space—the space of puzzles, the space of the bedroom, the space of the bathroom—in the game evokes queer sentiments in response to the false logics of compulsory heterosexuality.

The concluding chapter of the collection, Chapter 16, provides one final analytical toolkit for examining sex and sexuality in games. Brent Kice typologizes kinds of sex acts in games based on their functional purpose—to sell the game via a "money shot" or to actually simulate sex—and their connection to player experience. He frames this analysis and the development of such a toolkit through Foucault's notion of biopower, drawing on a rich scholarly history of exploring the video game as a biopolitical form. Kice suggests that games witnessed the end of death-as-power, left behind in the money-sucking arcade machines of the 1980s and 1990s, and now see power operate in its biopolitical form: sex and the power over life. Understanding sex as power in this sense, Kice argues for the importance of examining how sex in games controls players, either by continuing to construct them as consumers or by affording emotive and agentic capacity to them as active participants in the medium.

All of the chapters in this collection push at the contemporary boundaries of game studies, employing innovative close-reading techniques, comparative-historical methods, and feminist and queer critique. In many cases, pushing the envelope in so many directions results in chapters that may not ultimately be commensurable. This collection is unified not by a single theoretical perspective but rather by an investment in expanding how scholars can and should approach the topic of sex and sexuality in video games. Despite divergent theoretical perspectives and disciplinary training, each chapter offers a new way of thinking about sex and sexuality. In doing so, we hope to push game studies itself to become "Rated M for Mature."

References

Alexander, Jeffrey. 2007. "'A Real Effect on the Gameplay': Computer Gaming, Sexuality, and Literacy." In *Gaming Lives in the Twenty-First Century*, edited by Cynthia L. Selfe and Gail E. Hawisher, 167–202. New York: Palgrave MacMillan.

Brathwaite, Brenda. 2007. *Sex in Video Games*. Boston: Thompson Learning, Inc.

Consalvo, Mia. 2003. "Hot Dates and Fairy-Tale Romances: Studying Sexuality in Video Games." In *The Video Game Theory Reader*, edited by Mark J. P. Wolf and Bernard Perron, 171–94. New York: Routledge.

Ouellette, Marc. 2013. "Gay for Play: Theorizing LGBTQ Characters in Game Studies." In *The Game Culture Reader*, edited by Jason C. Thompson and Marc Oullette, 47–65. Newcastle upon Tyne: Cambridge Scholars Publishing.

Pulos, Alexis. 2013. "Confronting Heteronormativity in Online Games: A Critical Discourse Analysis of LGBTQ Sexuality in World of Warcraft." *Games and Culture* 8 (2): 77–97.

Shaw, Adrienne. 2009. "Putting the Gay in Games: Cultural Production and GLBT Content in Video Games." *Games and Culture* 4 (3): 228–53.

Zimmerman, Eric (@zimmermaneric). 2012. Twitter post. 11:41 a.m., July 2, 2012.

Games cited

Anthropy, Anna. 2008. *Mighty Jill Off*. Anna Anthropy.

Atlus. 2008. *Shin Megami Tensei: Persona 4*. Atlus.

Bethesda Game Studios. 2011. *The Elder Scrolls V: Skyrim*. Bethesda Softworks.

Big Blue Box. 2004. *Fable*. Microsoft Game Studios.

BioWare. 2007. *Mass Effect*. Microsoft Game Studios.

BioWare. 2009. *Dragon Age: Origins*. Electronic Arts.

Maxis. 2000. *The Sims*. Electronic Arts.

Molleindustria. 2004. *Queer Power*. Molleindustria.

Obsidian Entertainment. 2010. *Fallout: New Vegas*. Bethesda Softworks.

Platinum Games. 2010. *Bayonetta*. Sega.

Quantic Dream. 2010. *Heavy Rain*. Sony Computer Entertainment.

Rockstar North. 2004. *Grand Theft Auto: San Andreas*. Rockstar Games.

SCE Santa Monica Studio. 2005. *God of War*. Sony Computer Entertainment.

Singapore-MIT Gambit Game Lab. 2011. *A Closed World*. Singapore-MIT Gambit Game Lab.

Yang, Robert. 2014. *Hurt Me Plenty*. Robert Yang.

PART ONE

The (r)evolution of video games and sex

1

Intergenerational tensions: Of sex and the hardware cycle

Rob Gallagher
(King's College London, UK)

The year 2013 saw the release of "next generation" consoles from Microsoft and Sony and, with them, the beginning of a new phase in the hardware cycle. Console gaming has long been defined by this annular rhythm, whereby a system plays out a "lifespan" of several years before being superseded. The relationship between outgoing and incoming hardware is often cast in terms of heredity, with names meant to connote evolutionary progress or quasiregal lineage: PlayStation to PS2 to PS3 to PS4. While these might appear to be empty metaphors, I want to suggest that they are indicative of the extent to which ideas about sex—and, more specifically, *hetero*sexuality—inform the discourse, history, and culture of gaming. As I will argue, both the stories games tell and the stories told about games reflect the cultural privilege afforded to what queer critics have called "repro-time" or "reproductive futurism," whereby the periodicity of heterosexual procreation becomes a template for understanding progress and success (Halberstam 2005, 5; Edelman 2004, 3). Thus games continue to cast players as heroes who overcome increasingly complex obstacles to rescue the princess/wife/child and secure the future, even as publicists and journalists mantrically repeat heady promises about "next gen" gaming technologies guaranteed to be fitter, faster, brighter, and better than their forebears.

Such promises are grounded in an opportunistic misreading of evolutionary theory. As Gillian Beer observes, Darwin's work has often been invoked "to yield the assurance of irreversible upward growth" over the last century and a half (2000, 106), and such is the case in gaming discourse, wherein evolutionary metaphors prop up the convention of "old games and gaming technologies [being] replaced and superseded by their updated and upgraded successors"—a convention which, while it has come to appear "natural," in fact exists chiefly to serve the commercial interests of publishers and platform holders (Newman 2012, 8). This essay seeks to challenge such modes of narrating history and framing play by looking at how particular games and game consoles disrupt or subvert the mythology of evolutionary progress and the heteronormative logic of repro-time.

In this respect, the essay adopts a slightly different approach to that of most queer and feminist critiques of gaming, which have tended to focus either on the images and messages that games contain or else on the marginalization of female and/or queer players and designers. With what follows, I hope to supplement such work by addressing gaming's role in fostering what Freeman calls "chrononormativity": the propagation of "tempos and routines, which . . . organize the value and meaning of time" along heteronormative lines (2010, 2–3). To be sure, in interrogating gaming's treatment of sex and sexuality we need to address how designers, publishers, legislators, and rating boards handle the representation of gendered bodies, sexual activities, and lesbian, gay, bisexual, transgender, intersex, and questioning (LGBTIQ) identities. As I hope to show, however, we also need to consider other, subtler manifestations of sexist and heteronormative bias. A generation of gamers has now reached the age of consent without ever knowing a time before PlayStation; it behooves us, as such, to address the ways in which the hardware cycle informs and is informed by the rhythms of biography, biology, and culture. I pursue this goal via a consideration of the PlayStation brand, looking at Sony's framing of the relationship between different generations of PlayStation hardware and at the *Metal Gear Solid* and *Siren* (or, as it is known in Europe, *Forbidden Siren*) series, two Japanese game franchises that manifest an unusual preoccupation with reproduction, mutation, inheritance, and infection—aspects of human sexuality that games often ignore. These thematic concerns can and should, I argue, be read in relation to the way that these series have functioned both as flagships for their genres and as vehicles for articulating the concept of a "PlayStation family" across multiple "generations" of hardware (Rubenstein 2010).

PlayStation's pygmalion

In heteronormative discourse, the patriarch—paternal male as owner, breadwinner, and protector—is imagined as the cornerstone of the family structure. In PlayStation's case, that role is played by Ken Kutaragi. Having led the development of the first three generations of Sony console hardware, the engineer is frequently described as the "father of the PlayStation" (Asakura 2000, xi)—an epithet that speaks to the continuing currency, within video game culture, of the kind of "traditional 'great men and their works' theories of history" that queer and feminist historians have long challenged (Huffer 2013, 90). Reiji Asakura's account of the PS1's development—the tellingly titled *Revolutionaries at Sony*—is typical in placing great stress on Kutaragi's "vision" (182). Reporting that the engineer drew up the blueprint for the console in the mid-1980s, confident that the "evolution" of transistor technology would have rendered his design feasible within a decade, Asakura demonstrates just how neatly the idea of technology steadily evolving in a single direction dovetails with a Pygmalionesque rhetoric of masculine creative power. Kutaragi himself, meanwhile, frames the project in suggestively sexual terms, speaking of "biorhythm[s] . . . building toward a critical juncture" (158–60). In both cases, the PS1's history becomes a gamelike quest narrative in which Kutaragi (whom Asakura unashamedly declares "the hero" of his book (xi)) conquers the resistance of a retrogressive old guard to produce a seminal work that singlehandedly pushes gaming forward—proof that if games themselves are rife with myths of lone male struggle, so too are discursive framings of the industry and its history.

This is not to deny Kutaragi's influence on the PlayStation's design. It is, however, to insist that, in spinning a tale about the marriage of masculine creative potency and cutting-edge technology, *Revolutionaries* minimizes the importance of the myriad coincidences, contingencies, and sociocultural factors that also shaped the project. The fact that the PlayStation was initially conceived as a CD-ROM-based add-on for Nintendo's Super Famicom, for example, and that Sony's decision to persevere with development had less to do with the irrefutability of Kutaragi's calculations than the wounded pride of executives stung by Nintendo's ditching of them in favor of Phillips, should remind us that design is at least as much about property rights and supply chains, corporate rivalries, cultural norms, and happy accidents as it is about brilliant individuals' inspirations (Asakura 2000, 37–8, 65).

This becomes still more evident if we consider the PS2's "backwards compatibility." Taking the sting out of upgrading by ensuring that PS1 games remained playable on Sony's "next generation" hardware, this feature helped the PS2 to inherit and increase its predecessor's lead over the competition and proved crucial in shoring up the console's identity as a kind of sequel to or evolution of the first PlayStation—scion of the same noble house. This, however, was the result not of "vision" but of happenstance: felicitously, Kutaragi's team realized that they could repurpose the original PlayStation's processor as an input/output controller for the PS2. That this was more a matter of luck than judgment is suggested by Sony's failure to make history repeat itself with the PlayStation 3. Where the PS2 played PS1 games, early PS3s were compatible with PS2 discs; where the PS2 was powered by the bespoke "Emotion Engine" processor, Kutaragi's "Cell" technology was at the core of its successor; where the PS2 had doubled as a DVD player, the PS3 played Blu-rays. Despite following closely in its forebear's footsteps, however, the PS3 failed to sustain Sony's grip on gaming culture. Developers found The Cell much harder to work with than Microsoft's PC-like Xbox 360 architecture, while Blu-ray, its triumph over the rival HD-DVD format notwithstanding, failed to replicate DVD's success. In the absence of a more elegant means of maintaining backward compatibility, meanwhile, Sony simply crammed an Emotion Engine into each PS3, inflating the console's already high price. The company soon abandoned the feature altogether. In this context the rhetorical brio that had served Kutaragi so well as Asakura's "hero" became a liability, and a series of ill-judged interviews saw him rechristened "crazy Ken" by satirists (Kuchera 2007); less a virile father figure, more an addled older relative.

The PS2's backward compatibility, then, begs to be understood not as proof of progressive technological "evolution" but as an example of what evolutionary biologists call "exaptation," the "process by which features acquire functions for which they were not originally adapted or selected" ("exaptation, n."). Svetlana Boym (2013) has exapted the concept of exaptation itself in service of what she calls "off-modernism"—a critical project that calls into question "narratives of modernization and progress" by drawing attention to "missed opportunities and roads not taken." If gaming discourse co-opts Darwinian rhetoric to frame history vertically and vectorially, as a straight (blood)line leading ever upward, Boym uses exaptation as a spur to think "laterally." This approach has much in common with queer accounts of time: from Stockton's (2009) work on the virtue of "growing sideways" in a world where "growing up" entails internalizing heteronormative routines to Freeman's (2010, 85–6) work on "temporal drag" and the politics of memory to Sedgwick's (2003, 148–9) and Halberstam's (2005) respective discussions of how queer subcultures and relationships defy our culture's "'normal' generational narrative," following "strange temporalities" of their own. In their insistence on finding images and terms better suited to addressing history's queer zigzags, switchbacks, and sprawls, these critics have much to offer video game historians—as I now want to show by addressing the *Metal Gear Solid* and *Siren* series' roles in the PlayStation brand's own generational narrative.

Everything old is new again

On the surface, the *Metal Gear* series would seem to support both the model of video game history as a succession of generational leaps forward and the myths of masculine heroism with which, as we've seen, that model is bound up. Fleshing out an imagined history of macho military melodrama, each installment of the series has also pushed the graphical limits of its host platform, spurring players to keep upgrading to the next generation of Sony hardware. In 2005, when the PS3 was, as it were, little more than a twinkle in Kutaragi's eye, *Metal Gear Solid 4* was already being touted as a "killer app" for the console. *Metal Gear Solid 2* had likewise been the PS2's most anticipated title, highlighting the technological strides made since the original *Metal Gear Solid* (itself a continuation of a series that had begun in the 1980s) debuted on the first PlayStation. That game's success saw director Hideo Kojima hailed as an auteur—tasked, like Kutaragi, with lending a face to myths of masculine creative potency. In response, Kojima has shown an increasing interest in leavening the series' trademark "tactical espionage action" with an engagement with more "mature" themes, claiming that he wants players to reflect on "what we should and ultimately do pass on to future generations" (Tamari 2008). If these bids for profundity have sometimes come across as incongruous, sophomoric, or even hypocritical, I want to suggest that this is, at least in part, an indication of the difficulty of offering a mature engagement with questions of temporality, heredity, and technology from within an industry whose only model of intergenerational exchange is one of manufactured obsolescence and the relentless pursuit of the cutting edge. In other words, to understand *Metal Gear*'s take on sex, gender, and history, we also need to understand the pressures exerted by the hardware cycle.

While Kojima's invocation of "future generations" echoes the hetero-normative logic of reproductive futurism, in which the "Child remains . . . the fantasmatic beneficiary of every political intervention" (Edelman 2004, 1–3), the *Metal Gear* games themselves are notable for featuring a queer cast of clones, twins, surrogate mothers, and cyborg doppelgangers whose relationships defy the neat geometries of the family tree and the oedipal triangle (Gallagher 2012). As spectacular standard-bearers for successive console generations, the games have continued to affirm the hardware cycle's doctrine of perpetual progress; as stories, however, they have become ever more melancholy explorations of fallibility, regret, and what Freeman calls "the uncontrollability of the past and its ability to endanger the present" (2010, 86). This tension is particularly apparent with *Metal Gear Solid 4*. The series' PS3 debut saw Kojima pressing the console's (then) state-of-the-art hardware

FIGURE 1.1 *Embodying the hardware cycle: Metal Gear Solid's Solid Snake as he appeared in his PS1, PS2 and PS3 incarnations.*

into service to render the ravages that time had wrought on his protagonist (Figure 1.1), now a white-haired old man racked by regrets and brooding over past glories. If game developers have often used heroic masculine bodies to incarnate the promise and potency of technology, Snake's newly lined visage at once continued and subverted this convention. Testifying to the PS3's ability to generate unprecedentedly detailed character models, it also conveyed incongruous connotations of entropy, impotence, and senescence, presenting a striking contrast with the console's immaculately finished metallic surface and the brighter, better future it promised. The game likewise struggled to tell a story about the burden of the past while offering an entertaining demonstration of a new console's capabilities. Its downbeat mood and retrospective bent jarred in an experience meant to affirm the pseudo-evolutionary idea that the best is yet to come. At the same time, this dark tone seemed to have been informed by the exigencies of the hardware cycle, with Snake's nostalgia and pessimism echoing Kojima's attitude in interviews preceding the game's release: even as Sony was bullishly talking up the PS3's "revolutionary" cell processor, he was expressing his fear that "if . . . evolutionary roads like the PS3 are closed off, the industry will no longer grow" (Gantayat 2006).

Inspired, presumably, by the PS3's troubled gestation and the threat posed by Sony's rivals, Nintendo and Microsoft, Kojima's comment gestures more generally at the extent to which games are shaped (and warped) by the imperatives, logic, and quasievolutionary rhetoric of the hardware cycle. Of course, technological considerations and commercial pressures have always been factors in the industrial arts. *Metal Gear's* struggle to offer a "mature" engagement with questions of heredity, masculinity, nationality, and technology while simultaneously acting as best-selling brand flagship and poster boy for technological progress, however, foregrounds the unusual degree to which video games are understood less as examples of "cultural practice" than as gateways to "possible technological futures" (Newman

2012, 10), suggesting that gaming's obsession with the next evolutionary step may be constraining its expressive scope.

Siren: Horror and horology

Questions of history, inheritance, and reproduction are also central to Sony's *Siren* series, a generation-spanning trio of survival horror titles that prove even more conflicted than *Metal Gear* when it comes to conceptions of sex, heroism, and progress. As befits a franchise about fractured chronologies and tangled bloodlines, *Siren* has itself had a complex, even involuted, history. Directed by Keichiro Toyama, best known for the influential PS1 horror game *Silent Hill*, the *Siren* games essentially transplant *Silent Hill*'s scenario from small-town America to rural Japan. Released on the PS2, the first two games won plaudits both for their eerie tone and for their implementation of an innovative "sightjacking" system that allowed players to look through the eyes of enemies. Their prohibitive difficulty, however, proved off-putting for many players, and Sony opted not to release *Siren 2* in North America. Following the release of the PS3, Sony announced a third game, *Siren: Blood Curse*. This, however, was not a sequel but a remake, which aimed to "evolve" the original *Siren* in pursuit of a wider audience (Inaba 2008). It is the nature of this attempted evolution that I want to discuss here.

Like much horror, the *Siren* games articulate a fear of the primitive, presenting communities wherein an adherence to "backward" sociocultural norms, rituals, and superstitions has unleashed a plague that turns humans into "*shibito*"—hideous hybrid creatures evocative of bugs, larvae, and lepidoptera (Figure 1.2). Miki Takahashi, *Blood Curse*'s creature designer, reasons that "insects disgust us in a way that mammals can't," presumably on account of their sheer phylogenetic otherness, while scenario writer Naoko Sato underlines the importance of the "very traditional Japanese setting" to the *Siren* games, which present tradition itself as a sinister, dehumanizing force ("Behind the Curtain of Terror" 2008). In these games it is not just the protagonists' lives that are at stake, then, but the very course of human evolution and enlightenment, and sex figures less as an element of interpersonal interaction or identity than as a factor in differentiating species, a mode of fostering genetic mutations, and a means of ordering our understanding of time.

Of course, the scenario of city slickers stumbling upon brutal rural rituals and/or communities of monstrously inbred degenerates has long been a staple of the horror genre, from Machen's *Three Impostors* (1895) to Hooper's *Texas Chainsaw Massacre* (1974). *Siren*'s Japanese setting, however, gives this trope

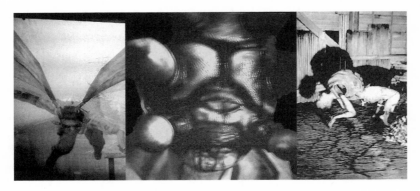

FIGURE 1.2 *Many of* Siren's shibito *boast insect-like characteristics.*

a distinctive inflection, with the game's ruined buildings and decaying bodies calling to mind the role of the atom bomb as a violent catalyst for change in Japanese culture—a subject that Kojima's games, which he hopes convey an "'anti-war, anti-nuke' message," also address (Tamari 2008). As this would suggest, if *Siren* plays on fears of regression, challenging the widespread Japanese tendency to pine for a bygone sense of collective identity (Allison 2006, 74), the games are by no means blithely optimistic about technology's potential as an engine of "progress." The monstrously overembodied *shibito* may articulate fears of degeneration and fleshly decadence, but they also incarnate the uncanniness of digital media, reflecting a long cultural history of seeing insects as a sinister, quasitechnological collective intelligence that threatens humanity's evolutionary preeminence (Parikka 2010, xi–xiii). Moving in stilted, repetitious loops, chattering mantrically to themselves, the *shibito* capitalize on the eeriness of artificial intelligence to hint at the way in which routines and traditions, "memories and . . . old habits" can gain parasitic sway over us ("Behind the Curtain of Terror" 2008). Intentionally "placed in an extremely weak and disadvantaged position" in relation to these creatures, players are encouraged to use "sightjacking" to piece together an escape route, so that—ironically—defeating the *shibito* means literally learning to see from their point of view ("The Making of *Siren*" 2004).

Both the game's scenario and its mechanics, then, work to establish an opposition between humanity (represented by the player and the player-characters) and the alien force, at once insectile, viral, and quasimachinic, which threatens to subsume it. This opposition, however, is structured less by Manichean notions of good and evil than by distinctions between reproduction and replication, individuality and collectivity, cyclical and linear time.

These are the same oppositions that underpin Baudrillard's essay, "Final Solution, or the Revenge of the Immortals," in which he portrays the human order of sexual reproduction as a miraculous evolutionary achievement poised precariously between two threatening kinds of replication: on the one hand the "the earlier order of the virus . . . of deathless things," which proliferate via copying; on the other the contemporary regime of "asexual, biotechnological modes of reproduction" enabled by computers, which, he argues, threatens to reverse "our" victory over deathless sameness and bring about the "nullification of differences" (2000, 7–10). For Lee Edelman there is something at once typical and troublingly homophobic about the way that Baudrillard, like "scientific discourse in general, celebrates the triumph of sexed reproduction over genetic duplication in a teleological narrative"—a stance that Edelman finds uncomfortably reminiscent of the still-potent Freudian cliché that individuals must "outgrow" regressive homosexual impulses in order to flower into full (heterosexual) maturity (62). Edelman's critique offers a useful way into *Blood Curse*, which, in seeking to evolve *Siren* into something more relatable, initially seems to fall prey to the same clichés Baudrillard affirms, focusing its plot on a heterosexual couple's attempt to save their daughter from a viral-insectile-machinic evil. In practice, however, the game offers a more complex message about sexuality and time, demonstrating that games can transcend or subvert myths of progress while also attesting to the power of those myths in determining notions of how games ought to be.

The most immediate difference between *Blood Curse* and the original *Siren* is an increase in visual fidelity; if nothing else, the game served to make visible how powerful Kutaragi's new baby was by comparison with its aging forebear. The developers also made a host of other changes, streamlining the game's interface, reducing the cast, and making certain characters American rather than Japanese (Figure 1.3). Intriguingly, this last decision has been explained both as a way to "present Western players with characters that are easier to relate to" (Inaba 2008) and as a means of evoking "the natural fear that arises when being faced with an unfamiliar culture" ("Behind the Curtain of Terror" 2008). In the game it is Westerners who have a horrifying encounter with Japanese culture, but the change also suggests a development team anxiously aware of the need to please foreign audiences during a hardware cycle that had seen Microsoft making considerable headway into a console market hitherto dominated by Japanese companies.

Perhaps the most important departure from the original *Siren*'s template, however, was the simplification of the game's narrative structure. In the PS2 games, players selected which episode to play next from a grid, with characters ranged along the X axis and points in diegetic time marked on the Y axis. Events were often encountered out of chronological sequence, with new episodes appearing in seemingly random positions on the grid. Once

FIGURE 1.3 Siren's *Kyoya Suda and his counterpart in* Blood Curse, *Howard Wright.* Blood Curse's *"evolution" entailed both an increase in graphical fidelity and the "Westernization" of certain characters.*

completed, episodes could be replayed, allowing players to complete alternate or additional objectives that would, in turn, open up new narrative possibilities for other playable characters—and thus new grid squares. If *Siren*'s "sightjacking" system fragmented gamespace into a series of partial views, this grid structure had a similar effect on narrative time: while it is possible to piece together an account of events, the resultant record remains, even after the game has been "completed," full of gaps, redundancies, and contradictions—a cubistic sketch rather than a comprehensive diagram. Moreover, where most game narratives follow either a single protagonist or a group united by a common goal, the priorities and motivations of *Siren*'s multiple playable characters would often come into conflict. While unlocking a particular door might help one character, for example, it could end up endangering another in a subsequent episode. In the vast majority of games, including horror games, the player is constantly making progress, however grueling; *Siren*, by contrast, rendered definitions of success relative and radically contingent, opening up queer gray areas in which apparently heroic actions might turn out to be futile, shortsighted, or counterintuitive—a move crucial in eliciting the sense of "despair" that the developers wanted players to experience ("Behind the Curtain of Terror" 2008).

It was, then, a significant departure for *Blood Curse* to abandon the grid system in favor of a narrative structured as a linear sequence of episodes subdivided into chapters (Figure 1.4). This narrative, moreover, was given a much tighter central focus, zeroing in on the travails of estranged couple Sam and Melissa as they attempt to rescue their daughter Bella and "avoid[ing]

FIGURE 1.4 *Top: The stage select grid from* Siren. *Bottom:* Blood Curse's *linear episode structure.*

anything that might slow down the pace" of the story ("Behind the Curtain of Terror" 2008).

Upon first playing *Blood Curse*, then, it seems that the goal of improving the first *Siren* has been pursued by way of a sexual and structural "straightening" process, with the designers foregrounding the heroic struggle to reunite a family by pruning away the original game's errant narrative branches. *Blood Curse* appears to be articulating exactly the kind of "reproductive futurism" that Edelman takes issue with, grounding in the figure of "the Child" a glorious, heteronormative future while justifying violence against monstrous "others" as necessary to secure that future (Edelman 2004, 2).

This conclusion is, however, challenged after the game's first six episodes. If these foreshadow reconciliation for Sam, Melissa, and Bella, such expectations are confounded at the end of episode six with the shock revelation that father and daughter alike have already fallen victim to the eponymous curse. Following this unexpected twist, diegetic time in *Blood Curse* folds back on itself, leaving players to negotiate the same events and encounters from different perspectives, in pursuit of other goals—a macro-scale recapitulation of the player's micro-scale process of progressing through a narrative game only by way of repeated retries. As Toyama has commented, "Replaying the same event while seeing it unfold in different ways is something I feel is an inherent characteristic of video games, so I wanted to take that unique element and weave it directly into the story itself" (Inaba 2008). One might predict that the second playthrough would be a matter of the player, now armed with hindsight, avoiding the mistakes they had made on their first playthrough in order to bring about the correct, "happy" ending. Again, however, (hetero)normative narrative expectations are frustrated. In an echo of Kafka's "Leopards in the Temple," in which what is initially experienced as the blasphemous interruption of a sacred ritual is repeated until it "can be calculated in advance, and . . . becomes part of the ceremony" (1983, 472), it becomes apparent that the only way to save Bella, and so fulfill reproductive futurism's imperative to protect "the Child," is to perpetuate the same temporal loop by ensuring that the ceremony with which the game begins is always interrupted. In other words, the "right" way to close the narrative (at least from the perspective of Bella's father) is to render closure—or progress—impossible. This means Bella cannot become a *shibito*, but it also means she can never grow up and (among other things) raise her own family. Ultimately, *Blood Curse* presents a scenario where the only choice is between perdition and repetition, the horror of finality and the horror of the perpetual, with Sam fighting to sustain a universe in which change, whether for better or worse, is simply inconceivable.

This vision of history repeating itself is, of course, at once apt and rather ironic, given the game's status as a remake intended to showcase another new PlayStation. Perhaps even more ironic is the fact that the plot of this M-rated video game (and stories of games corrupting, desensitizing, or traumatizing "little ones" with "mature" content remain a staple of mainstream media reporting (Hern 2013)) should turn out to hinge on an overprotective father's determination to keep his child forever innocent rather than see her "corrupted." In this respect, the game highlights a contradiction that lies at the very heart of reproductive futurism: if the Child's virginal innocence remains unsullied *forever*, the character will never attain sexual maturity, and the generational cycle will be terminated. Reproductive futurism, in short, can be understood as a kind of parlous sociosexual calculus, directed toward staking out a vanishingly small space within which the Child could "grow up" (i.e., be initiated into heterosexual "maturity") at a pace that is neither too fast nor too slow but, as Goldilocks would have it, *just right*.

Offering a welcome departure from the trope of the lone male hero saving the world, *Siren*'s imagination of a temporality of nightmarish, Sisyphean repetition also reminds us that—as Judith Butler's account of performative gender insists, and as Sony found to its cost with the PS3—maintaining the status quo, far from being a matter of leaving things as they are, requires ongoing effort (1993, x). True of gender norms, this is true too of generic conventions, and *Siren* and *Metal Gear* are notable for pioneering genres (survival horror and stealth action) that some now consider evolutionary dead ends. If early 3D games were often disorienting, hard to navigate, and visually crude, stealth and horror games capitalized on this, using the fact that players could neither see clearly nor move fluently to cultivate anxiety and suspense. In trying to keep up with technological advances, changing audience expectations, and "evolving" design practices, however, some commentators have argued that these genres have "evolved [themselves] into extinction," compromising the very qualities that made them compelling in the first place (Sterling 2008). This conclusion is supported by the fact that although *Blood Curse* is better-designed than *Siren*—if, that is, we understand good design to be a matter of enabling, orienting, motivating, and informing users—the original is arguably all the more effective as a horror game for being difficult to play and hard to follow.

This apparent contradiction gestures at the complexities of game design, in which pretensions to expression are inextricable from questions of interface design, technological optimization, and ludic balancing. Can a game decenter or perturb players while still being easy or user-friendly? Can it challenge teleological thinking while simultaneously motivating gamers to upgrade their console? Where does "evolutionary" streamlining shade into devolutionary "dumbing down?" If the readings above have not settled these questions, they have, I hope, highlighted the broader truth at which such questions gesture: that if gaming is to become more "mature" and more inclusive, it will involve thinking not just about the terms on which games incorporate sexual content and portray hitherto-underrepresented communities but also about temporal structures, routines, rhythms, and habits—and the way that these are at once gendered and shaped by commercial interests. We need to recognize that when self-described "hardcore" gamers express contempt for "noobs," late adopters or casuals who might play an iPhone game for fifteen minutes on a commute but would balk at investing the tens of hours required to finish many PlayStation games, they are enforcing gaming culture's own chrononormative ideas about "the value and meaning of time" (Freeman 2010, 3). We also need to recognize, however, that even dominant rhythms like that of the hardware cycle can leave room for queer kinds of syncopation: here we might think not just of *Siren* and *Metal Gear Solid*'s incongruously queer plotting but of artist Rachel Weil's story of being captivated by secondhand 8-bit games

discarded by boys who had moved on to "next generation" 16-bit systems—
an anecdote that suggests how cycles of obsolescence can unexpectedly
foster opportunities for participation among those who, whether for reasons
of gender, age, sexuality, or economic status, are excluded from gaming's
vanguard (Alexander 2014).

To look at how the hardware cycle has been narrativized, and at how it
has informed both games' narrative structures and their representations of
gender and sexuality, is then to confront the dispiriting fact that masculinist
and heteronormative attitudes may be even more pervasive than we assume,
manifesting not just at the levels of representation and simulation but also at
those of rhythm and structure. It is also, however, to discover that video games
have already begun to develop novel ways of mediating and even interrogating
the complex, often contradictory attitudes to sexuality, technology, and time
characteristic of the moments and cultures that produce them.

References

Alexander, Leigh. 2014. "Girly Video Games: Rewriting a History of Pink." *The
    Guardian*, June 5. http://www.theguardian.com/technology/2014/jun/05/girly-
    games-history-of-pink-rachel-weil.
Allison, Anne. 2006. *Millennial Monsters*. Berkeley: University of California Press.
Asakura, Reiji. 2000. *Revolutionaries at Sony: The Making of the Sony PlayStation
    and the Visionaries Who Conquered the World of Video Games*. New York:
    McGraw Hill.
Baudrillard, Jean. 2000. *The Vital Illusion*. New York: Columbia University Press.
Beer, Gillian. 2000. *Darwin's Plots: Evolutionary Narrative, George Eliot and
    Nineteenth-Century Fiction*. Cambridge: Cambridge University Press.
"Behind the Curtain of Terror" (documentary short). 2008. *Siren: Blood Curse*.
    Sony Computer Entertainment.
Boym, Svetlana. 2013. "The Off-Modern Mirror." *E-Flux Journal* 19: n. pag.
    http://www.e-flux.com/journal/the-off-modern-mirror/.
Butler, Judith. 1993. *Bodies that Matter: On the Discursive Limits of "Sex."*
    New York: Routledge.
Edelman, Lee. 2004. *No Future: Queer Theory and the Death Drive*. Durham:
    Duke University Press.
"exaptation, n." 2014. *OED Online*, June. http://0-www.oed.com.mercury.
    concordia.ca/view/Entry/258776?redirectedFrom=exaptation.
Freeman, Elizabeth. 2010. *Time Binds: Queer Temporalities, Queer Histories*.
    Durham: Duke University Press.
Gallagher, Rob. 2012. "No Sex Please, We Are Finite State Machines: On the
    Melancholy Sexlessness of the Video Game." *Games and Culture* 7 (6):
    399–418.
Gantayat, Anoop. 2006. "Nomura and Kojima Talk PS3." *IGN*, June 29.
    http://ca.ign.com/articles/2006/06/30/nomura-and-kojima-talk-ps3.

Halberstam, Judith. 2005. *In a Queer Time and Place: Transgender Bodies, Subcultural Lives*. New York: New York University Press.

Hern, Alex. 2013. "*Grand Theft Auto 5* Under Fire for Graphic Torture Scene." *Guardian*, September 18. http://www.theguardian.com/technology/2013/sep/18/grand-theft-auto-5-under-fire-for-graphic-torture-scene.

Huffer, Lynne. 2013. *Mad for Foucault: Rethinking the Foundations of Queer Theory*. New York: Columbia University Press.

Inaba, Tsubasa. 2008. "Developer Q&A: *Siren: Blood Curse*." *PlayStation Blog*, June 30. http://blog.us.playstation.com/2008/06/13/developer-qa-siren-blood-curse/.

Kafka, Franz. 1983. *The Complete Stories and Parables*. New York: Quality Paperback.

Kuchera, Ben. 2007. "We Come Not to Bury Kutaragi but to Praise Him." *Ars Technica*, April 26. http://arstechnica.com/gaming/2007/04/ken-kutaragi-steps-down-from-scei-leadership-role/.

"The Making of *Siren*" (documentary short). 2004. "Demo Disc 44". *Official PlayStation Magazine*. March.

Newman, James. 2012. *Best Before: Videogames, Supersession and Obsolescence*. New York: Routledge.

Parikka, Jussi. 2010. *Insect Media: An Archaeology of Animals and Technology*. Minneapolis: University of Minnesota Press.

Rubenstein, Jeff. 2010. "Media Molecule Officially Joins the PlayStation Family." *PlayStation Blog*, March 2. http://blog.us.playstation.com/2010/03/02/media-molecule-officially-joins-the-playstation-family/.

Sedgwick, Eve Kosofsky. 2003. *Touching Feeling: Affect, Pedagogy, Performativity*. Durham: Duke University Press.

Sterling, Jim. 2008. "How Survival Horror Evolved Itself into Extinction." *Destructoid*, December 8. http://www.destructoid.com/how-survival-horror-evolved-itself-into-extinction-114022.phtml.

Stockton, Kathryn Bond. 2009. *The Queer Child, or Growing Sideways in the Twentieth Century*. Durham: Duke University Press.

Tamari, Etsu. 2008. "Hideo Kojima Interview." *Konami*. http://www.konami.jp/mgs4/uk/interview/03.html.

Games cited

Kojima Productions. 2008. *Metal Gear Solid 4: Guns of the Patriots*. Konami.

Konami Computer Entertainment. 1999. *Silent Hill*. Konami.

Konami Computer Entertainment Japan. 1998. *Metal Gear Solid*. Konami.

Konami Computer Entertainment Japan. 2001. *Metal Gear Solid 2: Sons of Liberty*. Konami.

Konami Computer Entertainment Japan. 2004. *Metal Gear Solid 3: Snake Eater*. Konami.

Project Siren. 2004. *Siren*. Sony Computer Entertainment.

Project Siren. 2006. *Siren 2*. Sony Computer Entertainment.

Project Siren. 2008. *Siren: Blood Curse*. Sony Computer Entertainment.

2

Beyond *Rapelay*: Self-regulation in the Japanese erotic video game industry

Jérémie Pelletier-Gagnon (University of Alberta, Canada) and Martin Picard (University of Montreal, Canada)

In 2010, Kyung Lah, a reporter for CNN, produced an alarming news story that would have important consequences for the industry of erotic digital entertainment in Japan. The heart of the issue was the existence and circulation of Illusion Soft's most controversial computer game title, *Rapelay*, a 3D erotic game where users are put into the position of a serial rapist (2010a). In this video game, the player embodies an unnamed protagonist who, after having been arrested and condemned for public groping, decides to take his revenge on the women who denounced him by stalking and raping them one by one. Released exclusively for Japan in 2006, the game's brief appearance on Amazon.com in 2009 was met with shock and incomprehension: how could a video game based around the concept of rape be featured by one of the most respected online retailers (Chalk 2009). The game had spawned some interest in the broader Internet gaming community shortly after its release (Zigfried 2006; Parsons 2007) before getting coverage in the mainstream media (Ashcraft 2010), culminating with Kyung Lah's report on the game and feminist activist association Equality Now's public campaign against its circulation (2010a, b). The point that Equality Now tried to make was very clear: games featuring violence toward women open the way for the banalization of discrimination and violence against women. As such, allowing their circulation would demonstrate a tacit acceptance of such discourse in society (Lah 2010a). The game was widely criticized for its immoral subject matter (Alexander 2009); countries such as Australia (Reist 2009, 27) and Argentina (IANS 2010) went as far as banning the game from their territories. Ultimately, Illusion Soft took the game off stores' shelves and retracted all mentions of the game from their website.

The issue sparked by the release of *Rapelay* on Amazon.com seems to be one of a difficult relationship between two different rationales. On the one hand, from a Western point of view, cultural products should, to some extent, embody the moral character of the commonly agreed-upon culture; products from a niche market cannot be exempt from the public sphere, and allowing even a single example of amoral discourse in circulation cannot be ignored for the sake of consistency within the social climate. On the other hand, Japanese authorities' silence on the circulation of such games suggests that, as long as such products remain over the edge of mainstream culture, the social climate of Japan itself will not be affected by them; taking for granted the already problematic gender relationships in a yet patriarchal Japanese society (Allison 1996).

Indeed, the nature of the debate also spanned concerns about the culture of representation of sex, not only in Japanese video games, but also in Japanese media in general. Originally contained within the borders of gaming culture, CNN's coverage of the controversy (Lah 2010b) allowed the debate to transform into a preconceived condemnation without investigating the circumstances of the manufacture and sale of products of this sort in Japan. The American news outlet went on to question the free circulation of these types of games in Japan and the lack of government policies to regulate this form of morally disputable media. What came out of this incident is the general understanding that discussions on pornography in Japan do not happen internally, because Japan is culturally different and has different norms regarding sexuality (Lah 2010b). While it is true that the Japanese government has not been particularly proactive in policing erotic video games, and that this can partly be blamed on the underrepresentation of women in governmental matters, this conclusion overlooks important aspects of the Japanese video game industry. Investigating the dynamics that regulate the circulation of erotic video games in Japan will help us reassess this complicated issue.

The objective of this chapter will be to provide a deeper understanding of the media ecology from which the erotic games (*eroge* or "hentai games" as they are often called in English) genre emerged. This will entail an exploration not only of the history of the genre, but also of the history of the difficult relation between Japanese video games and government, police forces, and mainstream society. After demonstrating how closely related the production of erotic content and computer software were in the early days of the media, spawning many subgenres and niche cultural practices in PC gaming communities, we will depict this history of the friction caused by the gradual introduction of pornographic content in games within mainstream media. This latter part will primarily focus on the analysis of the events surrounding two game releases—*177*, published in 1986 by Macadamia, and *Saori—Bishoujo-tachi no yakata* (*Saori: The House of Beautiful Girls*), published by Fairytale in 1991—and their influence regarding the reevaluation of criminal law on the production and circulation of obscene material. It is only then that an understanding of the self-regulatory system that now governs Japanese pornographic game releases and its impact will be possible. This historical evolution will provide a more accurate perspective on the relation between Japanese society and sexual censorship in digital games.

1980s—computer hobbyists and teenage fun

As mentioned above, computer game production has been tied to erotica since the very beginnings of the game industry in Japan, where erotic content was typically used as reward and incentive for playing. Hudson's *Yakyuken*, a strip version of the rock-paper-scissors game, is probably one of the earliest examples of this design (Miyamoto 2013), although the Akihabara computer shop Tsukumo released its own version around the same time. The most well-known example of early erotic games in Japan is *Night Life*, an edutainment software conceived as an aid for intimate conjugal relations, where the users' bed experience would reflect the result of a series of questions, such as the physical condition of the users or to what extent they feel adventurous. Interestingly, this game was made and released by the game company Koei, best known today for their *Dynasty Warriors* and *Nobunaga's Ambition* series. However, *Night Life* was only the first of their early erotic game series; they would go on to release other noteworthy erotic games under their label "Strawberry Porno Game Series" such as *Danchi tsuma no yuuwaku* (*The Temptation of Housing Complex Wives*) and *Oranda tsuma wa denki unagi no yume wo miru ka?* (*Do Dutch Wives Dream of Electric Eels?*)—role-playing game (RPG)/adventure game hybrids in which players explore environments, seduce women, and sometimes engage battle sequences similar to *Wizardry*. In 1984, following other companies such as PSK, they would also release a game inspired by the *lolicon* (Lolita complex) artistic movement of the

1980s entitled *My Lolita*, an erotic surgery simulation game starring a naked underage character.[1]

Far from being the only company that released erotic games in its early years, Enix, best known for the very popular *Dragon Quest* series, published its first erotic game entitled *Marichan kiken ippatsu* in 1983, in which the objective is to save Mari-chan from a violent stalker by playing *janken* (rock-paper-scissors). Should the user win, Mari-chan congratulates him by stripping. The same year, Enix also published *Lolita Syndrome*, a *lolicon* erotic game where the player must help girls escape a house full of dangers. The better the user does at helping all ten characters, the more stripping scenes he is able to see. It should be noted that both Enix games *Lolita Syndrome* and *Marichan kiken ippatsu* are the result of computer hobbyist contests, part of a competition for aspiring game programmers that the publisher organized in order to look for prospective employees (Miyamoto 2013). It should also be noted that the designers chose to create pornographic games; this was not a requirement of the contest. The grand prize included the publication of the winning game. As computer schools were not such a common thing at the time, this was a way to both train new people and gather new software to put on the market. Nihon Falcom, also a very reputable game company, which later created the *Ys* series, published *Joshi daisei private*, an erotic puzzle game. As shown by the development of those studios, as well as other Japanese computer game makers at the time such as PSK, CSK, Championsoft, ASCII, Ponyca, dB-soft, Jast, Cocktailsoft, and many others, the production of erotic games was an integral part of the software business in the 1980s.

177—*eroge* enter the public discourse

However, it is not until 1986 that the issue of the legitimacy of the presence of pornographic content in video games was formally raised, and it is the computer game *177* that would first trigger national concern over the phenomenon. The game, created by Macadamia Soft for the NEC PC-8801, is a rape simulation game comprised of two main screens: a first screen where the player must rapidly press keys to catch a woman running away from the game's protagonist within a set time frame, and another one where the user, if successful in catching the woman, must quickly press keys in order to rape the woman in the bushes. Should the player perform well in the second screen, the protagonist marries the woman, in what is probably meant to be a "happy ending." Otherwise, the protagonist gets arrested, represented in the game-over screen. The game itself was a remake of a game unofficially circulated as *Pascale* with a similar premise (Miyamoto 2013). Until the release of *177*, most erotic games that hit the market did not represent rape or sexual abuse by putting the player in the role of an offender. To make matters worse, the title *177* refers to the article number 177 within the Japanese criminal legislation that forbids rape, transforming the game into a cynical farce whose meaning is to promote rape itself with a twisted message on the consequences of sexual assault.

Similarly to the case of *Custer's Revenge* in the United States during the 1980s, *177* became a case for concern at the national level; *eroge* would not be able to go back to a relative state of anonymity in the country. The game was introduced by Kômeito political advisor Kusakawa Shôzô to the reporting committee of the lower House of Representatives at the Japanese National Diet on October 10, 1986 as an example of hurtful game software whose sales should be restricted (Japan National Diet 1986). This was presented as a case study illustrating how unregulated use of computers and game consoles, a technology also initially thought to be useful in an educational context, could have negative side—effects for the development of children in Japan. In an age where the potential of those technologies was still unknown, and where young people were more proficient in its manipulation than their parents, video games could easily be framed as a public nuisance. The speaker stressed the fact that while people can read about or look at illustrations of such situations, the context of rape transformed into a game was far more problematic. As the first case of a harmful video game to be officially designated as such in a political context in Japan, this intervention resulted in the Ministry of International Trade and Industry (METI) suggesting that the industry self-regulate its content. No concrete steps were initially taken, but it would prepare the terrain for other developments in the erotic game scene. The introduction of *177* into the national public discourse, however, ironically accelerated its sales, and the software has become something of a highly sought-after collectable object (Miyamoto 2013).

At the time of this incident, Japanese society was apprehensive of video games' sudden popularity among the youth. Discourse on the bad influence of computer games was starting to develop in the media in response to this growing concern (Katou 2011). What this event highlights is that, at the time, protecting the younger population from video games—then perceived as an engrossing entertainment with devious effects—was a social priority. We also see a first example of the reluctance of the Japanese government to strongly impose censorship on these types of software, instead suggesting that the industry should regulate itself. The second major incident related to the circulation of adult games would expand on those two precedents.

The *Saori* incident—protecting the youth

Saori—Bishoujo no Yakata is an adult game released by FairyTale, under the brand name Xshitei (X-Rated), on October 18, 1991. The game presents the story of Saori, who gets abducted into a Western-style mansion by two strange men wearing white masks. Trapped in the property, she experiences erotic visual hallucinations of all kinds, including acts of incest, homosexual love, and sexual encounters between teachers and students. The game is notable for not being subject to censorship through the implementation of mosaics or any sort of screen deformation technique to hide the explicit content from the viewer as required by Article 175 of the Criminal Code of Japan (da Silva 2009).

While the game could be worthy of note in regard to its high level of sexually explicit content alone, it became controversial for a different reason. The game attracted attention when it became the object of a shoplifting incident by a middle school student of the Kyoto metropolitan area (Miyamoto 2013). Subsequently, in light of the amount of graphic content in the software, the authorities decided to bring the issue to another level by authorizing a search warrant at the software parent company, Jast, as well as four software resellers in the vicinity. As a result, the presidents of both Jast and Kirara (the company that owned the FairyTale brand) were arrested by the prefectural police on charges of possession of obscene material with the intent of resale (Miyamoto 2013). FairyTale then recalled all copies of the game, along with several others that were found to be at fault in the eyes of the law such as *Dragon City X Shitei*. The company rereleased them afterward with heavy self-censoring; male protagonists were erased from the images, and users could no longer see female genitals due to mosaics.

However, to understand why such seemingly drastic actions were enacted against the adult game company in question, we must shed light upon the Miyazaki serial murder case, an event that made a huge impression on the Japanese public and authorities in the 1980s. Between 1988 and 1989, Tsutomu Miyazaki targeted and murdered young girls in the locality of Saitama in the Tokyo metropolitan area. In the media coverage of the tragedy, news outlets emphasized the discovery of a videotape collection of about 5,700 items, which included horror and pornographic material. This coverage quickly attributed Miyazaki's actions to media fanaticism, a development that had a long-term negative effect on the perception of *otaku* among the Japanese population (Galbraith 2010; Kinsella 2000). As a feeling of mistrust toward *otaku* that would linger for years to come started to spread in the population, authorities started to inquire more vigilantly about the representation of sexual content in fringe media, including video games. Adult games, after being introduced to public concerns with *177*, were back on the radar of the authorities, this time with a greater sense of urgency.

This event had many ramifications for other studios as well as for the then flourishing adult game market. In 1992, Gainax—the anime studio best known for the creation of the anime television hit *Neon Genesis Evangelion* (1995–96)—was targeted by a lawsuit concerning the circulation of the video game *Dennou gakuen Scenario I Ver2.0* (*Cybernetic High School Scenario I Ver2.0*), released in 1990 (Miyamoto 2013, 9). *Dennou gakuen*, a quiz game with clothes stripping elements, was seen as guilty of breaking Miyazaki prefectural law on harmful books by depicting uncensored pubic hair. While Miyazaki Prefecture did not win the case, the issue was brought forward to courts of appeal until 1999, when the final appeal was rejected by the supreme court of Japan (Natsui 2001). In fear of retaliation, other game studios started to self-censor their games by applying conventions of adult video censorship, such as mosaics, to new releases more consistently. Adult game magazines such as *Technopolis* stopped publishing articles on games targeted for audiences over eighteen years of age and instead started to focus on rebranding itself as a *bishoujo* (beautiful girls) game magazine, leaving the adult game magazine and its pejorative meaning behind (Miyamoto 2013). Arguably, this quick succession of events led the entire adult game industry to adopt new guidelines that would allow its products to at least circulate more discreetly and avoid direct criticism.

Sofurin—self-censorship as a system

In 1992, a revolution occurred in the world of the Japanese pornographic game industry. Following the incident involving the producers of *Saori*, the industry group responsible for the creation and circulation of adult computer software formed the Ethics Organization of Computer Software (EOCS) (*conpyuuta sofutowea rinri kikou*, or *sofurin*). *Sofurin* is an association of adult game manufacturers that evaluates the morality of erotic content in pornographic computer games. Membership is nonmandatory; there is no official penalty for companies that do not wish to have their games inspected. It provides sticker labels for individual products that signal the attributed rating. While the organization initially provided two labels—"General software" and "18 and above"—in 1992, other categories have gradually been added such as the "15 and above" rating in 1994. The association then completely rebuilt its rating system in 2011 in favor of five ratings: "General," "12 and above recommended," "15 and above recommended," "15 only," and "18 only," each bearing their specific label (EOCS 2013b). Other standards were also established, such as for the size of the mosaics as well as for the depiction of violent and disgraceful material. *Sofurin* was also in charge of building a network of resellers that would support products inspected by the EOCS in order to strengthen a self-regulated production and distribution of software (EOCS 2013a). A number of studios joined the organization in its beginnings, including Gainax, which was under a lot of pressure from its legal conflict with the Miyazaki prefecture (Miyamoto 2013). The industry had finally taken METI's 1986 recommendation to heart.

The introduction of the association transformed the landscape of *eroge* in the years following its creation. *Eroge* publishing and sales increased significantly; the share of erotic game production as a portion of the total computer game market rose from 17.7 percent in April 1993 to 35 percent in April 1994 (Geemu Hihyou 1994, 72). However, since organization membership was not mandatory for publishers to put games on the market, final rating decisions could be influenced by other factors, such as the market presence of a specific publisher or game series. An example of the situation is the controversy around the initial release of the game *Sotsugyou 2 Neo Generation* (*Graduation 2: Neo Generation*), a nurturing simulation for the PC platform originally rated 18 and over at its release for reasons related to the depiction of underage consumption of alcohol and tobacco. After the company JHV quit the association and reluctantly released the game with an 18 and over label, the organization adjusted its evaluation method to create a compromise: the creation of a 15 and over rating and the reevaluation and release of a modified version of *Sotsugyou 2* (Geemu Hihyou 1994, 75). The possibility for publishers to release their game despite having no affiliation to the association thus creates a very malleable system of evaluation where pressure from developers could lead *Sofurin* to adjust its rating method.

While this provides a frame for studios to guide their approach to erotic content creation, this model is not without its issues. It is, however, the model that still prevails for the regulation of erotic content in computer games: the model to which *Rapelay* was subjected.

Otaku and the reinvention of pornography in games

From the mid-1990s onward, a very prolific period for the genre, the adult game market would see the release of multiple groundbreaking titles that would bring the production of *eroge* in a new direction. Leaf—at the time a relatively unknown studio of the publisher Aquaplus—released three major games within a two-year period as the "Leaf Visual Novel Series": *Shizuku*, *Kizuato*, and *To Heart*. The first two titles were more similar to older conventions of *eroge* insofar as they contained horror elements combined with sexploitation. However, they are notable for being the first titles to combine the form of the "Sound Novels" trademark developed by Chunsoft on the Super Famicom, in titles such as *Otogirisou* and *Kamaitachi no yoru* (*Banshee's Last Cry*), with erotic content. A notable feature of this game style is to put emphasis on reading by having the text occupy the whole screen instead of a small rectangular box at the bottom. Players see the character sprites appearing and disappearing behind the text, depending on who is talking. The software also presents a relatively linear story punctuated by choices where the player can steer the course of events in a desired direction, often to achieve a story-related goal such as saving a character or solving a murder. From a narrative perspective, this formed the frame of current visual novels.

However, it is with the release of *To Heart* and the new focus on character-based stories that the genre found its niche with *otaku* consumers and PC enthusiasts. For the first time in the *eroge* genre, the emphasis was not purely on sexual rewards, but also on the development of a romantic narrative with one of the protagonists (Miyamoto 2013). A single playthrough, if played correctly, ended up in a positive outcome with only a single female character. The game presented a more joyful story of romantic adolescent love. *To Heart* was a financial success, and since the focus on the game was not specifically on its pornographic appeal, it was possible to adapt the game for the general market to enjoy on traditional game consoles, such as the port by Aquaplus on the Sony PlayStation in 1999; this followed the trend set by other successful *eroge* such as *Dragon Knight II*, *Sotsugyou—Graduation*, and *Doukyuusei*.

With classics such as *Kanon* and *Clannad*, Leaf, and its competitor, Key, were the main representatives of the new *eroge* trend—one influenced by the sensibilities of the *otaku* market on character development and storytelling, termed the *nakige* form. The *nakige*, literally, "crying game," usually refers to a dramatic story whose purpose is to profoundly touch the user on an emotional level, usually with a bittersweet or sad ending,[2] generally using pornography as yet another connecting agent between the user and the story. While still considered adult games because of their erotic content, games in the *nakige* tradition, it is fair to say, have been able to go beyond the simple pornographic text rhetoric and also provide thought-provoking content and stories that use pornography to enhance their impact.

At the other end of the spectrum, there still exists a subgenre of *eroge* that strictly focuses on the depiction of pornography for its own sake. The entire purpose of these games, commonly called *nukige*, or "fap game," is more similar to many of the first examples of adult games from the 1980s, where sexual fantasy and the user's arousal take primacy over romance or narrative development. While some *nukige* studios can be part of the EOCS and provide content that is in compliance with their rules, other studios and publishers can market their games without the need for approval from the association, resulting in the creation of products that can be openly deviant. Lilith—founded in 2003—is one such publisher. With flagship series such as *Taimanin Asagi* (*Anti-Demon Ninja Asagi*) and *Kangoku Senkan* (*Prison Battleship*), most stories focus on the introduction of strong women characters of high social standing set against a resentful male protagonist whose sole purpose is to exact his revenge by sexually exploiting them through means of social isolation or brainwashing. While the situations depicted in such products are problematic from a moral point of view, the circulation of such games is not totally unregulated per se. Indeed, Lilith is not part of the EOCS, but the Contents Soft Association (CSA) (*contentsu sofuto kyoudoukumiai*), an alternative business cooperative association that regulates the depiction of pornographic material in PC video games, among other things such as software piracy control and business development promotion (Eizourinrikikou 2014). Integrated within the greater Motion Picture Regulation and Ethics Committee (*eizourinrikikou* or *eizourin*) since 2012, the CSA (originally *mediarinrikikou*) started to integrate PC game ethics review into their activities in 2003 when several game studios left the EOCS after disagreeing on review rules, thus breaking the EOCS monopoly on the practice (Miyamoto 2013). This focus on self-regulation and the multiplicity of moral safeguard organizations make it difficult to firmly establish where the line for moral representation of pornography lies on a national level. Indeed, with the coming of the CSA reviewing erotic content in PC games, the EOCS had to adapt stricter rules to retain association members. There is evidence that as early as 2005, the EOCS started to relax some of their regulation related to the depiction of sexual practices such as incest and bestiality, a phenomenon that further disqualifies the idea of a firm rule set for ethics review (Miyamoto 2013, 199). While there seems to be a lot of free space for studios to make games that depict problematic acts of a sexual nature, many of which present women in a demeaning way, the flexibility of a self-regulated system of ethics also allows for the creation of games that use the representation of sex in order to enhance the game experience beyond simple sexploitation.

Concluding thoughts—a difficult relationship with the international scene

As we have observed, the relationship between Japanese society and the production of erotic video games is not one that can be explained simply. Official authorities have acknowledged the presence of pornographic video games in the past, but their censorship and circulation are not subject to official regulations per se. What is also clear is that the orientation of the debates on censorship was mainly focused on preventing underage children's access to such products; fantasy-filled situations were seen as a bad influence for children whose "healthy" perception of male-female relationships would be at risk.

It is understandable that in a world where transnational circulation of cultural goods is so prevalent through official and unofficial channels, it is not possible to separate Japan's interpretation of ethics in regard to pornography from the rest of the world's. Political frictions due to differences in interpretation of moral issues, such as the one that *Rapelay* created, are more than ever bound to happen. Indeed, the reaction to the *Rapelay* controversy has been not to reinforce the guidelines in regard to pornographic content in Japanese video games but to better hide it from foreign eyes. As Illusion Soft put it, in its message to foreign customers, the games are not available in foreign countries and therefore should not be played there. The company Minori, in its statement regarding the blocking of its website to foreign Internet Protocols after the *Rapelay* debacle, explains that it is to protect freedom of speech and Japan's culture that such steps have to be taken (Ashcraft 2009). Taking a more cynical approach to the debate over the presence of Japanese *eroge* in Western countries, Tenco, the studio behind the erotic strategy RPG *Eiyuu*Senki*, published a promotional video where a fake English professor introduces the game as an imaginative strategy game with historical undertones while the Japanese subtitles transform his speech to put emphasis on the depiction of all the attractive underage girls and the arousing content that the game promises. While the joke is obviously on the discrepancies in what is being emphasized for each customer of different cultural belonging, it could also be seen as an effort to stir up pride toward the culture around *eroge* in reaction to the bad press they get in the West.

Indeed, the game was clearly marked for Japan release only, and Tenco first seems to have been very vocal about its desire not to publish the game outside Japan, sending a Digital Millennium Copyright Act letter to an unofficial translation group who wanted to make the game available to an English public (Visual Novel Translation Wiki 2013). However, further complicating the matter and emphasizing the desire for *eroge* publishers to expand their product to foreign markets, the company Fruitbat Factory, specialized in localizing Japanese indie games, announced in May 2014 that they were bringing *Eiyuu Senki* to North America and Europe for the PlayStation 3 (Elonen 2014).

It is this very internationalization of Japan's cultural products and the foreign pressure to reform moral boundaries in pornographic representation that seems to be the next challenge for Japan's *eroge* industry, an element that has never been brought up before the *Rapelay* controversy. While for some the issue of foreign pressure to regulate pornographic games more strongly is akin to a new form of cultural colonization, to which the proper reply is isolationism, others see this newly born interest as a business opportunity. Indeed, Jast and Nitroplus, through their international distribution companies Jast USA and Mangagamers.com, are relatively new players that seem to tap into the foreign erotic game market while taking the opportunity to shape public perception on Japanese pornographic games in a way that better takes account of the mainstream production of *eroge*.

Indeed, not all games of this genre are problematic, and the most popular ones are not really discussed in Western media, presumably because their content is no more questionable than pornographic or erotic material made in the United States. By controlling the flow of circulation of those products outside Japan, then, it is probable that representative products from those companies might be able to attain a more prominent position in the discourse surrounding erotic games, avoiding many of the misunderstandings that characterized the media outrage of *Rapelay*. While this game features themes that are very much questionable from a moral standpoint, reducing the production of erotic games in Japan to *Rapelay*—with headlines such as "Why Would *Rapelay* Thrive in Japan?"—is also problematic and misleading. Deeper knowledge of the context pertaining to these games, as well as close readings of their content, is needed to better understand how these games are produced, marketed, and consumed.

Notes

1 For further discussions on the *lolicon* phenomenon, please refer to Kinsella (1998) and Lam (2010).
2 This is why it is also known as *utsuge*, or "depressing game".

References

Alexander, Leigh. 2009. "And You Thought Grand Theft Auto Was Bad: Should the United States Ban a Japanese 'Rape Simulator' Game?" *Slate*, March 9. http://www.slate.com/articles/technology/gaming/2009/03/and_you_thought_grand_theft_auto_was_bad.html.

Allison, Anne. 1996. *Permitted and Prohibited Desires: Mothers, Comics, and Censorship in Japan*. Berkeley: University of California Press.

Ashcraft, Brian. 2009. "Erotic Game Developer Explains Foreign Access Web Blocking." *Kotaku*, June 26. http://kotaku.com/5302747/erotic-game-developer-explains-foreign-access-web-blocking.

Ashcraft, Brian. 2010. "Why Is CNN Talking About Rapelay?" *Kotaku*, March 31. http://kotaku.com/5506016/why-is-cnn-talking-about-rapelay.

Chalk, Andy. 2009. "'Rape Game' on Amazon Triggers Anger, Outrage." *The Escapist Magazine*, February 12. http://www.escapistmagazine.com/news/view/89398-Rape-Game-On-Amazon-Triggers-Anger-Outrage/.

da Silva, Joaquín. 2009. "Obscenity and Article 175 of the Japanese Penal Code: A Short Introduction to Japanese Censorship." April 21. http://redsiglo21.com/eiga9/articulos/obscenity.html.

Eizourinrikikou. 2014. "Eizourinrikikou kihon koudo." http://eizorin.or.jp/eizorin/rules/kihon.html.

Elonen, Jakke. 2014. "Fruitbat Factory to Localize Eiyuu Senki for PS3." *Fruitbat Factory*, May 6. http://blog.fruitbatfactory.com/2014/05/06/fruitbat-factory-to-localize-eiyuu-senki-for-ps3/.

EOCS. 2013a. "Honjin gaiyou—mokuteki to kigyou." (Summary of Corporate Body—Organization and Objectives). Ethics Organization of Computer Software. http://www.sofurin.org/htm/about/purpose.htm.

EOCS. 2013b. "Honjin gaiyou—reitingu shoukai." (Summary of Corporate Body—Introduction to the Rating System). Ethics Organization of Computer Software. http://www.sofurin.org/htm/about/rating.html.

Galbraith, Patrick. 2010. "Akihabara: Conditioning a Public 'Otaku' Image." *Mechademia* 5: 210–30.

Geemu Hihyou. 1994. "H geemu no tsumi to batsu." (H-Games' Sins and Punishments). *Geemu Hihyou*, 2. Tokyo: Micro design shuppankyoku.

IANS. 2010. "Argentina Bans Japanese Rape Video Game." *The Gaea Times*, April 20. http://law.gaeatimes.com/2010/04/20/argentina-bans-japanese-rape-video-game-21608/.

Japan National Diet. 1986. "Dai hyaku nana kai kokkai kessan i'inkan dai ichi go." (First Meeting of the 107th Members' Committee of the Balance of Account of the National Diet). *Kokkaikaigisen kensa shisutemu*, October 21. Transcript. http://kokkai.ndl.go.jp/SENTAKU/syugiin/107/0410/10710210410001a.html.

Katou, Hiroyasu. 2011. *Geemu centaa bunkaron: media shakai no comunikeshon* (Treatise on the Culture of Game Centers: The Communication of Media Society). Tokyo: Shinsensha.

Kinsella, Sharon. 1998. "Japanese Subculture in the 1990s: *Otaku* and the Amateur Manga Movement." *Journal of Japanese Studies* 24 (2): 289–316.

Kinsella, Sharon. 2000. *Adult Manga: Culture and Power in Contemporary Japanese Society*. Honolulu: University of Hawaii Press.

Lah, Kyung. 2010a. "'RapeLay' Video Game Goes Viral Amid Outrage." *CNN.com*, March 31. http://www.cnn.com/2010/WORLD/asiapcf/03/30/japan.video.game.rape/.

Lah, Kyung. 2010b. "Why Would *Rapelay* Thrive in Japan?" *CNN.com*, April 2. http://edition.cnn.com/2010/WORLD/asiapcf/04/02/rapelay.japan/index.html.

Lam, Fan-Yi. 2010. "Comic Market: How the World's Biggest Amateur Comic Fair Shaped Japanese Doujinshi Culture." *Mechademia* 5: 232–48.

Miyamoto, Naoki. 2013. *Eroge—bunka kenkyuu gairon (Adult Games: Introduction to Cultural Studies)*. Tokyo: Sougou kagaku shuppan.

Natsui, Takato. 2001. "Dennou gakuen shinario ichi baajon ni jiken dai ichiban hanketsu." *MeijiUniversity*, April 3. http://www.isc.meiji.ac.jp/~sumwel_h/doc/juris/.

Parsons, Zack. 2007. "Rapelay." *Something Awful*, January 25. http://www.
somethingawful.com/hentai-game-reviews/rapelay/.

Reist, Melinda Tankard. 2009. *Getting Real: Challenging the Sexualisation of Girls*.
North Melbourne: Spinifex Press.

Visual Novel Translation Wiki.2013. "Eiyuu Senki" http://tlwiki.org/index.
php?title=Eiyuu_Senki.

Zigfried. 2006. "Rapelay (PC) Review." *Honest Gamers*, May 27. http://www.
honestgamers.com/4775/pc/rapelay/review.html.

Games cited

Chunsoft. 1986. *Dragon Quest*. Enix.

Chunsoft. 1994. *Kamaitachi no yoru*. Chunsoft.

Chunsoft. 1992. *Otogirisou*. Chunsoft.

Elf. 1992. *Doukyuusei*. Elf.

Elf. 1990. *Dragon Knight II*. Elf.

Enix Corporation. 1983. *Lolita Syndrome*. Enix Corporation.

Enix Corporation. 1983. *Marichan kiken ippatsu*. Enix Corporation.

FairyTale. 1991. *Saori—Bishoujo-tachi no yakata*. FairyTale.

Gainax. 1990. *Dennou gakuen Scenario I Ver2.0*. Gainax.

Headroom. 1992. *Sotsugyou—Graduation*. Japan Home Video.

Headroom. 1994. *Sotsugyou 2~Neo Generation~*. Riverhill Soft.

Hudson Soft. 1981. *Yakyuken*. Hudson Soft.

Illusion Soft. 2006. *Rapelay*. Illusion Soft.

Key. 2004. *Clannad*. Visual Arts.

Key. 1999. *Kanon*. Visual Arts.

Kōei. 1985. *Danchi tsuma no yuuwaku*. Kōei.

Kōei. 1997. *Dynasty Warriors*. Kōei.

Kōei. 1984. *My Lolita*. Kōei.

Kōei. 1982. *Night Life*. Kōei.

Kōei. 1983. *Nobunaga's Ambition*. Kōei.

Kōei. 1984. *Oranda tsuma wa denki unagi no yume wo miru ka?* Kōei.

Leaf. 1996. *Kizuato*. Leaf.

Leaf. 1996. *Shizuku*. Aquaplus.

Leaf. 1997. *To Heart*. Aquaplus.

Lilith. 2007. *Kangoku Senkan*. Lilith.

Lilith. 2005. *Taimanin*. Lilith.

Macadamia Soft. 1986. *177*. Macadamia Soft.

Mystique. 1982. *Custer's Revenge*. Mystique.

Nihon Falcom. 1983. *Joshi daisei private*. Nihon Falcom.

Nihon Falcom. 1987. *Ys*. Nihon Falcom.

Sir-Tech. 1981. *Wizardry*. Sir-Tech.

Tenco. 2012. *Eiyuu*Senki*. Tenco.

X Shitei. 1991. *Dragon City X Shitei*. FairyTale.

3

Assuring quality: Early 1990s Nintendo censorship and the regulation of queer sexuality and gender

Evan W. Lauteria (University of California, Davis, USA)

In the late 1980s and early 1990s, Japanese video game producers and developers largely dominated the console-based gaming market in the United States. Classic video game series from *Super Mario Bros* to *Final Fantasy* were staples of American console gaming culture. Notably, however, these games do not immediately conjure up images of their Japanese origins. Mario's status as an Italian plumber and *Final Fantasy*'s iconographic roots in Tolkienesque and *Dungeons and Dragons* genre fantasy reflect Japanese design and marketing practices that yield "culturally odorless" artifacts through *dochakuka* or "glocalization" (Iwabuchi 2002; Robertson 1995). That is,

> [Japanese products], in contrast to American export icons, such as Coca-Cola or McDonald's, do not immediately conjure images of the country of origin in the minds of the consumers. . . . Japanese cultural industries tend to be less concerned with the direct exporting of Japanese cultural products than with selling the know-how of "indigenizing" the West, particularly America. (Iwabuchi 2002, 256)

The practices and applications of glocalization with regard to Japanese video games, however, are varied and, as I argue in the course of this chapter, have changed over time. Indeed, according to Carlson and Corliss (2011), "the day-to-day work of localizers typically involves a much more nuanced negotiation of contradictions, dilemmas, and interests" (65). That is, globalization of popular culture, as it occurs and is managed at the local level, involves an interplay of institutional power and individual action grappling with issues common to translation and transnational exchange—incommensurability, cultural views of respectability, and institutional variation in censorship and distribution.

Regarding translation, however, games offer issues that are different from those offered by televisual or novelistic media. While "accurate" translations are committed to "fidelity"—truthful representation of the original—this fidelity is in the context of representational language. That is, translations are designed to reflect the verbal/written meaning of the original with minimal deviation. Fidelity in game translation is, however, about fidelity to gameplay experience, not to linguistic commensurability (Mangiron and O'Hagan 2006, 12). Thus, localizers tend to take linguistic liberty perhaps less commonly taken in purely visual, written, or auditory media in an effort to facilitate gameplay rather than audiovisual meaning-making. Players must be able to traverse the game as text; its ergodic features, to borrow the language of Aarseth (1997), mandate a different orientation to meaning-making across regional difference. This, combined with the technological basis of video games—that is, that their coding produces a more malleable final product than traditional film—produces a field of translation practice that necessitates different kinds of translation choices from industries, their organizations, and their employees. Video game localizers are confronted with choices that may otherwise not be choices under a more typical translational rubric of linguistic commensurability versus fidelity alone. For example, Di Marco (2007) highlights the case of *Fatal Frame*, wherein US and European localization changed the physical makeup of the protagonist Miku to better facilitate gameplay based on cultural expectations of womanhood, age, and the horror genre. Because players must adopt roles in order to traverse the text—in this case, the role of the protagonist—the localization process must account for cultural difference to secure the possibility of such role adoption.

As suggested by Di Marco's study, this focus on commensurable play over representational fidelity comes at a cost. Cultural constructions of gender, sexuality, and nation become expendable when lacking an immediate "gloss" or sociolinguistic equivalent when shipped across the Pacific. This becomes particularly troublesome for queer gender and sexuality, which are both contestable in a "children's medium" in the context of the United States and vary widely by distinctly local, cultural imaginings of sex and sexuality. While in the United States, queerness is often neatly divided into sexual orientation (lesbian, gay, bisexual) and gender identity (transgender, or trans*), such a division is not so clear in the Japanese context. Terms such as *gei boi, danshō,* and *okama,* all of which denote gender nonconforming men or trans* folks who have sex with men (McLelland 2004), are not able to so distinctly divide sex, sexuality, and gender; nor does "gay" or "trans*" effectively encompass their meanings in Japanese. Indeed, in his analysis of Flea in *Chrono Trigger,* Michael P. Williams suggests that *okama* alone "can mean anything from a careless synonym for 'gay,' to a man in women's clothing exhibiting stereotypically effeminate mannerisms. Often these two concepts are conflated" (2014, 72–73). This is to say nothing of the performative dimensions of *okama,* which, as described in Williams' analysis, rely on particular linguistic referents and use of feminine first-person pronouns like *atashi* or *atai,* none of which have equivalents in English.

Video game localization practices, which have to confront these problems of incommensurability even as they attempt to sidestep them, illuminate the politics of globalization, the resilient power of local culture, and the social and institutional forces that structure and organize transnational popular culture production, regulation, and distribution. In the context of gender, sex, and sexuality, approaches adopted by localizers highlight the structuring forces that limit and confine, but also permit, queer representation in video games. To that end, this chapter turns to two cases of video game translation and localization for the Super Nintendo Entertainment System, focusing on the exclusion and inclusion, respectively, of two transgender women characters: (1) Poison in Capcom's *Final Fight*; and (2) Flea in Square's *Chrono Trigger.* In this analysis, I suggest that glocalization practices, especially translation and localization of video games, and the organizations that utilize those practices for market gains, are shaped by social-structural forces, particularly industry regulation and perceptions of national cultures. It is my hope that, through analysis of these two cases, this chapter offers game studies scholars interested in representation, particularly queer representation, a beginning argument for the importance of the production of cultural perspective within sociology for examining sex, gender, and sexuality in video game content.

A brief history of Japanese video games

The history of video games is a complex tale of the production of technologies for military force, market rises and failures, and the spread of transnational popular culture exchange. Many scholars address the shared history of video game production and military technology at length (Crogan 2011; Mead 2013), and these scholars suggest that the military-industrial-entertainment complex is a mutually constitutive system best evidenced by video games. From military scenarios to the very dynamics of all video games as "simulations," there is ample evidence that video games are intimately tied to military technology.

An overemphasis on this point, however, obfuscates the rise and fall of the American video game market in the 1980s. There is a point of sudden rupture in the Atari-led industry that complicates the relationship between military technology and video game enterprise, if only because it is the US military that is regularly cited as the source of these technological innovations in the absence of other military powers. Dyer-Witheford and de Peuter (2009) recount the abrupt change in the North American video game market in their introduction to *Games of Empire*:

In 1983, the mix of incompetent management, employee discontent, overproduction, and rampant piracy exploded. When Atari failed to reach projected profits, its stock fell—and the company abruptly plunged toward bankruptcy. It carried with it the entire industry it had previously drawn upward on its ascent . . . the North American game industry annihilated itself in one of the most complete sectoral disasters of recent business industry. (13)

Why, exactly, is this a moment of disconnect between American military and the video game industry? Because the market is quickly taken over by game designers and producers in Japan, a country without a standing army in need of military technologies or a militarized citizenry. Indeed, the very *kinds* of game developed by Japanese designers changed the market substantially.

Japan's game artistry transformed the new media. U.S. games, made primarily by computer scientists and engineers, had created lively, diagrammatic worlds of stick-figure shooters, mazes, sports, and puzzles. But from the moment of *Pac-Man*, the first game with an identifiable *character*, Japanese developers added something else: graphics and narrative. These images and stories came from a distinct tradition: *manga*— broadly, Japanese comics. (15; italics in original)

While Dyer-Witheford and de Peuter suggest that "the irony of U.S.-Japanese postwar relations was that the defeated culture excelled in adopting the victors' techno-cultural innovations" (215), this adoption was a complicated reworking of Japanese popular culture into an American video game market. Similarly, Chris Kohler (2005) argues that the insertion of cinematic elements, particularly nongamic cutscenes, distinguishes today's video games from early ones, and that these began with Japanese video games such as *Final Fantasy*. By producing games that have characters rather than just first-person scenarios, Japanese designers solidified the capacity of video games to be both representational and simulative media rather than simply (dis)embodied technological simulators.

This distinction between American simulations and Japanese manga-infused representational games is perhaps a bit misleading, however. Unlike home console systems, which allow consumers to purchase cartridges or cassettes in order to play new games on the same system, arcade machines often tie their software directly to their hardware, limiting the malleability of the physical device. "Conversion kits" or "mod kits" were designed by some companies to alter arcade games in a way that made them seem new, often altering the gameplay of other companies' products to create an entirely new (or seemingly new) game. General Computer Corp (GCC) developed such enhancements, but after an out-of-court settlement with Atari for making these enhancements without permission, GCC sold their then-in-development enhancement to *Pac-Man* to Midway, a licensee of Japan's *Pac-Man* production company, Namco. This new game, originally titled *Crazy Otto*, was released in US arcades in 1982 as "*Ms. Pac-Man*." Even prior to the decline of Atari and an American-dominated market, Japanese companies held notable influence on the American scene, and their collaboration—sometimes unintended—with American producers was not unheard of.

By contrast, video game companies such as Capcom and Square attempted to stick to a mostly-Japanese employee base in the 1980s and early 1990s, either sending Japanese managers and employees overseas to the United States or only hiring American marketers and quality assurance testers in the US companies left to do the work of programming, design, and translation in Japan. Indeed, even a company like Namco treated its relationships with its licensees like Midway as unidirectional; despite the market success of *Pac-Man* in both Japan and the United States, the American-produced *Ms. Pac-Man* and the later *Jr. Pac-Man* never made it across the Pacific.

Tracking changes: Two cases

These employment and distribution trends, however, changed by 1995. And my goal here is to track, at least partially, the causes of such changes. As mentioned before, this chapter addresses two cases—the production and localization of *Final Fight* and *Chrono Trigger*—with particular respect to their transgender characters. I stumbled across *Final Fight* as a result of another project I proposed earlier in graduate school. That project was initially aimed at illustrating the limits of discourse surrounding how "inclusive" BioWare games like *Dragon Age* or *Mass Effect* are because they have queer romance options. Driven by an interest in content analysis of queer content in a large swath of the game market, I attempted to code gamic and representational features of games to analyze queer inclusion by genre, region, and console over time. But I hit a brick wall with all of this when trying to grapple with one of the earliest characters in particular: Poison.

Poison is a low-ranking enemy character in Capcom's 1989 arcade game *Final Fight* and is arguably (and I'm arguing "for") a transgender character. While not the first trans* video game character to appear in the United States from Japan, Poison is controversial among American audiences because of the ambiguity and unknowable-ness about her persona. This unknowable-ness, perhaps, began with the erasure of her character and her palette-swap Roxy from the US Super Nintendo console versions of *Final Fight*. While Poison appeared in the arcade version of the game in 1989, she and Roxy are replaced by visually/presumably male characters Sid and Billy in the Super Nintendo port in 1991 (Figure 3.1).

By contrast, Flea, or "Mayone" in Japanese, in the 1995 American localization of Square's *Chrono Trigger* does not undergo the same sort of editing process between her Japanese and US appearances. While Ted Woolsey, the primary translator for *Chrono Trigger*, did change her name and the order of her speech (more on this later), she still appears in the Super Nintendo game and, indeed, addresses her gender outright (Figure 3.2). While *Final Fight* and *Chrono Trigger* differ in terms of genre, production company, and year of release, Poison and Flea share many commonalties: they are both

Roxy & Poison **Billy & Sid**
(Arcade, 1989 & SFC, 1990) **(Super Nintendo, 1991)**

FIGURE 3.1 *Poison & Roxy's Replacements*, Final Fight, *Capcom.*

FIGURE 3.2 *Flea addresses gender,* Chrono Trigger, *Squaresoft.*

named, but relatively unimportant enemy characters, and they share many physical features—pink hair, relatively revealing clothing, and names that echo the "culturally odorless" approach to global(izing) Japanese pop culture. Further, both games were released on the same console: the Super Nintendo Entertainment System. What, then, caused these changes in translation and localization practice? What sort of structuring features of the sociocultural context produced two starkly different outcomes between 1991 and 1995?

Poison: Nintendo censorship and gender

Drawing on limited historical and archival data, we are forced to rely on largely secondhand accounts of the production and localization processes for *Final Fight* and *Chrono Trigger.* Sheff (1993), however, attempted to paint a picture of the Japanese video game industry in the late 1980s and early 1990s through interviews with game designers, producers, and marketers. Regarding Poison and Roxy,

> When a Capcom USA representative suggested that it was tasteless to have the game's hero beat up a woman, a Japanese game designer responded that there were no women in the game. "What about the blonde named Roxy?" the American asked. The designer responded, "Oh, you mean the transvestite!" Roxy was given a haircut and new clothes. (225)

Nothing in the context of the video game itself suggests Poison or Roxy are transgender. Indeed, aside from their visual representations—as women—there is no indication as to their gender. They do not speak, nor does the game itself provide any background information for game enemies.

Table 3.1 Poison's character profile included in the Japanese Super Famicom *Final Fight* instruction manual. Translation is mine, with generous help from fellow sociologist Yuko Fujino.

■ ＰＯＩＳＯＮ（ポイズン）
身長：１７５ｃｍ　　　　体重：５２ｋｇ　　　　ニューハーフ
Ｂ８８・Ｗ６６・Ｈ８９。ロサンゼルスの孤児院で育つ。美容のためにも闘いはやめられないと彼？は考える。フライドポテトが好物。
■ POISON (Poison)
Height: 175cm　　　　Weight: 52kg　　　　New-Half
Bust 88 · Waist 66 · Hips 89. Poison grew up in an orphanage in Los Angeles. Poison thinks that he(?) can't stop fighting, even for the sake of being beautiful. French fries are Poison's favorite food.

Poison's status as a ニューハーフ or "new-half," a Japanese-English neologism term to collectively refer to male-to-female transgender women in Japan (McLelland 2004), is only revealed to the player through the instructional manual included with the Japanese Super Famicom version of *Final Fight* (Table 3.1). This, in part, explains why Poison is visible in the game when it was originally shipped to US arcades. No such instruction manual was included with the arcade machines; prior to its home release in 1990, there was no public, written indication that Poison was transgender.

But it is the phrasing of the Capcom USA representative's statement that is most striking. While Sheff's tale suggests that Roxy—and thus Poison, as well—were removed in their entirety once they were "outed" as transgender, the initial concern that sparked this conversation was over violence against women. Why, then, would this issue not have arisen during the arcade localization of the game? The primary difference between the arcade and console version is, quite obviously, the hardware used to play it: an arcade machine versus the Super Nintendo Entertainment System. Nintendo in the 1980s and 1990s had a particularly strict censorship policy for any games made by third-party vendors, and Capcom was subject, then, to this policy when moving the game from its own arcade machines to Nintendo's hardware.

Brathwaite (2007) outlines Nintendo's censorship guidelines in her game design book *Sex in Video Games*. Drawing on the 1993 Congressional hearings regarding video games, Brathwaite suggests that "other video game hardware makers such as Atari and Sega had seen their systems attracting games with increasingly sexual and violent content. By creating its 'Seal of Quality' and adopting content standards, Nintendo hoped to reassure customers of both the playability and suitability of its games" (132). Brathwaite goes on to cite the summary of the censorship policy delivered by Nintendo of America's vice-president, Howard Lincoln, though this summary was truncated for the hearings. Schwartz and Schwartz (1994) provide a more thorough account of the censorship policy. The guidelines, as they relate to sex, sexuality, and gender, were as follows:

> Nintendo of America's priority is to deliver high quality video game entertainment for our customers. When those customers are children, parental involvement in their game playing is recommended. Nintendo is concerned that our products do not contain material that society as a whole deems unacceptable.
>
> Consequently, since 1988 we have consistently tested the content of all games developed for Nintendo systems against our evolving game standards. As our business has matured, we have adapted our guidelines to meet the concerns of the members of our target age group and their parents. Although we realize that definitions of social, cultural and political views are highly subjective, we will continue to provide consumers with entertainment that reflects the acceptable norms of society.
>
> The following Game Content Guidelines are presented for assistance in the development of authorized game paks[1] (i.e., both Nintendo and licensee game paks) by defining the type of content and themes inconsistent with Nintendo's corporate and marketing philosophy. Although exceptions may be made to preserve the content of a game, Nintendo will not approve games for the NES, Game Boy or Super NES systems (i.e., audio-visual work, packaging, and instruction manuals) which:
>
> - include sexually suggestive or explicit content including rape and/or nudity; (1)
> - contain language or depiction which specifically denigrates members of either sex; (2)
>
>   . . .
>
> - depict domestic violence and/or abuse; (5)
>
>   . . .
>
> - reflect ethnic, religious, nationalistic, or sexual stereotypes of language; this includes symbols that are related to any type of racial, religious, nationalistic, or ethnic group, such as crosses, pentagrams, God, Gods (Roman mythological gods are acceptable), Satan, hell, Buddha; (7) (23–4)

One might assume that the emphasis on cultural and social acceptability would, given the climate regarding gender and sexuality and panic over children and pedophilia in the United States in the late 1980s and early 1990s, result in the removal of Poison from the game. But it is only guideline 5—domestic violence or abuse—that might have informed the Capcom USA representative's concerns regarding violence against women directly. And such concerns seem strange, given that *Final Fight* was originally designed to be a sequel to *Street Fighter*, a series that by the same year as *Final Fight's* Super Nintendo port first featured well-known female fighter Chun-Li.

Games journalists and fans have suggested that Capcom Japan made Poison transgender in the hopes of dodging the potential problem of Nintendo of America's strict and unwavering censorship policy, in particular number 5— that domestic violence and/or abuse were not permitted in what Nintendo envisioned as a "children's medium." It is possible, then, that Capcom Japan, wrapped up in the spectacle politics of the "new-half" that did not acknowledge those folks as "real women," made Poison transgender with the expectation that would sidestep the concerns that Capcom USA had about hitting a woman. Obviously, this failed to account for the social and cultural climate regarding transgender folks in the United States, and such an approach—if the tale is correct—backfired substantially.

Japanese data, however, does not support this claim. In numerous design documents and magazine articles, Poison's gender—new-half—is not ambiguous. It is quite clear that from the start that Poison was designed to appeal to a rising Japanese fascination with the spectacle of the new-half, which had gained media popularity in the 1980s (McLelland 2004). But both Sheff's account and the journalist/fan hypothesis regarding Poison's gender hold weight in the context of other game designers' frustrations over the Nintendo of America policies. For instance, the port of Lucas Arts' *Maniac Mansion* from the PC to the Nintendo Entertainment System in 1990 offers a prolific case of Nintendo cracking down strongly on censorship. Douglas Crockford, responsible for the technical aspects of moving the game to the Nintendo hardware, chronicled his frustration with Nintendo's nit-picking and often unexplained concerns with *Maniac Mansion's* content. Crockford expressed immense frustration with the expectations of Nintendo, which resulted in the removal of any statue or painting with a woman in a reclining pose, among many other changes (see Figure 3.3). He recalls the experience:

> The statue was a classical reclining nude. I told one of the Nintendo minions that it was a Michelangelo (the sculptor, not the turtle). There was a glimmer of hope that we could keep it if it was really art, so I sent Gary to find a book of Michelangelo's work, in the hope that he had made a statue that was similar. In fact he had, a work called *Dawn*, for the Medici Chapel.

FIGURE 3.3 *Classical reclining nude statue in* Maniac Mansion, *removed as per the feedback provided by Nintendo of America's censorship team.*

Nintendo's minions said we could keep the statue if we did something about the crotch. But if they could see pubic hair where there is none, what would they see if we tried to hide it?

We removed the statue.

So, the story behind Poison may have played out as such: Capcom Japan was aware of the limitations placed on the game industry in the United States under Nintendo's censorship policy. By fan and journalistic accounts, Poison was made transgender to bypass such policy; the solution was to design the only "female" characters in the game as "male" new-halfs: fully feminine in appearance, but categorically able to bypass Nintendo of America's domestic violence censorship policy given the gendered ideologies surrounding what counts as domestic violence. More likely, however, Poison was imagined as a new-half much earlier on in the design process, and Japan's own understandings of gender and sexuality rendered her gender expression and identity incommensurable with Nintendo of America's censorship policy. Despite Capcom USA's knowledge of Nintendo of America's strict guidelines, the cultural differences between Japan and the United States regarding transgender folks resulted in her elimination from the Super Nintendo Entertainment System console port of *Final Fight*. In place of Poison and her palette-swap Roxy, Capcom USA's localizers and quality assurance teams inserted Billy and Sid, and any character profiles at all were purged from the American *Final Fight* instruction manual. In an effort to "assure quality" under Nintendo's guidelines, transgender representation was not permitted.

Flea: Square shifts localization practices

The disconnect between Capcom Japan and Capcom USA in the above scenario is reflective of another Japanese game company's translation and localization snafu: Square's American release of *Final Fantasy IV* as *Final Fantasy II*. Though Square had already released a handful of games in the United States, including the original *Final Fantasy* in 1990, Square did not set up a substantial localization team or process in the United States by 1992. According to Ted Woolsey, primary translator for Square for their releases from 1993 to 1996,

> They really didn't have one [a localization process]. They had a person who spoke some English and she did her best with *Final Fantasy II*, which was her game. I didn't have a chance to work on that game. When I talked to the guys that [sic] hired me, the senior VP and then the finance guy, they basically had spent some 24-hour blocks of time late into the evenings, trying to rewrite the text as best they could without ever having played the game. (2007)

Final Fantasy II's manual, in-game text, and overall narrative are, at times, incomprehensible. Woolsey highlights a typo in the game manual in this same interview where the casting of magic is referred to as "blows wizard." These translation and localization problems seem to emerge, by Woolsey's story, from the organizational structure of Square in Japan and the United States. Localization and translation were conducted by the Japanese side of the firm, with quality assurance, marketing, and related finance housed in the United States. This same sort of organizational structure would have facilitated the misunderstanding at Capcom during *Final Fight*'s localization, as hypothesized above. That is, the American teams of these companies had little say in the translation work conducted in Japan, but were tasked with adherence to Nintendo of America's censorship policies and general quality assurance of the product. This created a situation wherein editing of the code itself—as in the removal of Poison and Roxy—would be necessary.

Ted Woolsey was hired for Square as a translator following the failures of the *Final Fantasy II* translation. Woolsey suggested that Hironobu Sakaguchi, creator of the *Final Fantasy* series, took the problems of *Final Fantasy II*'s English script as evidence of a necessary reorganization of the company's localization team and strategies. And, indeed, Woolsey's hiring marked the first time an American would work on the localization side of Square's game production. Woolsey and a handful of other Americans were hired to translate games such as *Final Fantasy III*, *Secret of Mana*, and, importantly for this study, *Chrono Trigger*.

While *Secret of Mana* was translated as a team effort, Sakaguchi put Woolsey to work on *Chrono Trigger* alone following his speedy and legible translation of *Final Fantasy III*. During his work on *Final Fantasy III*, Woolsey developed some translation techniques that would later become the industry standard, appropriately named "Woolseyisms." For instance, in *Final Fantasy III's* Japanese release as *Final Fantasy VI*, the main character was named "Tina"; Woolsey presumed the name sounded mysterious and foreign to a Japanese audience, and so, in turn, named her localized counterpart "Terra" to evoke a similar sentiment in American players. The focus was on experiential fidelity rather than linguistic fidelity. Square was interested in maintaining a gameplay experience rather than just a narrative or plot-based one. These techniques figured heavily in Woolsey's translation of *Chrono Trigger*. So while Poison vanishes from her localized game, Flea, a minor antagonist in the context of the entire *Chrono Trigger* narrative, appears twice in the game with minimal alteration from her original Japanese manifestation as "Mayone."

Woolsey employed his translation strategies oriented toward "experience" in some important ways, which shaped how Flea came to be represented within the game space. First, *Chrono Trigger* is the first and, to my knowledge, only video game produced by Square to feature character design and artwork by Akira Toriyama of *Dragonball* fame. Toriyama often found it humorous to name human and humanoid characters after English names for food and condiments, and so Woolsey opted to rename Flea from her original Japanese name "Mayone" (for Mayonnaise) alongside her allies Ozzie and Slash (Vinegar and Soisō, or Soy Sauce, respectively). In lieu of condiment-based names, the American localization features 1980s rock references. This did cause Woolsey's translation to lose some linguistic features unique to the Japanese version. For instance, Mayone ends most of her statements with "ヨネ〜" or "yo-né~," both as a sociolinguistic means of denoting her "cuteness" (a performance of gender attributed to new-half expression) and as a reference to her name "Ma-Yo-Né." There is, however, no direct equivalent to this in English language.

Second, and more importantly for this study, Woolsey reordered the grammatical and paragraphic structure of Flea's dialogue with the player's party to bypass some more subtle references to Flea's gender or the Japanese "new-half" identity category (Table 3.2). The sentences of line number 4, Frog's line of dialogue in this selection from the script, are ordered differently in the Japanese and American versions. In Japanese, Frog's comment "She's

Table 3.2 Comparison of Japanese versus American script for Flea, *Chrono Trigger*, Square.

Translation of Original Japanese	Woolsey's English-translated American Script
[Mayone] Hu, hu, here, here...	[Flea] Mwa ha . . . Here, over here . . .
[Mayone] Give it up, Frog-chan!	[Flea] Giving up, little tadpole?!
Lucca: Who're you!?	Lucca: Hey! Who ARE you?!
Frog: Don't get careless! This one's the Void Mage Mayone! She's not a normal woman.	Frog: Keep your guard up! This is no ordinary woman! Meet Flea, the magician!
Mayone: Mukiiii! Anyhow, I'm a guy!	Flea: What the . . .?! Hey, I'm a GUY!
Lucca: Geh! A guy, YOU!?	Lucca: Say what?! That's a guy?!
Mayone: *giggle*, but male, female, either way, the strong are beauuuutiful.	Flea: Male . . . female . . . what's the difference? Power is beautiful, and I've got the power!
Translation from Chrono Compendium (http://www.chronocompendium. com/Term/Retranslation.html)	

not a normal woman" hails Mayone's response, "Mukiiii! Anyhow, I'm a guy!," which interpolates "normal" in Frog's dialogue as a comment on normative gender. In English, however, "This is no ordinary woman" hails the following sentence "Meet Flea, the magician," and "normal" becomes interpolated as "nonmagical." Her magical abilities, rather than her gender or sex, are rendered suspect. This sets up Flea as a feminine man rather than a transgender woman, potentially dodging the issues Capcom USA dealt with by means of altogether erasure. In the context of game translation, this technique still facilitates gameplay, as Mayone and Flea both employ confusion-oriented magic spells in the battle following this banter. That is, both confusion regarding her gender and Frog's warning regarding her magic inform the player of strategies to use in the following battle, even if the representational logic of why such a strategy might be necessary differs by version.

Conclusions

What we find with Flea, then, is an altogether different approach to translation and localization than the techniques employed by Capcom just four years prior. The restructuring of Square's organization and its orientation toward localization in 1994 and 1995, which I suggest are different than Capcom's in 1991, facilitated a type of "glocalization" that was more capable of adhering to the goal of a "culturally odorless" product, ironically, perhaps, through the hiring and privileging of culturally-informed "locals" like Ted Woolsey. Partly in response to the demands placed upon companies through a culturally-specific censorship policy like Nintendo of America's "Seal of Quality" standard, businesses like Square shifted their orientation toward glocalization practices in an effort to improve them. In response, the image of the "new-half" goes from complete erasure in the American localization of *Final Fight* to a subtle and more nuanced linguistic reconfiguration in *Chrono Trigger*.

This chapter works with limited data on a very small number of cases, however. In terms of transgender characters in Japanese-to-English video games, only one other character—Birdo from *Super Mario Bros 2*—might be included in the population of cases before 1998. Adding in queer characters only brings the potential number of cases to between five and seven, depending on the parameters defining the population. As such, further research beyond the scope of these cases is necessary to make a more general claim about localization, translation, and marketing practices in the context of the early 1990s video game market and queer representation. What I have proposed here, though, is that glocalization is a changing process and that Japanese companies responded to their social, cultural, and environmental conditions in shaping that process. And, further, queerness and its representations are inherently bound up in those conditions and that process. Indeed, both Poison and Flea make subsequent appearances in other Capcom and Square games, respectively, indicating a potential trend toward "inclusive" glocalization (as opposed to "exclusive," or the erasure measure used for Poison originally).

But I do not wish to suggest that Woolsey's translation techniques, though facilitated by organization responses to environmental factors, were uniquely responsible for this change. Alongside Woolsey's initial hire, the 1993 Congressional hearings yielded a standardized rating system for video games known as the Electronic Software Rating Board (ESRB), still in place today. While Nintendo maintained a particularly strict censorship policy even after the establishment of a standardized rating system, the establishment of the ESRB potentially afforded game designers a comparative policy upon which to argue for the inclusion of particular content in their games. Indeed, this may have softened concerns about the inclusion of a new-half character like Flea, whereas that was not an option for Capcom USA when thinking about Poison.

What this and my sample suggest is that further research is necessary. O'Hagan (2009a, b, 2012) leads the charge on examining video game translation at the contours of video game studies. She argues that "the study on the reception of localized games will contribute fresh insights into game studies, which is currently largely limited to a single language mode. The focus on the localization process of Japanese games is productive in bringing in fresh perspectives to broaden the horizons of games studies" (2009a, 161). Such studies illuminate the cultural expectations of game design and marketing, the nature of games as playable, and the ways in which globalization and cosmopolitanism are at work in game localization. Indeed, Consalvo (2012) argues a similar point, illustrating that Japanese video game fandom amongst non-Japanese players is indicative of, and productive of, contemporary cosmopolitanism and transnational cultural flows. In this sense, scholarly work on games translation and localization has much to say about the contemporary condition of video games, especially with regard to queer representation and inclusion across national boundaries.

This chapter, however, emphasized the sociocultural conditions under which translation and localization occur. To properly and effectively come to understand queer representation in video games—that is, how sex, sexuality, and gender manifest within industry-produced video games—we as scholars must adopt a production of culture perspective that accounts for censorship policy, company organizational structures, and translation practice. With Poison and Flea, such terrain changed rapidly over the course of half a decade, and, as I have argued, those changes yielded quite different results. Further research on queerness, even when examining inclusion in acclaimed games like *Dragon Age* and *Mass Effect*, must take into account the factors that constrained and/or permitted such inclusion.

Note

1 This was colloquial terminology for game cartridges.

References

Aarseth, Espen. 1997. *Cybertext: Perspectives on Ergodic Literature*. New York: Johns Hopkins University Press.
Brathwaite, Brenda. 2007. *Sex in Video Games*. Boston: Thompson Learning.
Carlson, Rebecca and Jonathan Corliss. 2011. "Imagined Commodities: Video Game Localization and Mythologies of Cultural Difference." *Games and Culture* 6 (1): 61–82.

Consalvo, Mia. 2012. "Cosmo-Play: Japanese Videogames and Western Gamers." In *Social Exclusion, Power, and Video Game Play*, edited by David G. Embrick, J. Talmadge Wright, and Andras Lukacs, 199–220. Lanham: Lexington Books.

Crockford, Douglas. n.d. "Now You're Really Playing with Power: The Expurgation of Maniac Mansion for the Nintendo Entertainment System—The Untold Story." http://www.crockford.com/wrrrld/maniac.html.

Crogan, Patrick. 2011. *Gameplay Mode: War, Simulation, and Technoculture*. Minneapolis: University of Minnesota Press.

Di Marco, Francesca. 2007. "Cultural Localization: Orientation and Disorientation in Japanese Video Games." *revista tradumàtica: Traducció i Tecnologies de la Informació i la Comunicació* 5. http://www.fti.uab.cat/tradumatica/revista/num5/articles/06/06.pdf.

Dyer-Witheford, Nick and Greig de Peuter. 2009. *Games of Empire: Global Capitalism and Video Games*. Minneapolis: University of Minnesota Press.

Iwabuchi, Koichi. 2002. "From Western Gaze to Global Gaze: Japanese Cultural Presence in Asia." In *Global Culture: Media, Arts, Policy, and Globalization*, edited by Diane Crane, Nobuko Kawashima, and Ken'ichi Kawasaki, 256–73. New York: Routledge.

Kohler, Chris. 2005. *Power-Up: How Japanese Video Games Gave the World an Extra Life*. Indianapolis: Brady Games.

Mangiron, Carmen and Minako O'Hagan. 2006. "Game Localisation: Unleashing Imagination with 'Restricted' Translation." *Journal of Specialized Translation* 6: 10–21.

McLelland, Mark. 2004. "From the Stage to the Clinic: Changing Transgender Identities in Post-War Japan." *Japan Forum* 16 (1): 1–20.

Mead, Corey. 2013. *War Play: Video Games and the Future of Armed Conflict*. Boston: Houghton Mifflin Harcourt.

O'Hagan, Minako. 2009a. "Putting Pleasure First: Localizing Japanese Video Games." *TTR: traduction, terminologie, rédaction* 22 (1): 147–65.

O'Hagan, Minako. 2009b. "Towards a Cross-Cultural Game Design: An Explorative Study in Understanding the Player Experience of a Localised Japanese Video Game." *The Journal of Specialised Translation* 11: 211–33.

O'Hagan, Minako. 2012. "Transcreating Japanese Video Games: Exploring Future Directions for Translation Studies in Japan." In *Translation and Translation Studies in the Japanese Context*, edited by Nana Sato-Rossberg and Judy Wakabayashi, 183–201. New York: Bloomsbury Publishing.

"Player One Podcast, Episode 16: Interview with Ted Woolsey Transcript." 2007. http://www.playeronepodcast.com/forum/index.php?showtopic=145.

Robertson, Roland. 1995. "Glocalization: Time-Space and Homogeneity-Heterogeneity." In *Global Modernities*, edited by Mike Featherstone, Scott M. Lash, and Roland Robertson, 25–44. Thousand Oaks: SAGE Publications.

Schwartz, Steven A. and Janet Schwartz. 1994. *Parent's Guide to Video Games*. Rocklin: Prima Publishing.

Sheff, David. 1993. *Game Over: How Nintendo Zapped an American Industry, Captured Your Dollars, and Enslaved Your Children*. New York: Random House Publishing.

Toriyama, Akira. 1984. *Dragonball*. Shueisha.

Games cited

Bally Midway. 1982. *Ms. Pac-Man*. Bally Midway.
Bally Midway. 1983. *Jr. Pac-Man*. Bally Midway.
BioWare. 2007. *Mass Effect*. Microsoft.
BioWare. 2009. *Dragon Age: Origins*. Electronic Arts.
Capcom. 1987. *Street Fighter*. Capcom.
Capcom. 1989. *Final Fight*. Capcom USA. Arcade.
Capcom. 1991. *Final Fight*. Capcom USA. Super Nintendo Entertainment System.
Gygax, Gary. 1974. *Dungeons and Dragons*. Lake Geneva, WI: TSR.
Namco. 1980. *Pac-Man*. Namco.
Nintendo R&D4. 1985. *Super Mario Bros*. Nintendo of America.
Nintendo R&D4. 1987. *Super Mario Bros II*. Fuji TV.
Square. 1990. *Final Fantasy*. Nintendo of America.
Square. 1992. *Final Fantasy II*. Squaresoft.
Square. 1993. *Secret of Mana*. Squaresoft.
Square. 1994. *Final Fantasy III*. Squaresoft.
Tecmo. 2001. *Fatal Frame*. Tecmo.

4

The newest significant medium: *Brown v. EMA* (2011) and the twenty-first century status of video game regulation

Zach Saltz (University of Kansas, USA)

In the first decade and a half of the twenty-first century, video games have established themselves as one of the top entertainment industries in the United States. In 2013, the Entertainment Software Association (ESA), representing software manufacturers and developers nationwide, revealed that the gaming industry had earned $20.77 billion in sales in the United States (ESA 2013). The American motion picture industry, by contrast, grossed $10.8 billion the year before (MPAA 2012), while the music industry recorded profits of $4.8 billion (Smirke 2013). Both of these latter industries have struggled to adjust to the proliferation of digital platforms and personal electronics, with Hollywood forced to increase cinema ticket prices and the music industry suffering net losses in both album sales and digital downloads. In other words, video games have not only arguably become more financially successful than music and movies combined, but market conditions for video game production and sales appear to be more optimistic too.

At this point, some 60 percent of North Americans regularly play video games. Instead of this being a male-dominated activity, the ESA revealed that more than four out of every ten video game players are actually female. The ESA also reported that the percentage of women aged eighteen or older that played games (31 percent) was considerably higher than the percentage of boys under the age of seventeen (19 percent) (ESA 2013). And, unlike the claim that the influence of video games is limited to specialized niches, planetary revenues for games soared to $57 billion by 2009 (up from $7.5 billion in 1999), indicating that video games form one of the largest global media industries. Although the United States remains the largest single market for game distributors, numerous Asian countries, such as Japan and South Korea, have experienced rapid video game expansion, giving the industry an unprecedented global territorial dimension (Dyer-Witheford and de Peuter 2009).

In spite of the wider use of games and gaming practices worldwide, there has nonetheless been significant skepticism and criticism continuously directed at the video game industry from parents, politicians, and the media in the United States. Then Senator Hillary Clinton famously introduced a bill into Congress in 2005 that attempted to "put some teeth into video game ratings" and characterized video games as going "against the values [parents] are trying to instill in their children" (Feldman 2005). Former vice-presidential candidate and senator of Connecticut Joseph Lieberman testified before Congress that "romanticized and sanitized visions of violence" in video games have "become part of a toxic mix that has actually now turned some of them [teenage users] into killers" (Cong. Senate 2000).

But the gaming industry has proven to be more than simply popular rhetorical fodder for opportunistic politicians. In its relatively short existence as a form of mass communication, the gaming industry has also come under attack by federal and state courts reluctant to grant games First Amendment protection. What is noteworthy is the fact that this reluctance did not come as a result of video games' observable depictions of sex and violence. Instead, it came as a result of fundamental opposition to acknowledging the medium's potential to communicate significant ideas. In 1983, the Supreme Court of Massachusetts ruled in *Caswell v. Licensing Commission for Brockton* that "any communication or expression of ideas that occurs during the playing of a video game is purely inconsequential" (Brown 2008). Likening video games to a more technologically sophisticated version of pinball, courts throughout the 1990s and 2000s showed ambivalence in unequivocally upholding First Amendment applicability to games. In the opinion of most, pinball's degree of interaction between game and user was considered at best negligible, and few legal scholars opted to seriously take on the task of arguing that pinball was capable of expressing and conveying ideas and information to the same degree as other games. Nevertheless, the pinball comparison is noteworthy insofar as it primarily characterizes the flippant attitude of courts toward video games as a valid form of expression—and this was not limited to the 1970s and 1980s. In 2002, a Connecticut District Court characterizing video games as "merely digitized pinball machines" concluded that not only did it not constitute protected speech, but games were also "analytically distinguishable" from protected forms of media (*Wilson v. Midway Games, Inc* 2002).

In 2011, the Supreme Court categorically asserted in *Brown v. Entertainment Merchants Association* that video games qualified for First Amendment protection. In doing so, the court concluded that "the basic principles of freedom of speech . . . do not vary" with a new and different communication medium (*Brown et al. v. Entertainment Merchants Assn et al.*). In stating this, the court was not establishing a new precedent, but instead invoking a decision from 1952: *Burstyn v. Wilson*, or what was popularly known as "The *Miracle* Decision." This ruling was integral in striking down the power of state motion picture censorship boards to prohibit displays of sexual content and afforded the medium of film First Amendment protection. Thus, the Roberts Court's invocation of such wording was not accidental, and in this essay, I examine the many historical, social, and legal parallels between the two cases. Both occurred at critical historical junctures in which the film and video game industries were not just evolving in adoptions of novel technological platforms, but were also at a point of unparalleled penetration of audiences and consumption. Both rulings granted the task of regulating content to be convened at an industry-wide level (rather than through federal regulation), and both decisions drew sophisticated considerations regarding how both forms of media constituted authentic artistic expression, which in turn merited uncensored depictions of taboo, nonobscene subject matter. In short, I argue that by looking at the repercussions of the *Miracle* decision, we can logically deduce some potential ways that the representation of sexual content in video games will continue to evolve and break social taboos while simultaneously being constitutionally protected.

"Video Games Can Never Be Art"

Ironically, at the center of this legal debate is a core question that has been primarily limited to social and intellectual circles: Do video games constitute a valid form of art? The answer to this question not only depends on one's definition of art, but also extends to the function of art and the creative industries that produce it in a hypertechnological society. Bourdieu (1993) writes that cultural production can be divided into the categories of large-scale production, designed for primarily short-term commercial success, and small-scale "restricted" production, where gradual artistic success eventually fuels financial benefits. For Bourdieu, there was little differentiation to be made between the production of legitimate art, as opposed to "illegitimate art," and the commercial imperatives that lay as the basis of each. The question of whether video games are a form of art is significant not only because art is constitutionally protected, but also because objects containing artistic value tend to be bestowed with greater cache—or what Bourdieu would call social capital.

In an April 2010 blog for his website, entitled "Video Games Can Never Be Art," the late Pulitzer Prize-winning film critic Ebert (2010) famously observed the following:

> Why are gamers so intensely concerned, anyway, that games be defined as art? Bobby Fischer, Michael Jordan and Dick Butkus never said they thought their games were an art form. Nor did Shi Hua Chen, winner of the $500,000 World Series of Mah Jong in 2009. Why aren't gamers content to play their games and simply enjoy themselves? They have my blessing, not that they care.

Ebert's logic appears at the onset to be the sound and reasonable attitude of an individual who does not play video games. It may have seemed unlikely to Ebert and other nongamers that legal users (teenage or older) of the top-selling video game of 2013, the M-rated *Grand Theft Auto V* (2013), would find aesthetic pleasure in the reckless destruction of human life at the hands of sniper rifles or artistic sensibility in the carnal sexuality of Los Santos' well-endowed female prostitutes. In addition, Ebert reduces the ability of video games to offer sophisticated forms of interactive user engagement in much the same way that courts drew comparisons to "vapid" pinball. Art is a uniquely human activity that, according to Tolstoy (1994), "one man, consciously by means of certain external signs, hands on to others feelings he has lived through, and that others are infected by those feelings and also experience them." It is now a cliché to observe that art is in the eye of the beholder, but the sentiments of Tolstoy and Ebert appear to relegate art appreciation to an infectious disease that renders its users and appreciators as victims rather than patrons. In the cases of users finding even scant hints of sexual gratification in computer-generated characters, popular attitudes have diagnosed such feelings as deviant, pathologically abhorrent, and certainly not a legitimate form of art appreciation. This derogatory attitude was palpable in *Newsweek* critic Jack Kroll's (2000) scathing opinion of Lara Croft in 2000— that her "top-heavy titillation . . . falls flat next to the face of Sharon Stone. . . . Any player who's moved to tumescence by digibimbo Lara is in big trouble."

Bogost (2011) counters these claims by arguing that the very history of art is one marked by disruption and reinvention and that any attempt to locate a singular definition of art throughout history is a lost cause. But Bogost is particularly apt in suggesting the roots of today's video game controversies may have historical antecedents. In the mid-1910s, when multireel motion pictures were replacing printed words, phonographs, and vaudeville as the primary entertainment outlet for American audiences, similar debates emerged within circles of the cultural elite. Fueled by the high ideals of modernism, the new medium of film represented the closest advancement toward the perfected fusion of personal expression and mass public spectatorship and even the potential for viewer interaction. Bowser (1990) observes that one director who worked under Thomas Edison, christening film as the "drama of silence," noted that motion pictures constituted art because each audience member was capable of "creating his own emotions and language for the characters before him on the canvas and they are according to his own mental and spiritual standard. . . . This, I fully believe is the reason for the phenomenal popularity of the drama of silence throughout the world today." Coincidentally, 1915 happened to be the year the Supreme Court concluded in *Mutual Film Corporation v. Ohio* that "the exhibition of moving pictures is a business, pure and simple, originated and conducted for profit . . . vivid, useful, and entertaining, no doubt, but . . . capable of evil, having power for it, the greater because of their attractiveness and manner of exhibition" (Randall 1968). Because movies were entertainment, and therefore considered to be devoid of substantive ideas and susceptible to the portrayal of vice, the guarantee of protected speech did not apply.

Moving ahead to a four-year period between 1948 and 1952, two significant cases were brought before the Supreme Court that had significant impacts on the industry. The first ruling, in *United States v. Paramount Pictures* (1948), found the film industry guilty of violating antitrust regulations through its vertically integrated model of the "Big Five" studios having unilateral control over motion picture production, distribution, and exhibition. Forced to divest their ownership of individual theaters, while also facing the new technological competition of network television, the film studios' profits plunged throughout the 1950s and 1960s, not becoming truly profitable again until the "blockbuster" films of the 1970s.

The second ruling, *Burstyn v. Wilson* (1952), involved the exhibition of a forty-one-minute Italian film called *The Miracle* (*Il Miracolo*). Upon its initial screening at the Paris Theater in New York City in 1950, film prints were seized, and the film was banned as a result of being "sacrilegious" and containing objectionable levels of sexual content. *The Miracle*'s American distributor, Joseph Burstyn, filed a lawsuit against New York's film licensing board, and nearly two years later, the suit having reached the Supreme Court, Justice Tom Clark declared that the industry had an "absolute freedom to exhibit every motion picture of every kind at all times and places" (*Joseph Burstyn, Inc. v. Wilson* 1952). The court ruled that law officials or censorship boards could not ban a film on the grounds that it was "sacreligious." Subsequent affirmations of this ruling led to a loosening of the censorial Production Code.

Although the *Miracle* decision afforded motion pictures First Amendment protection, local censorship boards and social groups were skeptical that Hollywood would sufficiently police its content using an anarchic Production Code as a litmus test. Subsequently, the Motion Picture Association of America (MPAA) established the film industry's first age-based classification system. Through a board of anonymous viewers assigning ratings, the film industry's model of self-regulation was able to effectively bypass government attempts at policing film content.

Obviously, the video game industry does not face the same precarious economic circumstances as motion pictures in the 1950s and 1960s. If anything, today's circumstances actually tend to more closely parallel those of the 1910s, with video games offering audiences the exciting potential for new forms of artistic expression and user interaction, but with equally forceful degrees of social resistance in conservative circles. Since their inception, video games, like motion pictures, have been subject to widespread hysteria over the social effects of violent and sexual depictions leading to delinquent behaviors in younger users. One-on-one fighting games such as *Street Fighter* and *Mortal Kombat* continually pushed the boundaries of violence en route to becoming all-time best sellers. Manufacturers such as Atari and Nintendo informally adopted a set of rules that prevented "no excessive blood and violence" as well as "no sex." But when Nintendo offered consumers a toned-down and noticeably less violent version of *Mortal Kombat*, while its competitor Sega offered the same violent version that had previously been available, the Sega version outsold the Nintendo game three to one, leading to the conclusion that violence in video games led to increased sales (Anderson, Gentile, and Buckley 2007).

In 1994, after several controversial games including *Wolfenstein 3D* and *Night Trap* prompted an upset response from parents and civic leaders for their depictions of violence and sex, the Entertainment Software Ratings Board (ESRB) was created. This was after Congress had applied pressure on the video game industry and the ESA to create an industry-wide, content-based classification system. The result was a ratings board that served as a compromise between the video game industry's unofficial claim to free speech protection and the government's mandate to regulate the trade and sale of potentially obscene items. The ESRB subsequently designed an age-based schematic resembling the movie rating system used by the MPAA. The ratings applied ranged from "Early Childhood" (suitable for ages three and older) to "Adults Only" (eighteen years and older), and additionally each rated game received content descriptors. But perhaps more significantly, the ESRB adopted another crucial component of the MPAA and its Classification and Ratings Administration: the members of its board were also kept anonymous. And it should be noted that instead of playing the games themselves on consoles, board members would watch videotaped game footage selectively pieced together and submitted by software companies, along with other pertinent but unspecified information, in analyzing which rating to assign for a given game.

Although the rating system was designed to be self-regulated, two years later Congress asked the National Institute on Media and the Family (NIMF) to conduct an annual *Video and Computer Game Report* to assess how well the industry was conducting its rating system. In its first years, the report noted how, in spite of the rating system being effectively used by gamemakers and distributors, the industry's advertising nonetheless targeted players under seventeen with advertisements for Mature (M)-rated games. In the midst of an unprecedented pushback by parents and social scientists, the Federal Trade Commission, asked by President Bill Clinton to investigate violent game consumption of youth in the wake of the 1999 Columbine High School shootings, concluded that 70 percent of M-rated games were indeed targeting children under seventeen as their primary audience (Anderson, Gentile, and Buckley 2007).

In 2007, the ESRB assigned ratings to a total of 1,563 games. 59 percent of games received an E for "Everyone" rating, 20 percent received a T for "Teen" rating, 15 percent received an E10+ for "Everyone 10 and up" rating, and 6 percent received an M for "Mature" rating. Only twenty-three games in total (or slightly more than 0.01 percent) received a rating of AO, or "Adults Only" (McCann 2009). The most notable games with these restrictive ratings were *Grand Theft Auto: San Andreas* and *Playboy: The Mansion—Private Party Expansion*. One year earlier, the NIMF once again put public pressure on the video game industry to enforce its ratings. Although the ESA maintained that parents were involved in 83 percent of all game rentals and purchases, NIMF concluded that only 40 percent of parents understood what the ESRB ratings meant, and only slightly more than half used them as buying guides (Irwin 2006). Two years later in 2009, seven of the twenty top-selling video games received ratings of M or T, including the top game of that year, *Call of Duty: Modern Warfare 2*. For computer games, the statistics released by the ESRB showed that all but two of the top twenty computer games of 2009 were rated either M or T.

In spite of widespread criticism, the video game industry was actually policing itself *better* than the music and film industries. In 2000, the Federal Trade Commission sent underage mystery shoppers to entertainment retailers to see if they could purchase R-rated movies and M-rated games. Of the monitored video game retailers, only 15 percent asked the underage shopper their age, and a staggering 85 percent of children were able to purchase M-rated video games (compared with 48 percent of retailers asking for age and 46 percent of children allowed to purchase tickets to an R-rated movie). In addition, the Commission confirmed what fevered industry critics had long suspected: that the industry routinely targeted children in their advertising and marketing of adult games, and children under age seventeen could purchase such games without great difficulty (FTC 2011).

But revealingly, by 2010, these figures had completely shifted. In the very same survey, the FTC revealed that a staggeringly low 13 percent of underage teenage shoppers were able to purchase M-rated games; this result looked sterling alongside the 64 percent of underage shoppers able to purchase explicit music and the 38 percent able to purchase R-rated DVDs. Additionally, the Commission openly praised the ESRB for continuing to "have the strongest self-regulatory code [by] prohibit[ing] the target marketing of M-rated games to teens and T-rated games to children under thirteen and enforce[ing] its code with fines and other sanctions" (FTC). Retailers such as GameStop, Target, and Kmart allowed fewer than 10 percent of underage mystery shoppers to purchase an M-rated video game without adult supervision. Furthermore, in 2010, the ESRB asserted that parents are present at the moment games are purchased or rented 93 percent of the time (ESA 2010). Whether this strong degree of uniform enforcement stemmed directly from the auspices of the ESRB and gaming industry, or from retailers or parents, remains questionable. But it is undeniable that it has become significantly more difficult for underage gamers to purchase any violent video games on their own.

In spite of the industry's assertion that it was sufficiently monitoring not only the amount of violent video game content, but also the ways in which children could access such content, grassroots legislation from both sides of the political aisle began to take shape in 2005. Earlier that year, a mild scandal had emerged when users of *Grand Theft Auto: San Andreas* uncovered a "Hot Coffee" mod in the beta version of the game, where the player could solicit sex from his girlfriend that would then be graphically depicted onscreen. Rockstar Games had not submitted images from this hidden mod to members of the ESRB, and the game received an M rating. In wake of the discovery of the "Hot Coffee" minigame, the game was pulled from shelves, and its rating was promptly changed from an M to the dreaded AO (the video game equivalent of an NC-17 rating).[1] More troublesome than the sexual intercourse displayed for users was the fact that Rockstar Games had intentionally circumvented the ESRB's authority in warning consumers of objectionable content, nullifying the video game industry's credibility in policing its content. In Rockstar's hurry to distribute an M-rated version of *Grand Theft Auto* without the "Hot Coffee" content, the company ended up losing money in the process (Egenfeldt-Nielson, Smith, and Tosca 2013).

Responding to the high-profile condemnation of graphic video games stemming largely from the "Hot Coffee" fiasco, on October 7, 2005, California became the first state in the United States to enact a bill prohibiting the sale or rental of violent video games—defined as ones that depicted "killing, maiming, dismembering, or sexually assaulting an image of a human being"—to minors under the age of eighteen, with a fine of up to $1,000 for violators. Legislators cited research conducted by scientists and medical associations alleging to establish a correlation between playing violent video games and an increase in violent, antisocial behavior. Although the bill was passed, a federal judge blocked it in 2006, beginning a lengthy chain of appeals regarding the statute's enforceability and constitutionality and ending with a decision by the Supreme Court on June 27, 2011, in *Brown v. Entertainment Merchants Association of America* (ESA 2013). In a 7–2 vote, the court struck down the California statute, to the relief of the video game industry and chagrin of video game opponents.

In his majority opinion, Justice Antonin Scalia (of whom it was widely reported that he is also the grandfather of thirty-two children and teenagers) draws strong parallels between video games and artistic expression protected by the First Amendment. He also maintains that the government has no free-floating power to entirely restrict the ideas to which children may be exposed. In a particularly revealing passage, Scalia writes "[Video games] communicate ideas, and the most basic principle of First Amendment law is that government has no power to restrict expression because of its content. . . . While sexually explicit speech has traditionally been restricted by law in this country, there is no such tradition for depictions of violence, even when conveyed to children" (*Brown et al. v. Entertainment Merchants Assn et al.*). There are three significant legal considerations that can be drawn from this passage. The first is the striking similarity between Scalia's words and those of Tom Clark, who in the *Miracle* decision five decades before famously concluded that "motion pictures are a significant medium for the communication of ideas." Reversing the *Mutual* court decision from 1915 that had prohibited film from First Amendment protection as a result of its inherent "capacity for evil," Clark and the Supreme Court in 1952 identified an important civic function in the exhibition of motion pictures: to convey ideas to the mass populace. The *Miracle* decision asserted that motion pictures could not be denied First Amendment protection on the basis that the medium of celluloid was less reputable than newspapers or printed journals. In the 2002 District Court ruling in Connecticut, video games were discriminated against because the medium was presumed to be inferior to that of "distinguishable forms" of media. But Scalia's words demonstrate a progression of the video game medium from "purely inconsequential" entertainment (as characterized by the Massachusetts court in the 1983 *Caswell* ruling) to a medium that indisputably communicates ideas.

The second consideration is Scalia's implicit contention in referring to the history of sexually explicit speech and its prohibition through the outlawing of obscenity. He notes the long-standing literary tradition in the United States, which has systematically exposed children to objectionable depictions. In his opinion, Scalia cites "high-school reading lists" chock-full of depictions of obscene acts in literature, ranging from Homer's *The Odyssey* to William Golding's *Lord of the Flies*. Although this comparison appeared to be a conventional argument in favor of protecting the freedom of creative expression, Scalia takes it one step further by examining the role of physical video game packaging. Arguing that, like the front covers of books, video game packaging serves as an extension of the narrative, through its use of iconic and indexical imagery referencing specific characters and plot points, prominent mandatory display of ESRB ratings on the front packaging obscures and objurgates the game manufacturer's ability to convey core speech. Since images from the game cannot be separated from the game's story, Scalia and the court reasonably concluded that video game cover packaging could be considered core speech, leaving real doubt whether ESRB ratings have a legal mandate to be boldly displayed on covers. Legally speaking, video games had now, for the first time, been essentially granted the status of art.

Finally, Scalia's point about sexually explicit imagery is notable, since in previous courts, attorneys for *Brown* attempted to use a precedent in *Ginsberg v. New York* (1968) that established the complete ban on material that would constitute obscenity. Crucial in the *Ginsberg* decision was the court's delineation that the legal definition of obscenity was limited to hard-core sexual content; portrayals of other potentially offensive material such as vulgarity, drug use, and violence were still permitted. Thus, in the numerous courts where the ESA defended itself, judges routinely threw out *Ginsberg* as a substantive precedent, in effect stating that depictions of sex in video games did not constitute objectionable explicit content. Additionally, Scalia and the other concurring justices refused to place any legal value on the scientific research submitted by *Brown* associating playing violent video games with an increase of violent behavior. This represented another substantive milestone in legal precedent, since the original ban on adult video games in California had been administered on the basis of submitted claims to the court attesting to scientific proof that sexual and violent video games spawned deviant behavior.

Another significant component of the *Brown* ruling was the dissent by Justice Stephen Breyer. Ironically enough, Breyer has been widely considered firmly within the "liberal" ideological wing of the court and has proven to be a dependable strong defender of free speech. But in his dissent, Breyer identifies contradictions in the types of content being protected. Specifically, like critics of the MPAA's rating system, he wondered why violence is so readily tolerated as free expression, while sexual content is, hypocritically, entirely shunned. He observes: "What kind of sense does it make to forbid selling to a thirteen-year-old boy a magazine with an image of a nude woman while protecting a sale to that thirteen-year-old of an interactive video game in which he actively, but virtually, binds and gags the woman, then tortures and kills her?" (*Brown et al. v. Entertainment Merchants Assn et al.*). Breyer's comment not only points to the pitfalls of subjectivity on the part of any content-regulation board, but also seriously questions Scalia's logic of denying the California statute based on its "overinclusiveness." Although Breyer could hardly be considered a moral crusader in terms of his judicial philosophy, his comments suggest that with the cost of encouraging a broad cross section of free expression comes the obligatory plurality of prurient content and obscenity. His words recall Garth Jowett's ambivalent conclusions on the broader cultural impact of the *Miracle* decision: in the film industry's bid to recover the financial losses sustained due to theater divestment and competition with television, the newly granted freedom by courts was subsequently squandered on cheap sexual exploitation and violence (Jowett 1996). In 1973, five years after the movie rating system was enacted, two of the year's ten top-grossing films— *Deep Throat* (1973) and *Beyond the Green Door* (1973)—were unabashedly pornographic features, promoting a culturally embraced (if only temporary) "porno chic." This plunged the film industry into the scorn of right-wing reformers and politicians, who blamed soft-core on the decay of widely recognized urban hubs such as Times Square. Justice Breyer's comments suggest the possibility that completely unregulated content—or regulations more favorable to the inclusion of violence instead of sex—may, in fact, sink the video game industry only deeper into public relations woes.

Self-regulation to save the industry?

If there is any lesson we can glean from the liberalization of sexual content in motion pictures, it is, ironically, that content regulation is needed now more than ever in order for sexual content to become more culturally accepted— even if such content regulation exists purely for symbolic purposes. Recalling the words of Franklin Roosevelt, the Supreme Court's ruling in *Brown v. EMA* illustrates that the only thing the video game industry has to fear is none other than itself—namely, the ESRB and its reputability among vocal critics of the industry such as Justice Breyer. While sexual and violent content are now protected speech, it is important to understand the vital role the ESRB still serves in the production and dissemination of such games. A voluntary regulation system, no matter how effective or ineffective it is, is required in order to protect the private companies comprising the ESA against surreptitious government attempts to regulate product and impose its own standards. Instead of criticizing the ESRB for its archaic rating process and capricious application of age-based classifications, game users must recognize that without the ESRB, the content of video games may be subject to regional courts with judges potentially not as amenable to free speech as Scalia. Game users need to recognize that when the credibility of the ESRB is compromised—as most visibly evidenced in the "Hot Coffee" scandal—the industry is more susceptible to criticism that it is not sufficiently regulating its own product. And most importantly, game users need to recognize the problematic contradiction inherent in the *Brown v. EMA* decision: with the increasing legal protection of sexual content comes the eroding importance and legal justification of content regulators such as the ESRB. In an era in which a simple Google search can yield hard-core content for even the most primitive of Internet users, sex can be more easily accessed and accepted than ever before. While this represents a victory for socially progressive media consumers, it also provides fertile ground for moral reformers to stir further compelling demand for the greater legal protection of minors.

Examination of the historical context of the *Miracle* decision provides media scholars with insight into the potential directions of the video game industry and depictions of sex in the wake of the *Brown* ruling. But the evidence here also demonstrates that the future of video game ratings and content regulation is crucially vague. The "Hot Coffee" scandal revealed glaring omissions in the ESRB's attempts to streamline and police all objectionable content; will even looser enforceability, as now proscribed by the Supreme Court, result in more hypersexualized games being put in the hands of underage consumers? While evidence from the Federal Trade Commission characterizes the video game industry as surprisingly responsible, social and political critics of the industry have only increased with the high-profile shootings in Newtown, Connecticut, and Aurora, Colorado. Furthermore, concerned parents and psychologists may still find the prospect of manufacturers selectively submitting videotaped game footage for the purposes of preventing children from exposure to harmful content extremely troubling. Within the MPAA's rating board, the raters screen feature films in their entirety. For the ESRB, by contrast, it is unlikely that reviewers see more than a handful of minutes from a game with playing time ranging from thirty-two to forty hours, on average.

What is more important for the gaming industry—even more so than initiating a wholesale overhaul of the existing vetting process—is the preservation of positive, nonthreatening public relations. If consumers, advocacy groups, and politicians remain convinced that the ESRB is effectively policing content for minors, then the video game industry will likely remain mostly immune from serious legal problems. But what if, as Justice Scalia suggested, the mandatory display of ESRB ratings on video game packaging is suddenly overturned as a violation of free speech? It may be ironic that defenders of sexual content, in their attempts to eliminate the ratings board mandate and forge an unregulated market of video game content, may actually be doing themselves more harm than good by eradicating the industry's credibility. It is here where, once again, the development of sex in motion pictures may provide an insightful historical corollary: Lewis concludes that in the wake of the *Miracle* decision, the film industry's ability to self-regulate succeeded in dissuading legal action over its sexual content. In this sense, it was Hollywood's tight-knit corporate conglomeration—not socially liberal District and Federal Courts—that truly paved the way for greater free speech (Lewis 2000). In a similar vein, the existing mechanism of video game ratings attempts to protect more than just underage users—in a roundabout way, it protects the very sexual content it ostensibly seeks to censor. This contradictory dynamic is vital in order to understand the sophisticated ways in which the *Brown v. EMA* ruling represents a much greater step toward wider social acceptance of sexual content in video games even as it represents a threat.

Note

1   For a more detailed examination of the "Hot Coffee" controversy, see Alphra Kerr, "Spilling Hot Coffee? Grand Theft Auto as Contested Cultural Product," in The Meaning and Culture of Grand Theft Auto: Critical Essays, edited by Nate Garrelts (Jefferson: McFarland & Company. 2006), 17–34.

References

Anderson, Craig, Douglas Gentile, and Katherine E. Buckley. 2007. *Violent Video Game Effects on Children and Adolescents: Theory Research, and Public Policy*. Oxford: Oxford University Press.
Bogost, Ian. 2011. *How to Do Things With Videogames*. Minneapolis, MN: University of Minnesota Press.

Bourdieu, Pierre. 1993. *The Field of Cultural Production.* Oxford: Blackwell
    Publishing.
Bowser, Eileen. 1990. *The Transformation of Cinema: 1907–1915.* Berkeley:
    University of California Press.
Brown et al. v. Entertainment Merchants Assn et al. 2011. 564 US. 08-1448.
Brown, Harry J. 2008. *Video Games and Education.* Armonk: M. E. Sharpe.
Dyer-Witheford, Nick and Greig de Peuter. 2009. *Games of Empire: Global
    Capitalism and Video Games.* Minneapolis: University of Minnesota Press.
Ebert, Roger. 2010. "Video Games Can Never Be Art." RogerEbert.com, April 16.
    http://blogs.suntimes.com/ebert/2010/04/video_games_can_never_be_art.html.
Egenfeldt-Nielson, Simon, Jonas Heide Smith, and Susana Pajares Tosca. 2013.
    Understanding Video Games: The Essential Introduction. 2nd edn. New York:
    Routledge.
Entertainment Software Association. 2010. "Essential Facts About the Computer
    and Video Game Industry." http://www.theesa.com/facts/pdfs/ESA_Essential_
    Facts_2010.PDF.
Entertainment Software Association. 2013. "2013 Sales, Demographic and Usage
    Data." October 31. http://www.theesa.com/facts/pdfs/esa_ef_2013.pdf.
Federal Trade Commission. 2011. "FTC Undercover Shopper Survey on
    Enforcement of Entertainment Ratings Finds Compliance Worst for Retailers
    of Music CDs and the Highest Among Video Game Sellers." April 20. http://
    www.ftc.gov/opa/2011/04/violentkidsent.shtm.
Feldman, Curt. 2005. "Clinton Calls for Federal Game Regulation." *Gamespot,*
    July 14. http://www.gamespot.com/news/6129040.html.
Irwin, Mary Jane. 2006. "Rated V for Violence." *PC Magazine,* February 15. http://
    www.pcmag.com/article2/0,2817,1924294,00.asp.
Joseph Burstyn, Inc. v. Wilson. 1952. 343. US. 495.
Jowett, Garth. 1996. "'A Significant Medium for the Communication of Ideas':
    The *Miracle* Decision and the Decline of Motion Picture Censorship, 1952–
    1968." In *Movie Censorship and American Culture,* edited by Francis G.
    Couvares, 258–76. Washington: Smithsonian Institution Press.
Kroll, Jack. 2000. "Emotional Engines? I Don't Think So." *Newsweek,* February
    27. http://www.newsweek.com/emotion-engine-i-dont-think-so-156675.
Lewis, John. 2000. *Hollywood v. Hard Core: How the Struggle Over Censorship
    Saved the Modern Film Industry.* New York: New York University Press.
McCann, Shawn. 2009. "Game Ratings Rundown." *Library Journal* 134 (3): 85.
Motion Picture Association of America [MPAA]. 2012. "Theatrical Market
    Statistics 2012." MPAA Industry Reports, December 31. http://www.mpaa.org/
    Resources/3037b7a4-58a2-4109-8012-58fca3abdf1b.pdf.
Randall, Richard. 1968. *Censorship of the Movies: The Social and Political Control
    of a Mass Medium.* Madison: University of Wisconsin Press.
Smirke, Richard. 2013. "IFPI 2013 Recording Industry in Numbers: Global
    Revenue, Emerging Markets Rise; US, UK, Germany Drop." Billboard, April 8.
    http://www.billboard.com/biz/articles/news/digital-and-mobile/1556590/ifpi-
    2013-recording-industry-in-numbers-global-revenue.
Tolstoy, Leo. 1994. "What Is Art?." In *Art and Its Significance: An Anthology of
    Aesthetic Theory,* edited by Stephen David Ross. Albany: State University of
    New York Press.

United States. Cong. Senate. 2000. Committee on Commerce, Science, and
    Transportation. *Marketing Violence to Children*. 106th Cong., 2nd sess.
    Washington: GPO.
Wilson v. Midway Games, Inc. 2002. 198 F. Supp. 2d 167, 181. D. Conn.

Games cited

Capcom. 1987. *Street Fighter*. Capcom.
Cyberlore Studios. 2005. *Playboy: The Mansion-Private Party Expansion*. Groove
    Games.
Digital Pictures. 1992. *Night Trap*. Sega.
id Software. 1992. *Wolfenstein 3D*. Apogee Software.
Infinity Ward. 2009. *Call of Duty: Modern Warfare 2*. Activision.
Midway Games. 1992. *Mortal Kombat*. Midway Games.
Rockstar North. 2005. *Grand Theft Auto: San Andreas*. Rockstar Games.
Rockstar North. 2013. *Grand Theft Auto V*. Rockstar Games.

5

Explicit sexual content in early console video games

Dan Mills (Georgia Highlands College, USA)

Declining moral value in video games remains a popular topic in mainstream media and politics, and, particularly in light of incidents like the Columbine massacre in 1999 and its alleged relationship to video games, this attention seems justified. However, one could argue that the evaporation of moral value in video games has been a slow progression downward, beginning with games like *Leisure Suit Larry* and *Mortal Kombat* and continuing with *Command and Conquer* and *Tomb Raider*. Video games have for quite some time served as a forum for depicting violent behavior, materialistic desire, and cutthroat competition, and as society becomes more tolerant of their content, video games will arguably strive to mirror a society in decline itself. Baudrillard (1994) argues that postmodernism relies upon a "model of decomposition to the whole of society, a contagious model of the disaffection of a whole social structure, where death would finally make its ravages" (150). Baudrillard's definition of postmodernism echoes complaints from many current anti-video game activists.

Most of the focus on potentially harmful content in video games has reacted to violent video game content, but recent research has begun to address a lack of analysis of sexual content. In their 2007 discussion of violence in video games, psychologists Anderson, Gentile, and Buckley note that despite governmental restrictions on children's access to pornography, research about potentially "harmful effects of exposure to pornography is less massive and less conclusive than the literature on harmful media violence effects" (150). Indeed, real-world violence potentially resulting from exposure to any kind of media makes much more of an immediate impact on the general public's lives than does aberrant sexual behavior. I wish to take particular issue with video game researchers Novak and Levy's (2008) assertion that "some early young adults might go for sex and violence" in video games because they understand the "difference between a game and real life" and merely want to play video games "for cathartic purposes" (131). Novak and Levy whitewash the potential problems that have come about from video games, as well as any future problems that may occur when video game technology can truly create a "virtual reality." Even early video games had the potential to create lasting negative effects on gamers, as most video games inherently require repeated play to master, creating a dangerous epistemological gaming experience through the repetition of transgressive acts. Deleuze (1994) argues that "repetition displays identical elements which necessarily refer back to latent subject which repeats itself through these elements, forming an 'other' repetition at the heart of the first" which signifies a "difference without a concept, non-mediated difference. It is both the literal and spiritual primary sense of repetition" (25). Repetition, therefore, leads to a literal and spiritual empty signifier in creating a "non-mediated" other, resulting in an epistemological dilemma for the subject performing the repetition.

This chapter will explore sexual content in video games, from the earliest console systems to present computer games, to argue that sexual content in video games needs to receive the same attention as does violent content in video games. By employing a theoretical framework that brings together Baudrillard's understanding of postmodernism and Deleuze's notion of repetition, this examination of sexuality in video games will seek to understand the ethical and epistemological implications of repetitive video game play, with a particular focus on sexuality in video games.

Sexual content appeared in games for some of the earliest home video game systems, including the very popular Atari 2600. First released in 1977, the Atari 2600 was *the* video game system that started the at-home video game craze that still grips America's youth today. Although the system was designed for use by children, unlicensed adult video games appeared as early as 1982, when the video game company Mystique, a subsidiary of the pornographic film company Caballero Control Corporation and American Multiple Industries, released the first pornographic games for the Atari 2600 system. In spite of the graphical limitations of the Atari 2600, many of these games depicted anatomically correct, though low-resolution, game characters that engaged in sexual intercourse within the game. Controversy surrounded many of these games, and they remained largely underground products; even if a major retailer carried the games, they typically kept them "behind the counter" and out of sight. Substituting virtual pleasure for real-world pleasure, early pornographic video games rely upon what Deleuze calls the "*idea* of pleasure obtained and the *idea* of the pleasure to be obtained" which "act only under the principle to form the two applications, past and future" (97, Deleuze's emphasis). Deleuze claims that this tension between immediate versus delayed gratification results in "passive synthesis," an unconscious alteration in the interiorization of both ideas of pleasure.

Although they generally demean women, many of these games, paradoxically, had companion games that switched gender roles. Nevertheless, the companion games reflect very little change in the graphics and appearance and are frequently as demeaning to women. In the game *Burning Desire* (1982), for instance, the player assumes the role of a naked air rescuer who attempts to save a woman from cannibals. The woman stands on a burning pedestal as the hero dangles out of a helicopter and extinguishes a fire with an arm-length rod protruding from his pelvis (Figure 5.2). *Jungle Fever* (1982) reverses the gender roles for *Burning Desire*, but nevertheless poses the question of what the woman hanging from the helicopter sprays onto the fire. The use of cannibals as the villains demonstrates a tangibly xenophobic attitude toward indigenous people, and the long noses of the blue-colored cannibals could be read as racist. In the box art for both games (Figures 5.1 and 5.3), a woman appears with little clothing and serves as the object of sexual desire, and, in spite of the gender reversal in having a female character in *Jungle Fever* performing the rescue, the game nonetheless depicts women merely as objects of sexual desire.

In Mystique's *Beat'Em and Eat'Em* (1982), the player plays a nude woman who must catch sperm falling from masturbating men (Figure 5.5). *Philly Flasher* (1982) reverses the gender roles but is otherwise identical to *Beat'Em and Eat'Em*. The title *Beat'Em and Eat'Em* ostensibly refers to masturbation, but it has connotations of physical violence directed at the women "catching" the male game character's semen. Again, the gender reversal in *Philly Flasher* poses the question of what the female game character has to shoot out at the male characters at the bottom of the screen. The box art of *Beat'Em and Eat'Em* (Figure 5.4) depicts a woman seductively eating an ice cream cone. Moriarty wrote in 1983 that the game scenario of *Beat'Em and Eat'Em* "is enough to send the most liberal sexual enthusiast staring at his/her shoes in embarrassment" (20).

Advertisers, of course, use sex to sell virtually anything, and even these early console video games employed such marketing in spite of the fact that most retailers selling Mystique's games kept them out of sight. According to Near (2013), "If publishers believe that the marginalization or sexualization of women in games and their box art will improve sales to their target audience, they will emphasize such portrayals, and so the prevalence of these portrayals

FIGURE 5.1 Burning Desire *(Mystique/Playaround) box art from atarimania.com.*[1]

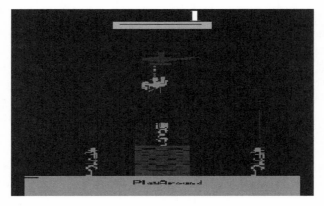

FIGURE 5.2 Burning Desire *(Mystique/Playaround) screenshot from archive.org.*[2]

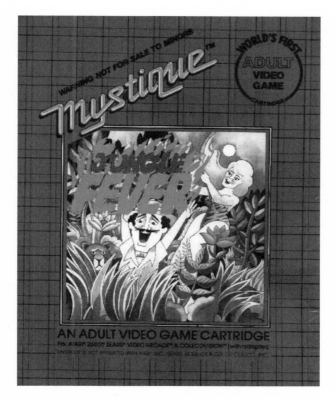

FIGURE 5.3 Jungle Fever *(Mystique/Playaround) box art from www.tomheroes.com.*[3]

will persist" (255). The depiction of sexuality on box art typically focuses more heavily on the depiction of women than on men: Burgess, Stermer, and Burgess (2007) note that on video game box art, "violence and sexiness was paired more frequently for female characters than violence and muscular physiques for the male characters" (1).

The attempts at gender equality on the part of Mystique's companion games do little more than perpetuate the oversexualized depiction of women. In *Bachelor Party* and *Bachelorette Party*, game play involves bouncing men and women against each other to "hit" on the opposite sex (Figure 5.6). As Moriarty notes, in *Bachelor Party*, "True to life, the women quickly disappear after he [the gamer] has hit on them" (20). In both games, the women appear aggressive, with their heads leaning forward as if welcoming the male character and his erect penis.

The box art for *Bachelor Party* (Figure 5.7) resembles one of the movie posters for the 1981 James Bond film, *For Your Eyes Only*. The James Bond

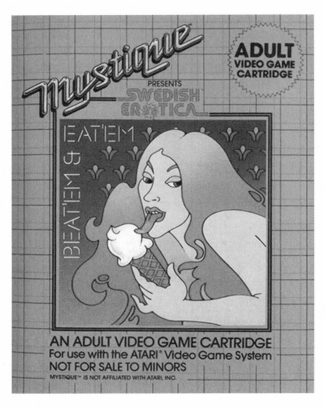

FIGURE 5.4 Beat'Em and Eat'Em *(Mystique/Playaround) box art from atariage.com.*[4]

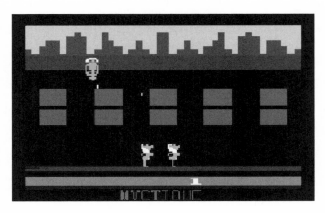

FIGURE 5.5 Beat'Em and Eat'Em *(Mystique/Playaround) screenshot from archive.* *org.*[5]

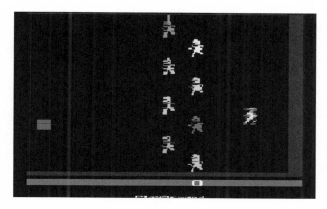

FIGURE 5.6 Bachelor Party *(Mystique/Playaround) screenshot from archive.org.*[6]

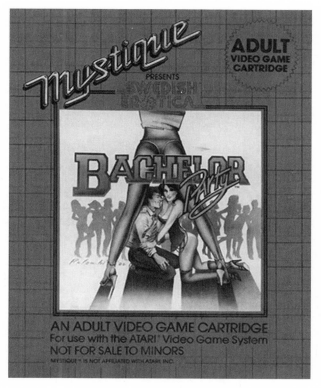

FIGURE 5.7 Bachelor Party *(Mystique/Playaround) box art from atariage.com.*[7]

franchise has long served as the ultimate manifestation of the male fantasy, with travel to exotic locales and numerous sexual encounters with exotic women. The *Bachelor Party* box art also portrays the woman we see between the faceless women's legs as the aggressor, and several other women wait for their turn with the bachelor in the background as mere silhouettes. The box art for *Bachelorette Party* (Figure 5.8) does objectify the male stripper, but nevertheless two women dominate the front of the image, and do so with a very seductive open-mouth expression.

Another woman on the box art for *Bachelorette Party* appears to reach out to touch the male stripper in the background. The effect, in the end, merely plays to male fantasies and not those of women: in both box covers women outnumber the men, and women play the role of the aggressor.

In *Gigolo*, the player assumes the role of a streetwalker who goes from door to door to engage in sexual encounters with women (Figure 5.10). Once the character is inside one of the various buildings, the screen changes to a

FIGURE 5.8 Bachelorette Party *(Mystique/Playaround) box art from atarimani.com.*[8]

blocky image of a man and woman having intercourse. The more encounters, the higher the score and thus the higher the amount of money you take to your pimp. *Cathouse Blues* reverses the gender roles in *Gigolo*, making the gamer a female prostitute. The box art for *Gigolo* (Figure 5.9) seems to allude to the finger touching scene in the 1982 Stephen Spielberg movie, *E.T. the Extra-Terrestrial*, as the dapper and debonair man touches index fingers with the woman appearing on the far left side of the image; such an allusion on the box of a pornographic video game to a popular, mainstream children's movie seems particularly in bad taste. In the bottom left-hand corner of the image appears one of the man's manicured fingers as he literally holds the woman in his hand; the effect of having a much larger image of the man than that of the woman places the man in a much more powerful position. The woman in the image appears to derive pleasure from merely touching the man's finger.

Mystique's games *Lady in Wading* and *Knight on the Town* (1982) depict chivalric scenarios with the goal of having sex with the other character. As in the other Mystique companion games, the graphics for these two games differed very little from each other; gameplay and appearance for *Lady in Wading* (Figure 5.12) and *Knight on the Town* (Figure 5.14) are virtually identical except for some changes in the colors of the elements on the screen. The box art for *Lady in Wading* (Figure 5.11) depicts the man, the object of desire for the woman who "wades" across the moat to reach him, coming out of the wall of the castle. The "wading" woman naturally wears very revealing clothing in addition to having access to a drawbridge, which would seemingly eliminate the need for her to go in the water.

The box art for *Knight on the Town* (Figure 5.13) depicts the main character in the game as a red-faced knight holding a large phallic lance pointing straight up. In this case, however, the knight attempts to reach a very buxom, red-faced woman who strokes the head of the horse the knight sits upon. This too carries with it sexual connotations. Scholars of chivalric romance have traditionally considered a knight's horse as signifying the knight's penis. Although clothed in the box art for both games, the characters appear naked in both *Lady in Wading* (Figure 5.11) and *Knight on the Town* (Figure 5.13). These phallic symbols both amount to what Deleuze calls a "virtual object," and when the virtual object appears as the phallus, "it is always located by enigmas and riddles in a place where it is not, because it is indistinguishable from the space in which it is displaced" (107). Deleuze's placement of the symbolic phallus (as opposed to the literal male sexual organ) at the site of its absence simultaneously places it in the "virtual" replacement of the sexual act, and this virtual replacement becomes as real as the real world act.

FIGURE 5.9 Gigolo *(Mystique/Playaround) box art from atarimania.com.*[9]

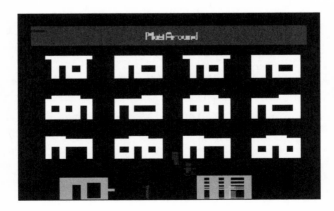

FIGURE 5.10 Gigolo *(Mystique/Playaround) screenshot from archive.org.*[10]

FIGURE 5.11 Lady in Wading *(Mystique/Playaround) box art.*[11]

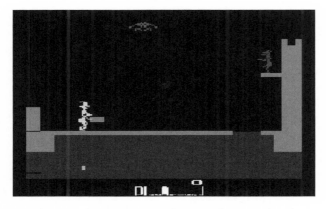

FIGURE 5.12 Lady in Wading *(Mystique/Playaround) screenshot.*[12]

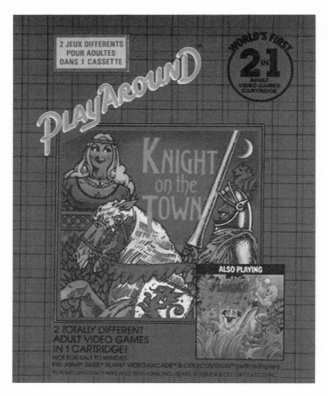

FIGURE 5.13 Knight on the Town *(Mystique/Playaround) box art.*[13]

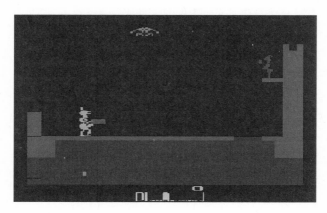

FIGURE 5.14 Knight on the Town *(Mystique/Playaround) screenshot.*[14]

Mystique was not the only creator of pornographic video games. In Universal Gamex's Atari 2600 game, *X-Man* the player moves through a maze in order to reach a door behind which he will have sex. Unlike Mystique's games, however, Universal Gamex did not create a companion game called *X-Woman*.

On the box art for *X-Man* (Figure 5.15), a woman begins to take off her bra while the "X-Man" fondles himself next to a mouth without a face and a crab, likely suggesting nameless, faceless oral sex and venereal disease, respectively. In one scene in the game the player can see the breasts of the woman he will have sex with if he wins the game (Figure 5.17). Considering the limitations of early video game graphics, the depiction of sexual intercourse in this game leaves little to the imagination (Figure 5.16).

The most notorious pornographic game designed for the Atari 2600 was *Custer's Revenge*, in which the player assumes the role of a nude General

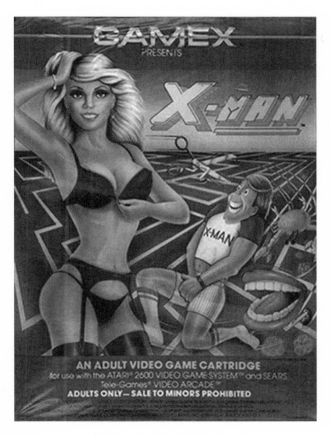

FIGURE 5.15 X-Man *(Universal Gamex) box art.*[15]

Custer with an erection who must dodge arrow attacks by Sioux Indians in order to rape a Native American woman tied to a cactus at the other end of the screen. Also known as *Westward Ho!* and *The White Man Came*, the box art for the game (Figure 5.18) depicts a Native American woman, less-scantily clad than in other pornographic games, but who appears to enjoy the much shorter General Custer performing oral sex on her while he ties her up. The naked Custer here is considerably unattractive, as saliva sprays from his mouth in his ravenous, beastly lust for the woman. Custer is naked in the game as well, except for his boots, and the nude Native American woman has a slightly darker skin tone than Custer. The designers of this game clearly spent more time on coding the intercourse component of the game than they did on the image of the cactus (Figure 5.19). Custer wears a pink scarf and a blue cowboy hat, and he and the naked Native American woman are both anatomically correct.

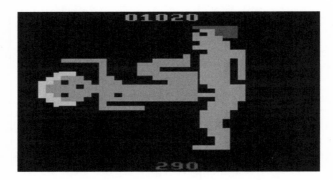

FIGURE 5.16 X-Man *(Universal Gamex) screenshot.*[16]

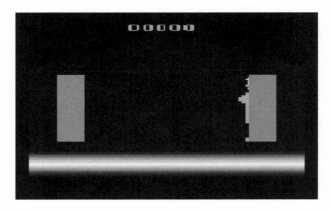

FIGURE 5.17 X-Man *(Universal Gamex) screenshot.*[17]

FIGURE 5.18 Custer's Revenge *(Mystique/Playaround) box art.*[18]

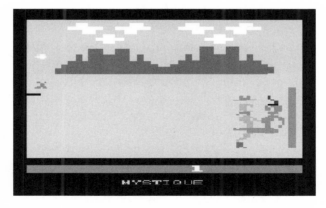

FIGURE 5.19 Custer's Revenge *(Mystique/Playaround) screenshot.*[19]

Even by 1982 standards, the game's graphics were weak. According to online video game reviewer Seanbaby (2002), in *Custer's Revenge*, "the graphics are so bad you can't tell you're playing a porno" ("EGM's Crapstravaganza Worst Games Ever" 160). Seanbaby (2003) also points out that the game's instruction manual in part reads, "If the kids catch you and should ask, tell them Custer and the maiden are just dancing" ("The 9 Naughtiest Games"). The representation of the naked characters and the rape equates to a simulacra, a representation that is only an imitation. In *Simulacra and Simulation*, Baudrillard writes that when Indians/Native Americans "returned to the ghetto," they became "the model of simulation of all the possible Indians from before ethnology," and this model gained "the luxury to incarnate itself beyond itself in the 'brute' reality of these Indians it has entirely reinvented" (8). Baudrillard continues by labeling the "savages" as "posthumous: frozen, cryogenized, sterilized, protected to death" because "they have become referential simulacra, and science itself has become pure simulation" (8). *Custer's Revenge,* therefore, depicts a stereotype of Native American character in addition to depicting a violent sexual act, both of which have the potential to become referential simulacra in Baudrillard's terms.

Atari filed a law suit to disassociate its game system from *Custer's Revenge*, as they reportedly "received up to 1200 complaints a day" about the game ("'Custer's Revenge' Removed" 1983). *Custer's Revenge* sold 80,000 copies, which amounted to twice the number of Mystique's other adult games (Kent 2002). In spite of a undoubtedly small target audience, the game received considerable negative attention; according to former *Electronic Games* editor-in-chief Arnie Katz, games such as *Custer's Revenge* "were games that most people wouldn't touch with a ten-foot pole" (Kent 2002, 556). Katz also noted that the organization Women Against Pornography picketed the game and that he told one of the organization's representatives to "ignore" the game to keep people from buying it (Marcovitz 2011). The controversy, however, according to Katz, ultimately doubled the sales of *Custer's Revenge* (Marcovitz 2011). In 1983, Kristin Reilly of the steering committee of Women Against Pornography said that, in response to the controversy over *Custer's Revenge*, the game company "denied it was rape" and "claimed that it was mutually consenting visual images, which is really asinine" (Moriarty 1983, 19).

Most of Mystique's pornographic games, including *Custer's Revenge*, came out in the same year. Incidentally, Atari had a "very disappointing" year in 1982, the year *Custer's Revenge* became available (Bernstein Research 1982), and as Wolf (2008) notes, at the release party of *Custer's Revenge*, "250 protestors gathered outside the New York Hilton" (284) to protest Mystique's official release of the game. To make matters worse, some Native American women reported being raped by men who referred to *Custer's Revenge* during the attack (Allen et al. 1985). The melding of pornographic content with what many perceived as sexual violence against a Native American woman in *Custer's Revenge* likely played the largest role in causing the disappearance not only of these video games but also of the company that produced them.

The company Playaround purchased Mystique when Mystique went out of business and created "double-ended" games out of Mystique's pornographic titles, which provided two games in one cartridge. In the bottom right corner of the box art of these games would appear the second game included (See Figures 5.1, 5.8, 5.9, 5.11, 5.13). Obviously not licensed by Atari, these pornographic games foreshadowed the 1990s' phenomenon of cybersex in their attempt to mingle a multimedia experience with erotic stimulation.

As video game technology advanced, however, themes and images once relegated to "behind-the-counter" games found their way into mainstream games played by gamers of all ages. In the case of games like *Custer's Revenge*, the strictures of the technology created an ambiguous series of visual images that allowed its designers to hide behind these limitations. Wolf argues that because of these limitations, games did not have the same impact and effect as later, more graphically developed ones, because earlier video games used "relatively simple graphics" that relied upon "iconic" and "abstract" depictions of reality or the experiences they sought to convey. But as technology advanced, according to Wolf, video games' "sophistication and verisimilitude" improved, and this led to a change in the gamer's experience. Wolf notes that whereas early video games' graphics were "so abstract and blocky that the game's manual had to describe what each was meant to be," more recent games have become more "real" and have created a more real-life simulation of reality (284). And as video game popularity spread, sex became more a part of mainstream games, with many popular games uniting sexuality with the gaming experience. As Hutchinson (2007) notes, in the case of the widely popular *Tomb Raider* game series, game character Lara Croft's "bodily form appears to have become ever-more sexualized, and her scantily clad dress (or lack thereof) ever more revealing" (16).

Video games such as *Tomb Raider* inherently involve an element of repetition, as no gamer can "finish" or "win" such video games on the first attempt. Deleuze likens repetition to representation and argues that it constitutes a transgression because it "belongs to humour and irony; it is by nature transgression or exception, always revealing a singularity opposed to the particulars subsumed under laws, a universal opposed to the generalities which give rise to laws" (5). Laws here can mean literal legislative laws, but more immediately, Deleuze's notion of "laws" suggests social mores, the "common-law" expectations of a society or community. Repetition of simulated, casual sex acts, in this context, constitutes a transgression of common Western social mores that traditionally expect sexual intercourse to take place only in the context of a monogamous relationship. Particularly in the context of Custer's rape of a Native American woman, the very act of playing *Custer's Revenge* repeatedly problematizes the epistemological experiences of seeking to win a game by raping a woman.

As with any consumer product, sex of course sells, but the beginnings of sexual content in video games appeared only in the context of video games specifically designed for adults, and retailers who sold these games typically did not display them with the other "kids'" games; forcing purchasers to have to ask specifically for the behind-the-counter adult games. Former *Penthouse* photographer Eugene Finkei claimed that the Mystique games were a "scam" and that they "must have been designed hastily" because there were "crude." He goes on to say that the "interaction between player and game was minimal," as was the "action," and that they were just "lousy games." The distributors and the public are wary of the product as a result of AMI's "Mystique games" (Moriarty). Eventually, however, mainstream video games in the early personal computer age began to incorporate sexual content, thus exposing such content to gamers aged under age 18.

As personal computers became standard household appliances in the 1980s, sexually explicit content followed soon after, including, for instance, Al Lowe's personal computer game *Leisure Suit Larry*. Released in 1987 by the now defunct video game company Sierra, the player in this game controls Larry Laffer, who attempts to have sex with the women he encounters in various hotels, casinos, and other lavish locales.

Like the box art for *Bachelor Party*, the box art for *Leisure Suit Larry* resembles the *For Your Eyes Only* poster, but in this instance, Larry looks between the faceless woman's legs while sitting in a presumably fancy sports car to go along with the exotic locales. Larry's leisure suit also appears very similar to Roger Moore-era James Bond clothing. *Leisure Suit Larry* spawned numerous sequels, the most recent of which appeared in 2009, but even in an early version, the game had taken on a certain self-conscious understanding of the game and its players with comments like "WHAT A PERVERT!!!" (Figure 5.20).

Even coin-operated arcade games began to depict graphic sexuality, a disturbing trend because an arcade could not hide such games "behind the counter." In the arcade game *Miss World Nude'96*, the player attempts to unlock areas on the screen to reveal a picture of a nude woman while creatures try to kill the player (Figure 5.22). During the game, the woman whose picture the gamer tries to uncover turns into a stack of bloody corpses (Figure 5.23). Screenshots from the game (Figure 5.22) depict either scantily clad or half-

FIGURE 5.20 Leisure Suit Larry *(Sierra Entertainment) screenshot.*

FIGURE 5.21 Miss Nude World'96 *(Comad Industry).*[20]

FIGURE 5.22 Miss Nude World'96 *(Comad Industry) screenshot.*[21]

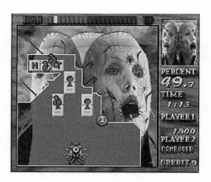

FIGURE 5.23 Miss Nude World'96 *(Comad Industry) screenshot.*[22]

naked women in very seductive and sleazy poses. This conflation of sex and death culminates in the fact that losing the game—that is, not successfully uncovering the image of the nude woman—results in the woman becoming something horrific, essentially implying that unless nude, a woman is horrific and ugly and signifies a failed attempt at sexual conquest.

Baudrillard sees a similar devaluing of sex in postmodernism, asserting that "sex and death are the great themes recognized for unleashing ambivalence and laughter." Baudrillard's remarks highlight the desensitizing to sex and violence that permeate most media in the Western world, and in the context of *Miss Nude World*, the implications of violence in place of failed sexual conquest has serious implications for failed sexual pursuits in the real world. The gamer might not be able to distinguish between the game world and the real world, as the gaming experience creates a type of repetition that Deleuze labels a "difference without a concept" and a "repetition which escapes indefinitely continued conceptual difference" (13). Particularly with early console games, gamers should have felt an overwhelming conceptual difference between game characters and real characters, but the attacks on Native American women prove otherwise. Popular belief holds that sexual violence results from sexual repression: Deleuze writes, "I do not repeat because I repress. I repress because I repeat, I forget because I repeat" (18). Deleuze's seemingly mindless subject engages in his conceptual repetition to the extent that it no longer remains a memory and essentially becomes a habit.

Criticized primarily for its violent content, *Grand Theft Auto III* features an army of streetwalkers, and predictably it generated ire from critics. In one of many possible images uniting sex and violence, Figure 5.24 shows the aftermath of the killing of one of these streetwalkers. In his explication of Freud's *Beyond the Pleasure Principle*, Deleuze writes that the union of sex and violence comes through a "narcissistic ego without memory"

FIGURE 5.24 Grand Theft Auto III *(Rockstar Games) screenshot.*

FIGURE 5.25 BMX XXX *(Acclaim Entertainment) screenshot.*

with a "death instinct desexualized and without love" (111). Death and sex, therefore, cannot coexist without sex becoming "desexualized and without love." The box art for *Grand Theft Auto V* shows a scantily clad woman making the "V" sign to signify both the Roman numeral for the game as well as, arguably, the female sex organ. The woman in this image also appears to be taking a "selfie," all while wearing little clothing and making an obscene gesture.

In Acclaim's arcade game *BMX XXX*, players collect cash on the competitive BMX circuit and then spend it in local strip clubs, complete with animated shots of topless dancers and half-naked bikers (Figure 5.25). This game received an "M" rating. In a combination of violence and sex, Tecmo's Xbox-only game, *Dead or Alive: Xtreme Beach Volleyball* displays a bikini-clad blonde on the box art. Again, in this image, there is the word "dead" over the top of three women wearing only bikinis.

Video games began their ascent to widespread popularity in the wake of the relatively recent second wave of feminism when in the United States antipornography groups began to appear, and academic and scientific studies coming soon after. In their 1981 study examining the effects of violent films on attitudes toward sex and violence, Malamuth and Check found that "males, relative to females, were more accepting of interpersonal violence[,] more accepting of rape myths [and] believed more in adversarial sex relations," while results for female test subjects "tended to be in the opposite direction" (441). While this may stand to reason for men watching pornographic, "X-rated" films in the early 1980s, Malamuth and Check found that the negative results happened after viewing movies that had aired on national television even if the theme of the movie was not about violent sexuality. It would seem that when watching mainstream adult movies, men should be able to compartmentalize the content and disassociate it from reality because their exposure to it came in a work of fiction. Nevertheless, according to Malamuth and Check, immediately after watching pornography the viewer may discount the images because they appeared as fiction, but over time the viewer can "disassociate" the fictive presentation and the initial "discounting"; this results in the viewer retaining the images but not the discounting, which can lead to a "long-term attitude change" (444). In a 1985 interview, Kirkendall pointed out that much pornography frequently contains violence, which typically "delineates the male or sets him up as a dominant figure in a relationship with the female as the subordinate" (24). In the same interview, antipornography activist Gina Allen called pornography a "symptom of a sick society" (29). Studies have also predictably shown that pornography can lead to misogyny. In their 1993 study of the effects of violent pornography versus those of nonviolent pornography, Demaré, Lips, and Briere similarly found that "sexually violent pornography" has direct effects on "self-reported likelihood of sexual force and rape, as well as on actual rape, and on coercive sexual behavior" in a manner that surpassed inherent "anti-women attitudes" outside of the context of viewing violent pornography (296–7). Demaré, Lips, and Briere blame pornography for antisocial and even criminal sexual attitudes and behavior.

Recent studies have also determined that video games largely portray women as subordinate to men. In their 2010 study about the effects of sexual video game content that objectifies women, Yao, Mahood, and Linz determined that "playing a sexually-oriented video game primes sex-related thoughts and increases accessibility to a negative gender schema of females as sex objects" (85). These and many other studies demonstrate how the viewer of pornography unconsciously interiorizes the pornographic content independent of any *a priori* misogynistic attitudes. Deleuze claims that the "interiority of repetition is always affected by an order of difference: it is only to the extent that something is linked to a repetition of an order other than its own that the repetition appears external and bare, and the thing itself subject to the categories of generality" (25). In other words, for Deleuze, repetition feeds a sense of generality in spite of its inherent reliance upon difference. Viewing any kind of pornography, whether on film, video, or video game, thus results in a "generalized" view of pornographic media in Deleuze's sense, a view that ultimately results in a one-size-fits-all view of women and sexuality. According to Stermer and Burkley (2012a), research demonstrates that misogynistic "video games paint a very narrow view of women, depicting them as subordinate to men and suggesting their primary role is as the object of men's desires" (2). Stermer and Burkley (2012b) also conclude that as video games become more and more popular for both children and adults, "important differences" may appear between how children and adults process video game stimuli, and this affects "behaviors in the context of existing knowledge" (533). For Stermer and Burkley, a child becomes particularly susceptible if he or she has not formed "rigid gender role expectations" (2012b, 533). In contrast to Mystique's simplistic pornographic video games, current mainstream video games include sexual content with much more detailed graphics and more powerful platforms, which suggests that current underage gamers playing such games are more susceptible to the negative effects of sexual content than were their adult counterparts playing Mystique's games in the 1980s.

Baudrillard argues that "only the doubling, the unfolding of the visual medium in the second degree can produce the fusion of technology, sex, and death" (117). In other words, we become what we see on the screen. Fueled by outrage over the Columbine massacre and the subsequent copycat incidents, the crisis of inappropriate games falling into the wrong hands led to the bipartisan Media Violence Labeling Act, introduced by Senators John McCain and Joseph Lieberman in 1999. This proposed bill requires enforcement of the existing rating system, with penalties up to $10,000 for violations. In 2000, Indianapolis instituted an ordinance that required retailers to place graphic games behind curtains and to limit access to gamers over 18 years of age. Increased cases of attention deficit disorder/attention deficit hyperactivity disorder, desensitization to real world violence, less sensitivity to pain and suffering of others, less socialization among children, stifled creativity, and a belief that the world is a mean and dangerous place are just a few of society's problems that anti-video game activists attribute to video games. The average age of a video gamer is 30, however—far beyond the age at which serious psychological or emotional damage can occur that would leave lasting effects. In Williams' (2003) influential study of television, the appliance that initially served as the "screen" for home video game systems, critical attention directed toward television has focused on sex, violence, "political manipulation," and "cultural degradation," which all "have to be seen in a whole social and cultural process" as aspects of ideology, that is, "a way of interpreting general change through a displaced and abstracted cause" (112). Deleuze sees a similar degradation in his notion of repetition, arguing that "in the infinite movement of degraded likeness from copy to copy, we reach a point at which everything changes nature, at which copies themselves flip over into simulacra and at which, finally, resemblance or spiritual imitation gives way to repetition" (128). A "spiritual imitation" giving way to repetition suggests the same kind of spiritual brokenness many of today's anti-video game activists decry. But unfortunately the outrage over violence depicted in video games has eclipsed any potential conversation about sexually explicit content in them, and this conversation becomes more and more relevant and immediately necessary in an age of concern over increasing sexual activity among younger children, a proliferation of reality TV shows about teenaged mothers, and increasing rates of sexually transmitted diseases in children.

Notes

1 Accessed March 24, 2015. http://www.atarimania.com/game-atari-2600-vcs-bachelorette-party-burning-desire_20269.html.
2 Accessed March 24, 2015. https://archive.org/details/atari_2600_burning_desire_1982_playaround_-_j.h.m._202.
3 Accessed March 24, 2015. http://www.tomheroes.com/Video%20Games%20FS/video%20games/Atari/2600boxes/J/jungle_fever.htm.
4 Accessed March 24, 2015. https://atariage.com/box_page.html?SoftwareLabelID=25.
5 Accessed March 24, 2015. https://archive.org/details/atari_2600_beatem_and_eatem_mystique.
6 Accessed March 24, 2015. https://archive.org/details/atari_2600_bachelor_party.
7 Accessed March 24, 2015. http://www.atariage.com/box_page.html?SoftwareLabelID=994.
8 Accessed March 24, 2015. http://www.atarimania.com/game-atari-2600-vcs-bachelorette-party-burning-desire_12087.html.
9 Accessed March 24, 2015. http://www.atarimania.com/game-atari-2600-vcs-bachelor-party-gigolo_12086.html.
10 Accessed March 24, 2015. https://archive.org/details/atari_2600_gigolo_1982_playaround_-_j.h.m._205.
11 Accessed March 24, 2015. http://www.atarimania.com/game-atari-2600-vcs-beat-em--eat-em-lady-in-wading_12088.html.
12 Accessed March 24, 2015. https://archive.org/details/atari_2600_lady_in_

wading_1982_playaround_-_j.h.m._204.

13 Accessed March 24, 2015. http://www.atarimania.com/game-atari-2600-vcs-jungle-fever-knight-on-the-town_12090.html.

14 Accessed March 24, 2015. https://archive.org/details/atari_2600_knight_on_the_town_1982_playaround_-_j.h.m._203.

15 Accessed March 24, 2015. http://en.wikipedia.org/wiki/File:Xman_atari.jpg.

16 Accessed March 24, 2015. https://www.google.com/url?sa=i&rct=j&q=&esrc=s&source=images&cd=&cad=rja&uact=8&ved=0CAcQjRw&url=http%3A%2F%2Fwww.youtube.com%2Fwatch%3Fv%3DOJCvxRCzk4g&ei=PYuQVP69N8mkNozAgJgC&bvm=bv.81828268,d.eXY&psig=AFQjCNFR_kuAlwlglOhzn573eOMPz-3xIA&ust=1418845341610448.

17 Accessed March 24, 2015. https://archive.org/details/atari_2600_x-man_1983_universal_gamex_corporation_alan_roberts_h.k._poon_gx-001.

18 Accessed March 24, 2015. https://archive.org/details/atari_2600_custers_revenge_1982_mystique_-_american_multiple_industries_joel_h._m.

19 Accessed March 24, 2015. https://archive.org/details/atari_2600_custers_revenge_1982_mystique_-_american_multiple_industries_joel_h._m.

20 Accessed March 24, 2015. http://cdn-www.cracked.com/articleimages/ob/seanbaby/header1.jpg.

21 Accessed March 24, 2015. http://cdn-www.cracked.com/articleimages/ob/seanbaby/naughty01b.jpg.

22 Accessed March 24, 2015. http://cdn-www.cracked.com/articleimages/ob/seanbaby/naughty01c.jpg.

References

Allen, Gina, Annie Laurie Gaylor, and Sol Gordon. 1985. "Pornography: A Humanist Issue." *Humanist* 45: 23–32.

Anderson, Craig Alan, Douglas A. Gentile, and Katherine E. Buckley. 2007. *Violent Video Game Effects on Children and Adolescents: Theory, Research, and Public Policy*. Oxford: Oxford University Press.

Baudrillard, Jean. 1994. *Simulacra and Simulation*. Ann Arbor: University of Michigan Press.

Bernstein Research. 1982. *The Video Game Industry: Strategic Analysis*, December 28.

Burgess, Melinda C. R., Steven Paul Stermer, and Stephen R. Burgess. 2007. "Sex, Lies, and Video Games: The Portrayal of Male and Female Characters on Video Game Covers." *Sex Roles* 57 (5/6): 419–33.

Demaré, Dano, Hilary M. Lips, and John Briere. 1993. "Sexually Violent Pornography, Anti-Women Attitudes, and Sexual Aggression: A Structural Equation Model." *Journal of Research in Personality* 27 (3): 285–300.

Deleuze, Gilles. 1994. *Difference and Repetition*. New York: Columbia University Press.

Hutchison, David. 2007. *Playing to Learn: Video Games in the Classroom*. Westport: Teacher Ideas Press.

Kent, Steven L. 2002. *The Ultimate History of Video Games*. New York: Random House International.

Malamuth, Neil M., and James V. P. Check. 1981. "The Effects of Mass Media Exposure on Acceptance of Violence Against Women: A Field Experiment." *Journal of Research in Personality* 15: 436–46.

Marcovitz, Hal. 2011. *Are Video Games Harmful?* San Diego: Reference Point Press.

Moriarty, Tim. 1983. "Focus On: Uncensored Videogames: Are the Adults Ruining It for the Rest of Us?." *Videogaming & Computergaming Illustrated: Uncensored Videogames: Where Do you Stand?* 10: 19–21.

Near, Christopher. 2013. "Selling Gender: Associations of Box Art Representation of Female Characters with Sales for Teen- and Mature-Rated Video Games." *Sex Roles* 68 (3/4): 252–69.

Novak, Jeannie and Luis Levy. 2008. *Play the Game: The Parent's Guide to Video Games.* Boston: Thomson Course Technology.

Seanbaby. 2002. "EGM's Crapstravaganza Worst Games Ever." *Electronic Gaming Monthly* 15 (1): 154.

Seanbaby. 2003. "The 9 Naughtiest Games Ever Made." *Electronic Gaming Monthly* 162: 134.

Skurnik, Jennifer "'Custer's Revenge' Removed: X-Rated Video Games Multiply." 1983. *Off Our Backs* 3 (27).

Stermer, Paul S., and Melissa Burkley. 2012a. "Sex-Box: Exposure to Sexist Video Games Predicts Benevolent Sexism." *Psychology of Popular Media Culture* 4 (1): 1–9.

Stermer, Paul S., and Melissa Burkley. 2012b. "Xbox or Sexbox? An Examination of Sexualized Content in Video Games." *Social & Personality Psychology Compass* 6 (7): 525–35.

Williams, Raymond. 2003. *Television: Technology and Cultural Form.* London and New York: Routledge.

Wolf, Mark J. P. 2008. *The Video Game Explosion: A History from PONG to Playstation and Beyond.* Westport: Greenwood.

Yao, Mike, Chad Mahood, and Daniel Linz. 2010. "Sexual Priming, Gender Stereotyping, and Likelihood to Sexually Harass: Examining the Cognitive Effects of Playing a Sexually-Explicit Video Game." *Sex Roles* 62 (1/2): 77–88.

Games cited

Comad. 1996. *Miss World Nude'96.* Comad.

Core Design. 1996. *Tomb Raider.* Eidos Interactive.

DMA Design. 2001. *Grand Theft Auto III.* Rockstar Games.

Midway Games. 1992. *Mortal Kombat I.* Midway Games.

Mystique. 1982. *Bachelor Party.* Mystique.

Mystique. 1982. *Bachelorette Party.* Mystique.

Mystique. 1982. *Beat'Em and Eat'Em.* Mystique.

Mystique. 1982. *Burning Desire.* Mystique.

Mystique. 1982. *Cathouse Blues.* Mystique.

Mystique. 1982. *Custer's Revenge/Westward Ho!* Mystique.

Mystique. 1982. *General's Retreat.* Playaround.

Mystique. 1982. *Gigolo.* Mystique.

Mystique. 1982. *Jungle Fever.* Mystique.
Mystique. 1982. *Philly Flasher.* Mystique.
Rockstar Games. 2013. *Grand Theft Auto V.* Take-Two Interactive.
Sierra Entertainment. 1987. *Leisure Suit Larry.* Sierra Entertainment.
Team Ninja. 2006. *Dead or Alive: Xtreme Beach Volleyball.* Tecmo.
Universal Gamex. 1983. *X-Man.* Universal Gamex.
Westwood Studios. 1995. *Command and Conquer.* Electronic Arts.
Z-Axis. 2002. *BMX XXX.* AKA Acclaim.

PART TWO

Video games and sexual (dis)embodiment

6

The strange case of the misappearance of sex in videogames

Tanya Krzywinska
(Falmouth University, UK)

Over the past few years, the popular press has made considerable capital from couching criticisms of video games in sensationalist rhetoric. One of the outfalls of the use of compellingly lurid rhetoric is the aggravation of fear; in this case the fear that games pose a significant threat to our peer-driven yet otherwise innocent children and teenagers, as well as more generally to our moral health and values. If the sensationalist rhetoric is believed, the impression gained is that video games are loaded with dangerous, corrupting, violent and sexual imagery.

"Computer games will carry cinema-style age ratings to protect children from violent and sexual images, ministers said yesterday," reports Tanya Byron in response to a UK government-commissioned report in 2007. Calls for greater regulation designed to gain the attention of the fearful are often served by yoking together sex and violence. British politics aside, this is a classic exploitation technique that thrives on lack of knowledge. Technology is presented as a portal through which will pour soul-eating terrors that threaten to undermine the pillars of civilization. Where violence or sex do appear in games—and why not, as these both play a core role in human imagination and experience—all sense that these are mediated and often highly contextualized in either gameplay or narrative terms (factors more likely to be taken into account in relation to the more established media such as film or television) is lost. For those looking for easy answers or wishing to exploit the fears of others without understanding, rhetorics of sensationalism enable games to be made responsible for the broader ills of society (Gauntlett 2005; Barker and Petley 2001).

And yet, the game industry has also benefited from sensationalist rhetoric in regard to sex, particularly in the perfumed promise of sexual utopia apparently offered by new digital and haptic technologies. During the 1980s, the term "teledildonics" fell like honey from the lips of the preblogging chattering classes. Promising a garden of delights, Virtual Sex emblemized the new frontier; throbbing and pulsating controllers provided only a tantalizing rumble of a future where bodies would be wired for perpetual orgasm, unfettered by relationships and sexually transmitted diseases. The pledge of ecstatic presence fizzled, however, in the cold light of a handful of pixels and a limited number of mechanized bleeps. Sexual promise is very often made in relation to new technologies, mobilized every time a new medium, interface method, or technological development is made—as for example, it was transferred to Microsoft's hands-free interface, Kinect, after the amatory disappointments of the Wii controller.

One of the most problematic aspects of sensationalist rhetoric when used as a tool to sway opinion is that it elides complexity. As psychoanalytic thought suggests, human sexuality is far from simply reproduction, with imagination as important as physiology and drives. Working with the erotic imagination (which does not acknowledge in its inherent putative state limiting realities), sensationalist rhetoric regularly promises far more than it actually delivers. However, once we look for the loudly denounced and promised sex in games, it is far less apparent than suggested. This point is very well made by Daniel Floyd's entertaining animated essay (2010), and Brenda Brathwaite makes a similar argument in her design guide, *Sex in Videogames* (2007). However, Floyd and Brathwaite, as well as making sensationalist claims, overlook a more subtle and erotic presence in gaming and games, which this paper seeks to demonstrate.

My plan is to take a more sophisticated and theoretically informed look at sex in games. While there is proportionally little sex in games in relation to other media, I will begin by showing that some games do have explicit sexual imagery; a necessary step, because it is important to ascertain the conventionalized types of rhetoric used within games to represent sex and sexual desire. Further, I aim to outline some of the context and conditions on which the explicit presence of sex seems to rest, and as well as addressing the wider and more subtle libidinal economies of games—a term I have adapted for use in this essay that is borrowed from psychoanalysis generally and Lyotard (1993) specifically. In a broader sense, such work is important if we are to move beyond the reductive model of "effects" theory. It is therefore a principal claim of this chapter that sex in games should not be measured simply by the use of explicit sexual imagery: broader concepts of sexuality and desire must be considered. I propose an approach to the study of sex and games that takes account of representation, rhetorics and conventions, game mechanics, and the libidinal economies at work in games and the act of gaming. Working in concert, game computing and mechanics, story structures, and representation constitute a game's aesthetic configuration, and all must be considered when regarding our libidinal investment in games. In so doing I draw on concepts and models that provide a libidinal understanding of sex and desire. I will start by examining some of the leading conventions used in the representation of sex in games, focusing on graphics and narrative. Going on to analyze the use of sex, overtly or implicitly, in terms of the design of game mechanics, I conclude with a section arguing for a more diffuse and sophisticated understanding of the "erotics of games."

For something to be sexually "graphic" in visual, pornographic terms, there has to be a certain level of detail so that the anatomical features involved in sex are apparent. Graphical fidelity is therefore important if an equivalent of a human body is to be constructed in a game—in fact, the development of sex in games hinges on such. That is not to say that game bodies need to be depicted stylistically in a photographic way, of course. Early 2D games managed to manipulate a few pixels to look like human breasts and erect penises in a highly crude graffiti-esque style. Mystique's *Custer's Revenge* is an example (Figure 6.1). The game's graphics are extremely "crude" in an overdetermined way and arise in part from their 8-bit, exploitation production context (indeed Atari sued Mystique for defaming their brand); and, while the intention might have been simply to garner attention through brutal crassness, the game's graphical crudeness makes explicit, through challenging rape imagery, the sexual agenda of American colonialism. Later developments in graphics technologies and particularly motion capture provide far greater expressive means in the representation of the sexual body. Bodies and their movements are now far more refined and subtle, allowing games to draw more readily on the types of images and representations of sex found in film-based media.

With the increased potential of graphics technologies, game bodies became tailored more tightly to please the gaze, although rarely do these idealized game bodies engage in sex. Sontag (1982) noted that in written fiction designed to be consumed as pornography, a style emerges where everything is exaggerated. The Marquis de Sade's stories, for example, are populated with huge male members and engorged female genitalia that

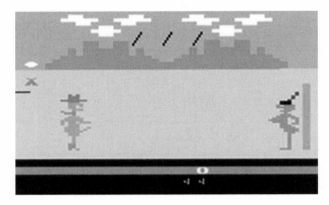

FIGURE 6.1 *From Pixels to Motion Capture:* Custer's Revenge *Screenshot.*
Source: http://upload.wikimedia.org/wikipedia/en/a/ae/S_CustersRevenge_1.png.

overpower subjectivity and rationality. Silicone implants and the fashion for bodybuilding are keyed into such an exaggerated mode—coded as they are in and through fantasy, and where tumescence and rigidity become an expressive form. Digitally produced bodies are sculpted straight from the imagination. Unencumbered by real-life physics, unrestricted by flesh and bones, game bodies are impossibly ideal. Yet, while anything is possible, a conventionalized and binarized picture emerges—large breasts, long legs, and tiny waists for women; bulked-out muscles for men. Archetypal sexualized avatars are deployed to create a seductive, connotation-based bestiary for the imagination to play with but which implicitly demonstrate the fallibility of and lack in our poor bodies.

Developments in graphics technologies allow designers and artists to create for players alluring characters, providing support for being in the world of the game by providing objects of desire and aspiration for players. However, the muscled, the agile, and the powerful represent sex—they do not have sex. Governed by the economics of the ideal and the forward motion of games (see Atkins 2006), iconic characters act as our fetishes, objects that bring desire into existence to keep it in play and hungry; as a result, sex itself must remain off-scene.

Given that games promise "action," it is a little surprising that sex is rarely integral to game stories. Where sex is present, it is likely to appear in a cutscene. The *Mass Effect* games included short sex scenes presented mainly as cutscenes. There is some player input, however, depending on verb choices and on which character the player has chosen to play and who the player chooses to interact with. Players can elect for their player-character to have sex with humans or aliens and differently gendered. For example, sex between a male Shepard and Liara, an alien, is a tender affair presented as an expression of intimacy and intensity. In many ways this pair conforms to the cinema equivalent of the "proper couple," except of course this is cross-species sex. Cutscenes enable the game to draw on the visual vocabularies used within cinema. Various camera angles can be utilized, marking a difference to the monolithic use of camera elsewhere. The framing pattern presents the encounter between Shepard and Liara in the first game as intimate and loving, using romance to legitimize the presence of sex. Implied sex through romantic liaison is common at the level of story in games, where sex tends to occupy the backstory. In an alternate scene in the first game between Ash (a human female) and a male Shepard, the encounter is presented in terms of fun and playfulness (with a hint of sadomasochistic-style power play)—a pastime framed as affectionate but not seemingly an expression of deep romantic love or passion. A further permutation is one that occurs between Liara and a female Shepard, again an intimate and passionate encounter, even if a classic pornographic trope designed mainly for male consumption. Importantly, all these encounters fade to black—another cinematic convention—once the idea of what is happening is established, even more quickly, in the case of those including the least human of the aliens.

Games draw on cinema, but game bodies are not those of actors—even if data on movement of real bodies is used. Lara Croft is made in the model of a pinup, but what does it mean to see her nude? Under the skin she is all wireframe, reminding us that our libidinal relation with game characters is the product of technological adept illusion tailored, like Pygmalion's Galatea, to the consumer's imagination. Lara's form, presenting a Sadean tumescent pornographic body in the pose of fifties cheesecake, is all tailored to the requirements of the action genre. We cannot see Lara nude, only the representation/simulation of nudity; very different, therefore, from physically nude actors in live-action cinema. Nudity is carefully managed in cinema and games, even if the status of nudity is very different. It might seem surprising, but before the introduction of the Production Code in the 1930s, Hollywood films presented a certain amount of nudity—present, for example, in D. W. Griffith's *Intolerance*. With the implementation of greater regulation in the late 1920s, actresses' breasts were covered, and framing and editing techniques were used to suggest but elide the physical sexual body. Such suggestive yet elliptical techniques are often simulated in games, as the fade-to-black in *Mass Effect* games shows. The effect of the suggestive elision, though, plays toward exploitation, rendering sex more dangerous and seductive.

Story types and tropes are also borrowed from cinema (as well as other media) and, as in many other forms of popular fiction, "romance" between two complementary people (class, race, age, aspiration, etc.) provides the condition that legitimizes the presence of sex. Where this trope is missing, sex becomes sensationalized or even unconscionable—a framework exploited by the *Grand Theft Auto* franchise. Romance also lends pathos in revenge or rescue scenarios but is rarely the major theme in the context of action-led games. Like film, many games also use the legitimizing and permissive effect of comedy, a framework that has often been used in popular culture to permit mentions of sex and desire. Games are generally less focused on sex and romance than action, however. It is rare for games to show sex as tragic, traumatic, or a form of self-empowerment, a trope found in soft-core movies with female central protagonists such as *Emmanuelle* (1974) or *Story of O* (1975); although in *Fable*, it does represent a rite of passage and helps to make the central character more rounded and believable. Symbolization is another common and suggestive device borrowed from film and fictional forms—the "dance" of two adult piñatas seen in cutscene as a prelude to the production of babies in *Viva Piñata* is a good example and one designed for children to play. Preexisting vocabularies are therefore deployed in games. These range from those derived from mainstream, art, and exploitation cinema, as well as soft-core and hard-core film. But, decisively, games also use sex in ways that extend beyond representation and narrative. It is to the place of sex as a game mechanic that I now turn.

It is helpful to make a distinction between games and virtual sex simulators (although the latter can be found in some games). While sex simulators (sims) have a relatively long history and are often found for free on the unregulated Net, in terms of market and form they are not "games," even as they may have similar interfaces and use conventions found in games. Sex sims are generally designed to be consumed as exclusively porn, while the situation with games that incorporate sex within the sphere of game mechanics is more complex. Most of the games looked at here are those where sex is integral to their internal and external design.

Playboy: The Mansion has as its lead designer Brenda Brathwaite, an advocate of sexually explicit games for adults. The game is made under the Playboy franchise, gamifying a well-known brand and making use of that brand to inform the game's representational dimensions. Social aspiration and a tongue-in-cheek humor prevail. In the guise of "Hef" (Hugh Hefner, the magazine's "playboy" owner), the player is tasked with building relationships with a range of visitors to his house in order to create copy (photos, articles, and interviews) for a magazine. Progress is made by holding parties, getting women to pose nude for Hef/player's in-game camera, and persuading minor celebrities to write for the magazine or be interviewed. In this way, status and cash are accumulated—both overtly measured and keyed into the game's internal winning conditions. The mechanics borrow in part from *The Sims* mixed with those of the *Tycoon* series. A drive meter is visible to the player for each nonplaying character (NPC), providing a means by which a player can see how happy they are: the aim is to do what keeps them happy. This is done by choosing from the various verbs provided by the game to compose a conducive conversation with those NPCs. Ego-soothing bunnies aid Hef/player's passage through the social encounters thrown up by the game, although if they are neglected they will leave the mansion, diminishing the player's route to success. Prestigious people are attracted to parties once the player spends money on hipper furnishings and on entertainment. Hef/player can also take photos of his well-managed female guests to place in his magazine. The player can cycle through various poses and site the model in a location with the click of a few buttons. The game also includes "factoids" from the magazine's history and images of (real) past "playmates."

The game provides a highly regulated tease; sex is clearly the core theme, and its most explicit articulation can be found when Hef/player persuades a female NPC to have sex with him. The persuasion process takes a while, but eventually sex ensues. The Playstation handset vibrates to indicate orgasm as the woman sits astride Hef, whom we see in third person; her climax is comically (ridiculously) indicated by an *in-situ* backflip and a shout of "weeeee," as if she was on a fairground ride. Both keep their pants on throughout, making naked breasts the focus of attention, as was mostly the case with the *Playboy* magazines. There are no sexually graphic cut-ins or close-ups of the type usual in hard-core film—inclusions that would place the game outside of regulatory systems. No risk is therefore taken with the franchise or investment. Women with whom player/Hef has built close relations are more likely to readily pose and have sex with him. Relationship building is therefore central even in the broader context of the business and commercialization of the sexual body. Sex here is unproblematic; that is, once appropriate smoothing devices are deployed. As such, sex becomes quantifiable, gamified, and, simultaneously constructed as a normal activity partaken of by consenting adults without deep emotional or marital ties. If you know the rules of the game you can "make out" for pleasure and business. *Playboy: The Mansion*'s version of sex is intended not to be read as perverse or transgressive. By virtue of this formulation, Brathwaite is able to make a game where sex becomes part of the gameplay mechanics and actively uses symbols and ellipses to mark it off from "hard-core" pornography.

By contrast, *7 Sins* takes a far less benign and normalizing approach to sex. Here, sex is associated with cynicism and transgression. Sex is certainly not legitimated by romance or even titillating playfulness. Unlike the *Playboy* game, the aim is not to manage the drives of others but to manage your own. You play an "unrepressed" (sexually psychotic) man, and your task is to keep the player-character's "sin" bars topped up, never letting one drive overwhelm the others. It is a far less slick and well-designed game than the high-profile, big-budget *Playboy: The Mansion*, underlining thereby *7 Sins'* grimy, exploitative qualities. The main game arc is supplemented with various minigames, accessible at any time, that are designed to help balance out the player-character's sin bars. Various possibilities are on offer: zooming in to "perv" portions of a cartoonish female body, stealing money from a woman's flat; and perhaps the most bizarre minigame of the lot is one designed to bring down the Anger bar, where the player-character urinates into a potted plant, aiming the flow to swat flies. The verbs that govern the game's internal design are composed of transgressive actions such as "steal," "grope," or "perv," and in-game conversation options range from clichéd chat-up lines to abuse. In the first level of the game, the player-character is tempted to transgress but compelled to manage his urges in order not to get fired from the shop where he is working. The odd good deed can be undertaken to rebalance close-to-bulging sin bars (the temptation for the player is to see what happens when the different sin bars maximize). The game's internal mechanic derives implicitly from a model of sexuality associated with unconscious drives, drawing on the powerful notion that the sexual drive is disruptive and compelling. This conceptualization of sex is one that informs older pornographic fiction, such as de Sade's monstrous fornicators. It is also a model that is found in psychoanalysis and the Lapsarian notion of sex as shameful. As a cross-medial genre, exploitation makes its capital from precisely this transgressive notion of sex and sexual desire. In this sense, a psychoanalytic model of sex as drive-based fits hand-in-glove in games where there is a need for quantification; a drive model of sex can therefore be easily translated into gamic terms through a device such as a progress bar.

"We are puppets of our hormones and genetic programs. But nature repays us with pleasure." (Blackburn 2004)

The games I have mentioned above are rare in their explicit use of sex whether in or at play in representation and gameplay mechanics, yet we might approach the topic of sex and games in a more subtle way by looking closely at the libidinal economy of the player-game relationship in games where sex appears to be absent.

Playing games appears to be a very rational and controlled activity. Many theorists of games have defined games in terms of their rules and the need for players to manage their performance, considering these their defining condition. I have argued elsewhere (2009) that a great deal of the pleasure of playing games lies in the sensations and rewards associated with becoming a more skillful and prudently responsive player of a given game. But management through constraint is not the only pleasure game in town; games are more than just these, and when addressing the erotics of play, we have to take rules into account not simply as procedural elements of a game but more generally as part of a libidinal economy—to use Lyotard's evocative phrase (meaning the psychic and emotional energy produced by drives). In pursuit of understanding the libidinal economy of games, our focus is on the relationship between the player and the game, and game designers deploy a large variety of devices to please, tease, and excite a player.

It has become quite common in text-based game studies analysis to regard games in terms of the verbs they proffer. As a means of aiding in the task to understand more deeply the pleasures of games, it seems helpful to also regard games in terms of adjectives. Appropriately, these knit syntactically with a game's mechanical verbs, making up a game's vocabulary. In chaining adjectives with verbs, my aim here is to show how "doing'" in a game becomes libidinally charged. The particular grain of a given act couched within meaning-producing contextual qualifiers is designed to resonate and evocate. Actions in games are cyphers or metonyms—not full acts as would be the case in the real world but instead actions made potent by imagination. Prompted by physical actions and the events on screen, the player conjures from memory and imagination what it feels like to be doing that action. The libidinal economy of game is then, in part, dependent on a creative engagement on the part of the player.

Table 6.1 lists verbs and adjectives that characterize our libidinal investment in games. Some of the words listed would be erotically charged in connection with any media, but some are specific to games, and some are drawn from the work of critics, as is the case with Espen Aarseth's evocative terms Aporia and Epiphany (1997). What is also notable here in terms of libidinal economics

Table 6.1 Libidinal characteristics in the gaming encounter

Expectation	Immersion
Intensity curves	Bodily control—condensed movements
Frustration/Aporia	Concentration/focus
Elation	Skillful
Release	Drive
Reward	Enigma/relevation
Feedback	Ephipany

is that they all carry a sexual connotation: words that we might find used in an artful yet nuanced description of a sexual encounter.

For a moment I ask you to take up the position of an artist or lover, observing with passion and attentive to all the nuances of line, form, and correspondence. Let's take *Assassin's Creed* (2007) as the object of such a mode of seeing; other games are possible, of course. In a general sense, the chief pleasure of this game is the kinetic energy afforded to the player through the player-character, renegade Assassin Altair. The player-character can scramble up buildings, jump gaps between them, and climb high pinnacles to survey the environment, as well as run, sneak, and wield various weapons. All these actions are necessary to progress through the game. What this verb-approach does not reveal are the qualities of how our pleasure in this is achieved. Throughout the game, characters are built and designed around the use of motion capture, which lends them a nuanced and fluid mode of movement. This invests vitality, animating them so they do not act in stilted or repetitive ways. Characters also move through intensively eye-arresting, detailed environments. There are no clean horizon lines to be seen here, nor simple graphical planes; instead, the eye dances across multilayered shapes, movements, colors, and textures. Altair himself moves with ultimate confidence and grace in this world (it is, after all, measured precisely to his computational and graphical physics). He is also the embodiment of contradictions: conundrums that arrest the gaze and intrigue. He is extremely agile, leaping weightlessly across impossible voids, yet also steadily weighted, with footfalls and arm movements seeming solid—connecting reassuringly with the world he so lithely inhabits. His chain mail presses downward into his body, yet sits in juxtapositioned contrast with the fluidity of the light cotton tabard that dances around his legs, emphasizing his movement and linking him to the free and transcendent breeze. The eroticized kinetic power in the free-floating cloth provides for the player a characterization of Altair, who moves in mysterious ways, particularly noticeable in cutscene sequences where he leaps in faith from some precipitous minaret, leaving the player to wonder at his physical assurance. Exotic and distanced by strong third-person characterization, he is briefly ours to hold, a fetish in the sanctioning of our mesmerized gaze. The same attention to kinetic detail is also found in Altair's fighting animations. Taking on a group, he whirls like a dervish, sword flying in balletic arcs. Killing softly, his primary mode is quiet assassination, an act shown as at once tender and brutal: slitting the throat of one victim with a spring-loaded blade, then stroking closed the eyes of his victim. His veiled face, silky, assured movements, the noticeable physical contact with those he shoulders past or fights, all work to evoke a complex, embodied, and tactile presence.

What can also be said to be present in this characterization is a libidinal coherence around what psychoanalysis calls a phallic economy, more accurately pivoting around the eroticization of the act of penetration. Sliding the knife in, slicing deep and intimately into the flesh of enemies; all this violent yet artful penetration balances with a more general economy of physical touch. There is therefore, clearly, an erotic dimension in play, perhaps just under the surface for some players, and of course as it is the player who puts the knife in, he or she, too, is implicated in this erotic, violent *danse macabre*. A certain type of sexual currency is apparent—one that links penetration with domination, sharpened by Altair's silken touch. This economy of domination is complex, forged on the anvil of homosociality, and brackets off any notion of penetrative sex as an expression of equality and intimacy.

I am not the only one to note the erotic economy at work in games that are not apparently about sex. In a rather different way, Hanna Wirman (2009) noted the erotic encouragements of the deep-voiced male narrator in *Bejewelled*, who encouragingly purrs the word "good," building to "excellent" and "awesome," at the player. Such sexualized encouragement sits alongside orgasmic explosions when lines are conjoined. This is a game that has proved extremely successful in the casual game market and may well have used such techniques to seduce a female market. In a more general sense, the act of designing a game as an orchestrated experience of a player can also be regarded in the same way that a theatricalized fetish or sadomasochistic scene may be choreographed; both are designed to take the participant on a journey, with the game/scene designer assigned power over the player/submissive, who must submit to exacting demands, through the contract of the game.

According to Blackburn (2004), the definition of lust is the "anticipation of pleasure" and the "pursuit of rapture" (16). These work equally well in describing playing a game. Designers aim to keep players playing—to tease them onward by constantly projecting players forward in time to what is yet to come (Atkins 2006). But many play to lose themselves in the heat of the moment, to feel the break in tension caused by the completion of a difficult task. Blackburn tells us lust is "desire that is felt, the storm that floods the body. That heats and boils and excites" (17). Gamers regularly speak of how they become immersed in a game and their perception of time distorted, suggesting that there is a link between a sense of immersion in a game and the medieval definition of ecstasy, where we transcend time and ourselves. While this might be a bridge too far for some who have a more prosaic approach to games, it is the case that games are loaded with textual seductions—prediction, revelation, progress, and feedback as well as kinetic and audiovisual pleasures. Cybernetic qualities are also libidinal qualities that become evident in a player's synergic relationship with a game, the mutual responses back and forth—a dance or conversation—resembling the reciprocity of engaging in (good) consensual sex. Like making music with others, playing a collaborative game in a group means riffing on real-time events, timing one's actions to synchronize with others, and guessing what they might do next; reciprocal sensitivities that create a strong and pleasing sense of synchrony, providing a particular kind of libidinally informed pleasure that is based on the twin pillars of ritual and mutuality. In addition to all this dancing, we are also offered impossible, idealized bodies to inhabit that promise to free us from our so fallible meat (fear not, I will refrain from the obvious extension here!). Yet at the same time, such escapes work counterwise to bring home the limitations and sensualities of the flesh.

Freud reminds us that human sexuality is complex, psychological, and diversely invested. Could it be that the suffusion of libidinal energy within games is symptomatic of constraints on a more direct or even truer expression of sexual desire in popular culture? Could it be that we are now inheriting the outfall from the fact that games have tended to avoid eighteen ratings because that would limit their market? Is the traditionally sexually conservative American market driving the sublimation of sex in games? The plethora of sexualized bodies and violent action that appear in games seem to be instantiations of the return of the repressed. Hollywood's Production Code in the early 1930s certainly produced a sublimation of sex into other charged images/themes, particularly in melodrama and screwball comedy, which often relied on innuendo to speak in code about sex to its audience. Freud argues that repressed sexual desires always find a way to be aired. Having said this, do we really want "groaning fornication" in games? Doesn't the erotic thrive on the veiled, the suggestive, the hidden and forbidden? The outcome of the veiling of sex does, however, reinforce inadvertently a "transgressive" rhetoric of sex, and perhaps is this symptomatic of an unconscious need to preserve the frisson of sex afforded by such rhetoric?

Games do demand control of "lust," and games regularly rely on deferred gratification. Yet the promise of pleasure is always there, keeping us playing, hungry for more. Desire slaked is desire no more; gone, its invigorating energy. Games provide us with machines for the perpetuation of desire. It is tempting to think that this is why there are quite a few sex management games on the market—these games make as their ludic mechanic the act of making, controlling, and manipulating lust. Isn't that what we do when we defer gratification and keep trying again when we play games? The lust-balancing mechanic of 7 Sins then slots neatly in as a conceit about the nature of games and gaming. But before this gets carried away too far, this game makes use of age-old rhetoric that sees sex as "lustful," in need of control lest we will somehow become unanchored, adrift in a sea of sensual pleasures, lost to work and family ties. Yet isn't this why we play games? To lose our anchors? To experience immersion and flow? There is certainly some capital here in seeing games as desire machines. They promise us pleasure, yet in return we subject ourselves to their rules and regimes of work. Many devices of compulsion get used in this process of seeking the ecstatic—allowing us to be beside ourselves, immersed in a game. And this is why it is valid to make claims that games have libidinal economies.

Game sex has conditions that are indicative of the main ways in which sex is shaped by contemporary commerce and cultural values. It is acceptable when it is wrapped in the silks of romance as theme, narrative, or activity motivator. Transgression seems less of a condition, yet a major way in which sex is shown in popular culture is as sinful, in terms of either exploitation or titillation, as carnival or comedy. These are generic means to render sex excitingly transgressive. We have also seen a more complex rhetoric of sex at work in games that do not show sex directly—the kinetic and gendered economy of tumescence and penetration. And in terms of playing games we subject ourselves to rules; we may think we are playing but we are played, our experience orchestrated as it might be in a bondage scene.

I hope that the increasing democratization of the tools used to make digital games results in greater diversity in the way they treat sex. Culturally, there needs to be more widespread acknowledgment that sex is more complex than an "act" and that it might be regarded in ways other than as governed by a quantifiable drive. Designers also need to get beyond the anodyne romance model and the myth of complementarity to address the disturbing otherness of sex, but without unreflexive recourse to clichéd rhetorics of exploitation. These moves will then provide an account of the complexity of human sexuality as a means of countering sensationalist moral panic rhetorics about games. Making game sex in more diverse ways further enables designers to explore the potentialities of game media in relation to a core part of human life. And, finally, more broadly, such work would be part of a more general cultural process of engaging with, rather than disavowing, the radical strangeness of sex, desire, and sexuality.

References

Aarseth, Espen. 1997. *Cybertext: Perspectives on Ergodic Literature*. New York: Johns Hopkins University Press.

Atkins, Barry. 2006. "What Are We Really Looking At? The Future Orientation of Play." *Games and Culture* 1 (2): 127–40.

Barker, Martin and Julian Petley. 2001. *Ill Effects: The Media/Violence Debate*. 2nd edn. New York: Routledge.

Blackburn, Simon. 2004. *Lust: The Seven Deadly Sins*. Oxford: Oxford University Press.

Brathwaite, Brenda. 2007. *Sex in Video Games*. Boston: Charles River Media.

Floyd, Daniel. 2010. Animated Lectures on Videogame Issues. http://unrealitymag. com/index.php/2010/04/23/daniel-floyds-animated-lecture-series-on-video-game-issues/.

Gauntlett, David. 2005. *Moving Experiences. Media Effects and Beyond*. 2nd edn. London: John Libbey.

Krzywinska, Tanya. 2009. "Reanimating HP Lovecraft: The Ludic Paradox of Call of Cthulhu: Dark Corners of the Earth." In *Horror Video Games*, edited by Bernard Perron, 267–88. Jefferson: McFarland & Co.

Lyotard, Jean-Francois. 1993. *Libidinal Economy*. London: Athlone Press.

Sontag, Susan. 1982. "The Pornographic Imagination." In *A Susan Sontag Reader*, 205–34. Harmondsworth: Penguin.

Wirman, Hanna. 2009. "And he said, gasping, 'Good . . . Excellent'." *Bad Games Colloquium*, July 18. Bristol: University of the West of England.

Games cited

Big Blue Box. 2004. *Fable*. Microsoft Game Studios.

BioWare. 2007. *Mass Effect*. EA.

Cyberlore Studios. 2005. *Playboy: The Mansion—Private Party Expansion*. Groove Games.

DMA Design. 1997. *Grand Theft Auto*. BMG Interactive.

Maxis. 2000. *The Sims*. Electronic Arts.

Monte Cristo. 2005. *7 Sins*. Digital Jesters.

Mystique. 1982. *Custer's Revenge*. Mystique.

PopCap Games. 2001. *Bejewelled*. PopCap Games.

Rare. 2006. *Viva Pinata*. Microsoft Game Studios.

Ubisoft Montreal. 2007. *Assassin's Creed*. Ubisoft.

7

Let's play master and servant: BDSM and directed freedom in game design

Víctor Navarro-Remesal (Centro de Enseñanza Superior Alberta Giménez (CESAG), Spain) and Shaila García-Catalán (Universitat Jaime I of Castellón, Spain)

In a sense, only a single drama is ever staged in this "nonplace" the endlessly repeated play of dominations. The domination of certain men over others leads to the differentiation of values; class domination generates the idea of liberty. . . . This relationship of domination is no more a "relationship" than the place where it occurs is a place; and, precisely for this reason, it is fixed, throughout its history, in rituals, in meticulous procedures that impose rights and obligations. It establishes marks of its power and engraves memories on things and even within bodies. It makes itself accountable for debts and gives rise to the universe of rules, which is by no means designed to temper violence, but rather to satisfy it. . . . the law is a calculated and relentless pleasure, delight in the promised blood, which permits the perpetual instigation of new dominations and the staging of meticulously repeated scenes of violence.

(FOUCAULT 1988, 38–39)

Video games are defined by player agency; that is, their discourse depends on player action to exist. This agency implies that the player has freedom and power, and, because of that, they are often seen both as power fantasies and as the next step in a linear evolution of media. But this freedom and power are never absolute; they obey a clearly defined set of rules with strict limits. We uphold the concept of "directed freedom" (Navarro-Remesal 2013) to explain the role of the player within the video game system and define games as a medium. BDSM practices are sexual activities related to domination, submission, and the whole range of power dynamics between two or more sexual partners. This focus on power and freedom seems to be a good match for the aforementioned nature of video games. We believe that a look at BDSM in gaming will provide us with a better understanding of the construction of freedom, agency, and discourse in this medium.

Although it is quite uncommon, some games have depicted BDSM not only as an aesthetic embellishment but also as a vital piece of the ruleset. Such is the case of the mainstream game *God of War III*, the independent productions *Bind Her* and *Consensual Torture Simulator*, and the commercial niche service *3DKink*. In this chapter, we analyze these works—and the codification of freedom and power within them—by combining game design theory and a philosophical approach based on the Hegelian figures of the Master and the Slave. This analysis illustrates some tendencies in the depiction of sex and alternative sexualities in games and shows the mechanisms of the tension between system and player and their role in creating a playable discourse.

The player in, or under, control: Directed freedom

As cultural texts, video games empower the reader, turning her into a player. To put it simply, without a player there is no video game. Interactivity is a main trait, but not every interactive product is a game—they can include websites or DVDs, for example—nor does every element of a game need to be interactive; authors like Newman (2002) and Aranda and Sánchez-Navarro (2009) have upheld the importance of noninteractive moments in playable texts. If a video game is a system that produces an experience for the player, it is implicit that every element of it adds to this experience—be it interactive, noninteractive, or aesthetic. Cutscenes, pauses, scripted events, and limits, among other devices, are tools of the gaming trade. Games use a very specific type of interactivity: a ludic one, with ludic rules, goals, and constraints.

Games create ethical, political, and aesthetic meaning, and the authorship of this meaning is still debated. Some authors understand them as tools for player expression, while others see the player as a mere enabler of a discourse created by the designers. Sicart (2011) labels these positions as "instrumental play" and "procedurality," respectively. Lövlie (2005) writes about a guided experience, willingly limited by the designers, that the player has to "reenact" in an active manner. He calls this "reenactment." This seems more accurate to the reality of game design: the final experience is the result of what the player can do within the game but also of what she can only witness, what she cannot do, and, even more importantly, what she cannot avoid doing. No matter how big the game is, the player will be in charge, but only within the margins of its ruleset, which she has to obey.

Voorhees (2013) writes about the "game/player problem," a dichotomy between two schools of thought that focus either on the player or on the game when conceptualizing control, and defends gameplay as an "economy of desire that operates between the player and the game itself" (16). Smith (2007) puts it under a more deterministic and proceduralist light: "A designer who wants to tell the story of how A leads to B while maintaining an interactive element will start going to great lengths to ensure the interactor that the choices he makes are important while making absolutely sure that they are not." The system enables a universe of visible desires and possible actions, and the player defines her own path within that universe. She is, then, in control but also a slave.

This is what we call "directed freedom," "the margin of action that the system allows for the player through communication with it" (Aranda and Sánchez-Navarro 2009, 23). The player has a certain degree of freedom in four different aspects of the game: (1) to explore and interact with the system elements, that is, actions and reactions; (2) to adopt several strategies when solving the problems posed by the system; (3) to customize and generate content; and (4) to modify the structure of the game, creating her own path from a wide array of combinations. This freedom can be summarized in two factors: player representation—her "avatarness," the way she is embodied within the gameworld and the role she has to adopt to play it—and structural flexibility— the possible paths the system can take and the ways the player can travel through them. We define directed freedom, then, as "the characteristics of the structural flexibility of the system modulated by the player representation. That is, the possibilities of agency within the game system: what the player can do, through what or who can she do it, how can she do it and what are the consequences of what she does" (Aranda and Sánchez-Navarro 2009, 33).

There is no game with absolute freedom, as games need goals, rules, and end states. The concept of directed freedom denies, or at least questions, the cultural enthusiasm of interactivity as something that is measured in quantity—the more interactive a game is, the better—and of games as the next step in a media genealogy, somehow surpassing the previous ones. From this genealogical point of view, the appearance of a new representation medium brings something the previous one lacked, setting the scene for the attractive but deceptive idea of games as "interactive storytelling." But video games are not just an evolution of other audiovisual forms; they were born from several origins, including analog games, role-playing, and theatrical and audiovisual representation, like cinema and television. Not every video game features a strong narrative—or any narrative at all—and, as we have shown, not every moment in a game is interactive. As Linderoth (2002) explains, video games have a "system"—the ludic ruleset—and "guise"—the fiction, the audiovisual representation—and narrative elements can be spread on both sides.

The expressive potential of games as a medium comes from the tension between the designers and the players: what is offered by the former and what the latter do with it. The discourse and its meaning are constantly negotiated in this interaction; in the dual gift of power and impotence. Negotiation, power, and impotence are ideas that also serve as the foundation of BDSM.

Concerning power and desire: The Hegelian myth of Master and Slave

In chapter IV of *Phänomenologie des Geistes* (*The Phenomenology of Spirit* or *Mind*, depending on the translation), Hegel reimagines the genesis of Humanity through the mythical situation of the Master and the Slave. Kojève (1980) interprets Hegel's ideas from the notion of Desire as the driving force of action. And action, as we have explained, is essential in video games: cultural texts whose novelty lies in putting the reader in an active position, turning her into a player, an actor. For Kojève, it is Desire, as opposed to knowledge, which maintains man in a passive calm, makes him restless and pushes him into action. But this Desire is not the desire for something definite—not for a body or for a possession—but rather the desire for a value. This is something clearly reflected in video games, where the assignment of a value to the actions of the player is essential for the text to be considered as *ludus*—a rule-based game—and not merely *paidia*—or a recreational, make-believe activity—a seminal distinction made by Caillois (1958). This desire for value is, fundamentally, a desire for acknowledgment. This is what allowed Lacan (2004), following Hegel and Kojève, to state that desire is the desire for the Other. This can be applied to video games: the player's desire—and thus, her action—is for the system as a fundamental otherness for whom, and against whom, the player acts.

Hegel imagined a mythical origin of the self-awareness of man as a cultural being in the shape of a confrontation for acknowledgment, just as the player confronts the game system. Without it, man simply cannot be understood as a cultural being. This confrontation is seen initially as a death struggle, so each competitor must put his own life at stake to be recognized by the other. In this way, agreement and symmetry are impossible; the only solution is the fight, or the game, with asymmetry and inequality. Someone must win to be recognized by the other. But, after the fight, both opponents must be alive; otherwise, the acknowledgment could never exist. Fighting is, then, dialectic; one must steal the other's autonomy, force him into submission. This is vital for BDSM practices and for zero-sum games.

One of the opponents must abandon his desire for acknowledgment to satisfy the other's desire and, therefore, identify himself as Slave, acknowledging the other as Master. "Man is never just a man. He is always, necessarily and essentially, Master or Slave" (Kojève 1980, 20). Because of this, the historical "dialectics" are the dialectics of Master and Slave. However, the Master is only Master as long as the Slave acknowledges him as such. But the Slave is not acknowledged by the Master as a man but rather as an animal or an object, whereupon the Master will not have his desire fulfilled by another man. Following this logic, satisfaction of Desire has failed: "Thereupon, if man cannot be satisfied but by acknowledgement, the man who behaves as a Master will never be satisfied" (Kojève 1980, 20). On the contrary, the Slave finds a vital advantage; his work makes him master of nature. He has, as Lacan puts it, "savoir-y-faire," know-how. And this knowledge that work brings is what transforms the world and civilizes man. As he has acknowledged the Master as an Other, it will be enough to impose himself on him to be acknowledged, whereas the Master can never invert his position. For all that, "all slavish work realizes not the Master's will, but the will—at first unconscious—of the Slave, who—finally—succeeds where the Master—necessarily—fails" (Kojève 1980, 30). Hegel invites us to think that freedom comes through slavery or, to put it another way, he leaves History in the hands of the Slave. This is the reason why Hegel's ideas and the subsequent interpretation by Kojève influenced Marx in a decisive way. The slave creates and maintains the conditions for the relationship to exist.

Forget all about equality: BDSM, domination, and submission

If the Master and Slave dynamics are the base of culture and civilization, BDSM can be seen as a reimagining or perversion of these dynamics; one that appropriates them and turns them into a game in which both roles obtain, as Foucault (39) said, "a calculated and relentless pleasure." BDSM is a vague acronym that combines many things: bondage, domination, submission, discipline, and S&M (sadism and masochism). As such, it functions as a broad container for many fetishes and alternative sexual practices, all united by the notion of sex as a power play. BDSM is often associated with certain tools and sex toys, like dildos, whips, paddles, floggers, gags, clamps, and handcuffs and clothing, accessories, and materials like leather, latex, masks, fishnets, necklaces, and collars. These props can act as proxies of sexual intercourse and as amplifiers of desire, reinforcing sex as a power play.

These practices are a staging of desire as a game of unbalanced power, where sexual intercourse may or may not be at the center of the stage. Both participants agree and accept their roles without a previous fight; fighting and violence, in BDSM, are just an act, part of the game. But this does not mean it is all just pretend: although a Slave wants to be a Slave and is never forced to take that role, he surrenders himself completely to the (consensual) domination. An S&M fetishist may define himself as top (dominant), bottom (submissive), or switch (likes to change between roles). Pain, which is often associated with S&M, is just a tool of power and does not have to be a compulsory part of the deal; what is important is the acceptance of the roles.

It can be argued that this lack of balance is inherent in the sexual act. As Grynbaum (2012) writes, "Both psychoanalysis and the blossoming of sexual diversity have shown that sex is not a full act in which the fusion of two complementary sexes form a complete unit." According to her, the dimension of the sexual act is present in the unconscious as an absence or a lack of something. This difficulty tends to be resolved "under various forms according to the game structure." BDSM is a game that makes the inner mechanisms of sex visible and leverages them.

Sadomasochism as a form of sexuality is, above all, a set of hierarchies, of power relations. The sadist—from Donatien Alphonse François or the Marquis de Sade—takes the role of the master, the dominator, and finds pleasure in the domination—and, moreover, in the devaluation—of the other. The masochist—from Sacher-Masoch—finds pleasure in his position of Slave, of the dominated. Between these two figures there is no chance of a relationship of equals, as that would break the power game, but there is dependence. As Uranga (2009) explains, "Both the sadist and the masochist are trapped by an interdependence that cannot be ignored." One cannot exist without the other; both are vital to the play.

The conditions—and limits—of the domination are established and negotiated in advance, and it is common to use safe words as a signal that the submissive wants to stop the game and is not just playing along. The master can punish and humiliate the masochist but never without consent or the option to be stopped. Moreover, for Lacan, the masochist neither wishes nor seeks the sadist's pleasure but rather his unrest; even if the masochist receives and accepts punishment and torture, in fact it is he who underlines the anguish in the sadist and, hence, imposes the rules of the S&M dynamic, revitalizing the play. By accepting being submissive, the slave holds the key to the whole game.

Sex and submission in a mainstream game: The case of *God of War III*

The *God of War* franchise, for PlayStation platforms, comprises six games that tell the story of Kratos, a servant of the Gods in a dark and stylized version of Greek mythology. They are mainstream action-adventure games with a heavy emphasis on action. Kratos, the main character, is brutal, both in the story and as a set of skills for the player. All of these games feature a brief sexual minigame, something that has become a staple or in-joke of the saga. This minigame consists of optional quick time event (QTE) scenes where the player has to press certain buttons in time or progress stops. Successful completion rewards the player with energy. The events always unfold in the same way: Kratos reaches a room with one or more girls in a bed, the player accepts or refuses their offer, and, if accepted, sexual intercourse takes place off-screen, usually in a very exaggerated and even self-parodic fashion.

In *God of War III*, Kratos visits Mount Olympus and is tempted by Aphrodite herself. When the player reaches her chamber, she is frolicking around with her two handmaidens in her bed. She then disposes of them and asks Kratos to "share her bed"—"Do you know how long it's been since a real man has come into my chambers?" Kratos is reluctant, blinded by rage as he is, but the player can accept the offer. Aphrodite then adopts a submissive position, but she very specifically asks the hero to please her. The camera pans to the right and shows the handmaidens watching. They serve as indicators of the player's performance. If he does well, they become aroused; if he fails, they frown and make funny remarks.

The "guise" of this minigame can be understood as a parody of the power fantasy and wish fulfillment that drive the whole franchise, where the player takes the role of an unstoppable, virile, and violent warrior. Aphrodite is shown scantily clad, breasts revealed, a clear image of lust. She refers to Kratos as a "real man" and dares him to please her. Although no BDSM elements, such as ropes or whips, are shown, she is negotiating domination, and this is where the "system"—the ruleset—comes in.

It would seem obvious that Kratos is the dominant and Aphrodite the submissive, as she lies in her bed surrendered and defenseless, but, to succeed, the player has to follow her orders to be dominated and pleased. If the player fails a command she complains, and the handmaidens become visibly embarrassed, even mocking Kratos. Too many mistakes and Aphrodite pushes Kratos out of her bed. She is in control, demanding, setting the rules and the goals. Kratos and the player are just toys for her to satisfy her lust for rough, satisfying sex. Kratos' pleasure and satisfaction are never mentioned; he is just fulfilling his orders like a "real man." Aphrodite's orgasm is the real goal.

This scene is only moderately explicit, and BDSM dynamics are only hinted at, but it is a clear game of submission, an unbalanced sexual relationship in which the player is asked—forced—to act in a dominant fashion while, in fact, being enslaved by the system and its rules. The player is only free to refuse Aphrodite's offer; once he accepts, he is bound by the rules and by the limited agency he is given. However, the sequence is not designed to make the player feel powerless. On the contrary, the system and the guise aim to manage the economy of desire in such a way that the player wants to participate.

The intercourse is barely interactive—just like all QTEs—and every time the player repeats it, the events are exactly the same. Few playable moments in the game are as noninteractive, as proceduralist, as this scene. The player's only task is to reenact a scene carefully scripted by the developers. This may be because it is a minigame with a touch of self-parody, but at the same time it reminds us of Lacan's identification of the desire for value with the desire for the Other and of Kojève's assertion that it is the Slave's will that succeeds, not the Master's. Kratos and the player are never free, and their only reward comes from the acknowledgment of the (falsely) submissive Aphrodite.

Independent consensual sex: The case of *Bind Her* and *Consensual Torture Simulator*

Bind Her is a short browser game designed by Arnott (2012) that asks the player to tie a constantly moving woman to a bed. Her limbs are moving continually, and the player has to separate them from her trunk by binding them with ropes. If the woman's limbs touch the ropes, they are broken. The system ruleset is very simple and clear, in a way similar to the table game *Operation*. The goal is to immobilize the woman, to submit her completely, and once that is achieved, the game ends, without any depiction of the implied subsequent intercourse. But the key to the discourse lies in its guise: the woman, shown in "cartoonishly drawn full-frontal nudity" as the game warns, winks and smiles every time the player succeeds, proving that she agrees with her submission and that her resistance to it is part of the role-play.

The ruleset puts the player in the role of the Master, but, once again, she has to follow clear rules with no possibility of escape. She may have more—and more significant—agency than in *God of War III*, but her freedom is as directed as it was there: her only possible action, and the only way of achieving rewards and a win state, is to pursue the satisfaction of the Slave. The power is in the hands of the bound woman, who constantly highlights the player's impotence and embodies the goal, the rules, and the obstacles. She is the game, and the game is always under control. The lack of a virtual body—an avatar, an embodiment—for the player makes this power dynamic even clearer; the intercourse is between the woman, who embodies the whole game, and the player, who lacks any fictional proxy. The woman can show emotions through facial expressions in the guise, while the player has no such indicators. Once more, the only signs of satisfaction belong to the Other, to the Slave. To have pleasure is something one can do alone, to desire is to be "condemned" to look for indicators of desire in the face of the Other, continuously asking oneself "what does the Other want from me?"

Another independently designed game, *Consensual Torture Simulator*, is a short text game written by Kopas (2013) that portrays a premeditated and negotiated encounter between a couple. The player, again, takes the role of the Master, and the girl asks to be punished until she cries. The intercourse has its origin in a request by the Slave, and everything is done with tenderness and affection. The couple seem to be very much in love, and their subtle interactions are a strong part of the text. They agree on a safe word, "tulip," that the Slave can use at any time to stop the game.

The player has to choose actions from a dialog tree to advance: the tool she wants to use to punish her lover, such as hands, feet, a flogger, or a cane, and how she wants to use it. After she has tortured the Slave long enough, the game informs her that she is tired and her arms hurt. The effort of the Master is a vital element of *Consensual Torture Simulator*, as well as the uncertainty that the Slave really wants to be punished and is finding pleasure in the violence. The game focuses on the physical pain often associated with S&M. Kopas presents it by stating that "there are a lot of videogames about violence but not nearly enough about consensual forms of violence and non-normative forms of intimacy." Game designer Anna Anthropy (2013) has also written about "this . . . game by my girlfriend" in her blog, stating, "as a designer, your role is more complicated than just the one who wields all the authorial power. . . . It's not as much about the experience that I want to create as it is about the experience the player creates. It's not about dragging a player kicking and screaming through my masterpiece." She compares this "dialogue" between designer and player with her S&M activities, stating "I am at my most attentive, my most reactive, when I'm topping. . . . When we're designing, we're creating a set of rules to act in our place when we may not be there. But I think it's useful to think of a game not as a show that the player is lucky to get to watch but as an experience we're allowing her to perform, a conversation." Anthropy, writing about Kopas' game, defines a dominant person as "someone who receives submission," arguing "while there isn't equal authority within a D/s [dominance and submission] relationship, there is an exchange."

For Anthropy—and, judging by *Consensual Torture Simulator*, for Kopas— the designer is the Master, but the Master depends on the Slave and has to pay attention to her, consider her needs, and allow her to be a part of the exchange that they consider D/s relationships to be. Even if *Consensual Torture Simulator* portrays the most violent acts of all the games analyzed in this chapter, it is also the one that shows a more loving and caring intimacy between the Master and the Slave. The player can decide to stop the torture at any time if she finds what she is asked to do unbearable; the Slave never pronounces the safe word, though. And, if the Slave does cry, the closing text describes the Master taking her to bed and comforting her.

Consensual Torture Simulator shows the interdependence that traps both the sadist and the masochist, as proposed by Uranga. The player is in control here, and she seems to be the one guiding the experience, but she has only a limited amount of actions available: the actions, one can conclude, that both characters agreed upon before engaging in the session. The economy of desire is carefully presented and delimited. There may not be equality in a D/s relationship, but the exchange cannot exist without consent and the voluntary renunciation of a certain amount of freedom to create a consensual imbalance of power. By agreeing to use only the mechanics and dynamics proposed by the game, the player gains power to be dominant. This game admits that the player's freedom is never absolute but highlights how this directed freedom allows power fantasies to exist and how this little freedom is precious and significant. Desire requires limits to restrict the vast totality that pleasure yearns for. Without limits there is no desire, no freedom.

BDSM as a dollhouse: The case of *3DKink*

Kink.com is a production company based in San Francisco that runs several websites dedicated to BDSM and fetishes, such as SexAndSubmission, MenInPain, DeviceBondage, FuckingMachines, and DivineBitches. All these sites feature videos and pictures of scenes produced by them. On their main website, they state that their mission is to "demystify and celebrate alternative sexualities by providing the most authentic kinky experiences." One of their products is *3DKink*, a virtual environment with faint ludic elements that can be described as a "porn director simulator." The website presents it by stating that the player will be "in the director's chair at a kinky video shoot." This "virtual world game" allows the player to create a wide variety of scenes by combining locations, models, poses, outfits, and toys. Everything can be directed and customized.

The player can choose up to three participants for each scene—"Myself," "SexMate," and "3SomeMate"—and, while in the scene, the SexMate has two bars in the Heads-Up Display (HUD)—one for Excitement and another for Pain. She makes specific requests—for oral sex, for "another position," for a change in pace—and, if the player complies, the Excitement bar goes up to 100 percent. She reaches climax, and sexcoins, in-game currency to unlock content, are earned, depending on the quality of the orgasm. The Pain bar goes from green to red after reaching 50 percent, and this negatively affects Excitement, unless the player buys and activates the "Likes Pain" option. The SexMate has to like being physically punished; otherwise, the player will not get any sexcoins. As in *God of War III*, the main goal is to please the partner and bring her to an orgasm.

In this case, however, the role of the player is more ambiguous. She may identify herself with the "Myself" character or, in a more general sense, with the director of the scene. This is because the avatarness in this game is ambivalent. Although it is implied that the player is always embodied by the "Myself" model, only in a few instances is this true. The rest of the time she simply takes the role of the director and is embodied by the camera itself, the menus, and the HUD.

There are four main modes: (1) Story Mode; (2) QuickMode; (3) FreeMode; and (4) Sequencer. The Story Mode features a couple of scenes preceded by a dialog tree where the player has to convince the girl to have sex with him. During this dialog, the player is assuming the role of the "Myself" model—in this mode, it has to be a man and the SexMate a woman—and, after bringing the SexMate to orgasm, the scene will appear with a star in the menu, implying that it has been completed. But, once the scene begins, the models are dolls that obey all the player's orders via a detailed in-game menu and HUD, and there is nothing to distinguish these scenes from QuickMode and FreeMode except for more possible combinations of genders. In these two, the SexMate can be a woman or a transsexual or "shemale." In all of them, the models reproduce predefined animations and poses, and the player can take pictures and record videos. The Sequencer mode is more similar to a video-editing program, with a timeline for each of the elements—including camera, lighting, and other technical aspects—in which the player can manually set the poses and animations.

3DKink is, therefore, closer to a virtual filmmaking tool than to a video game. It is a detailed tool for the fantasy fulfillment of people openly into BDSM practices. As such, it is almost a BDSM catalog or encyclopedia. But its ludic elements do not differ much from what we explained about *God of War III*: the goal is the woman's or transsexual's orgasm to an even greater extent than in Kratos' adventure. The sex partner gives instructions to the player, demanding to be pleased in a specific manner, and the player's pleasure is seemingly never taken into account. The player's pleasure arises from the pleasure of representation through the classic mechanisms of spectatorial identification. Although the player can decide and act, she is still bound to her scopic drive, attached to her gaze. In all the games analyzed here, there is a mirror effect that serves as a metaphor of the structure of desire: I desire what the Other desires, I want to be where the Other is.

The true pornographic component of *3DKink* is the extensive collection of items that allow the player to recreate her fantasies: the body is fully available, all objects are purchasable, and the player can design her partner down to the smallest detail: Foucault (1988) classified this as positive power. The player seems to be fully in control of her "dollhouse," but to build her collection she has to obey the system, represented by the SexMate's desire. The female orgasm is the challenge and boredom the obstacle. The player's merits are only acknowledged and rewarded by satisfying the desire of the Other. This desire, contrary to the dynamics of most goals in games, remains ambiguous, elusive, almost ungraspable. Female "jouissance"—sexual enjoyment—is codified via bars and sound outputs, but it remains partially indecipherable, made metonymy in the orgasm: the player's duty.

This desire of the Other is instrumentalized in a perverse way; the player needs to satisfy a woman—an iconic Other—to obtain more assets to build her own dollhouse and fantasy scenes. In this regard *3DKink* features a strong sense of instrumental gameplay, but it demands the submission to the Other's desire to gain permission to fulfill one's own desires. In terms of economy of desire, the player has to buy access to her own desires by satisfying the desires of the Other. Player freedom is subject to a superior will.

Domination is the name of the game: Final thoughts on BDSM and directed freedom

The question of freedom and control is a centerpiece of sex, game design, and BDSM. By analyzing their intersections, we can achieve a better understanding of both the role of the player in video games and the specifics and motives of BDSM practices. In both fields, the distribution of power is unequal but consensual. The Slave accepts losing her freedom just as the player accepts acting within the limits of the directed freedom proposed by the system; the Master takes control, acknowledging her dependence on the Slave, in the same way as the player takes control, acknowledging her dependence on the system ruleset.

In the cases we have studied here, BDSM elements are present not only as audiovisual ornaments but also as key elements of their rulesets, their fiction, and the ideas that build their discourses. It is very telling that all four games more or less overtly put the player in the dominant role and never make her play the slave. Video games are based on action, and, accordingly, the player is expected to be active. "Submit," as an action, is very hard to codify and measure with a system of rules, goals, and rewards.

But, as we have maintained, these games enslave the player in the sense that they force her to follow very clear and limited rules. Only the Master—the player—can succeed or fail; only she is responsible for her actions. Being active means the player has to accept her agency and put it to good use. In this respect, we can find an important difference between BDSM and video games: while the former is mostly make-believe—*paidia*—with rules of behavior, the latter adds goals, rules of success, and mechanics—*ludus*—to it to achieve this success. This extra layer turns video games—and BDSM in them—into a more layered set of dynamics. When the player engages in a game, she is, in some measure, a slave to the designer's intentions. At the same time, she is mastering the game and its fictional elements; overcoming obstacles is an active, dominant process that also implies playing the role of the master.

Freedom in a video game is always limited, but it does not mean blindly following the system's demands. While Hegel, Lacan, Kòjeve, and BDSM show us that there is always power and freedom in slavery, video games make this power even more explicit, turning the player into a kind of active slave expressing herself within the limits of the game's directed freedom, constantly negotiating the meaning of the game. Playing is a dialogue with the game designer in which the game itself acts as a proxy. These constant negotiations and dialogues ultimately function similar to the way meaning is negotiated and mutually agreed in a BDSM session, and, as we've illustrated here, a useful framework for game analysis.

References

Anthropy, Anna. 2013. "auntie pixelante > consensual torture simulator." http://auntiepixelante.com/?p=2185.
Aranda, Daniel and Jordi Sánchez–Navarro, eds. 2009. *Aprovecha el tiempo y juega*. Barcelona: Editorial UOC.

Caillois, Roger. 1958. *Les jeux et les homes. Le Masque el Le Vertige*. Paris: Gallimard.

Foucault, Michel. 1988. *Nietzsche, la Genealogía, la Historia*. Valencia: Pre-Textos.

Grynbaum, Ana. 2012. El acto masoquista. http://www.ecole-lacanienne.net/documents/actualites/926/argumento-cultura.pdf.

Kink.com. 2014/n.d. October 10. http://www.kink.com/k/values.jsp.

Kojève, Alexandre. 1980. *Introduction to the Reading of Hegel. Lectures on the Phenomenology of Spirit*. New York: Cornell University Press.

Lacan, Jacques. 2004. *El Seminario, Libro 10, La angustia, 1962–3*. Buenos Aires: Paidós.

Linderoth, Jonas. 2002. "Making Sense of Computer Games: Learning with New Artefacts." Paper presented at *International Conference on Toys, Games and Media*. London: London University, Institute of Education.

Lövlie, Anders Sundnes. 2005. "End of story? Quest, Narrative and Enactment in Computer Games." *Proceedings of DiGRA Conference: Changing Views—Worlds in Play*.

Navarro-Remesal, Víctor. 2013. Libertad dirigida: análisis formal del videojuego como sistema, su estructura y su avataridad. http://hdl.handle.net/10803/111168.

Newman, James. 2002. "The Myth of the Ergodic Videogame. Some Thoughts on Player–Character Relationships in Videogames." *Game Studies* 2 (1). http://www.gamestudies.org/0102/newman/.

Sicart, Miguel. 2011. "Against Procedurality." *Game Studies* 11 (3). http://gamestudies.org/1103/articles/sicart_ap.

Smith, Jonas Heide. 2007. The Road Not Taken—The How's and Why's of Interactive Fiction. http://game-research.com/index.php/articles/the-road-not-taken-the-hows-and-whys-of-interactive-fiction.

Uranga, Mitxelko. 2009. "El hombre sadomasoquista. Una nueva mirada oblicua a Nietzsche." *Antroposmoderno*. http://antroposmoderno.com/antro-articulo.php?id_articulo=1223.

Voorhees, Gerald. 2013. "Criticism and Control: Gameplay in the Space of Possibility." In *CTRL-ALT-PLAY: Essays on Control in Video Gaming*, edited by Matthew Wysocki, 9–20. Jefferson, NC: McFarland.

Games cited

Arnott, Leon. 2012. *Bind Her*. Leon Arnott.

Kink.com. 2009. *3DKink*. Thrixxx.

Kopas, Merritt. 2013. *Consensual Torture Simulator*. Merritt Kopas.

SCE Santa Monica Studio. 2010. *God of War III*. Sony Computer Entertainment.

8

Countergaming's porn parodies, hard-core and soft

Diana Pozo (University of California, Santa Barbara, USA)

In October 2009, SF Media Labs, a Bay Area startup run by Randy Sarafan and Noah Weinstein, demonstrated a hacker project they called the "Joydick" (Figure 8.1) at the sex and technology conference Arse Elektronika. This wearable device, designed to be built at home by hacker-fans of the Atari console, could transform a gamer's dick into a joystick-like controller. A Velcro strap could be wrapped around the base of a phallic object—represented by a blue dildo in Joydick's demonstration videos—allowing the phallus of the gamer's choice to replace the joystick's four-directional movement. A stroking action of the gamer's hand, wearing a specialized ring, took the place of the controller's single red button. At the conference, two demonstrators stood silhouetted behind a white sheet, while a large monitor showed a vertical shooter on Atari Flashback 2, a 2005 emulation console. As the two labored in their makeshift tent, the facilitator announced with a mixture of glee and embarrassment, "so basically what's happening is, they're masturbating back there!" (Nosedef 2009, "The Joydick"). The audience erupted with laughter.

Joydick's designers presented it as a unique innovation. Unquestionably the future of gaming, Joydick would finally bring together the allied realms of "video gameplay and male sexual stimulation," Weinstein and Sarafan argued in the conference catalog (2011, 137). Yet Joydick is also ambivalent about these startup claims of innovation and being the technology of the future. Despite attracting an article in tech blog *Kotaku* (McWhertor 2009), Joydick was never designed as a commercial product. A "hacker project," Joydick exists chiefly as a set of instructions for modifying the Atari Flashback console,

FIGURE 8.1 *Left: the Joydick as an Atari controller. Right: a still from Joydick's demonstration video.*

both on SF Media Labs' website and in the Arse Elektronika catalog. So while some may compare Joydick to the "bodily interfaces" (Parisi 2009) that gained commercial success in the 2000s, including Wii and Kinect, Joydick is more similar to the "artist mods" that Alexander Galloway (2006) says are part of a "countergaming" movement.

Joydick, and projects like it, including Heather Kelley's sex-education game concept "Lapis" (2005), and the many projects including SeXBox (2005) detailed on Kyle Machulis's blog *Slashdong*, are part of a 2000s countergaming movement devoted to creative uses of game hardware and part of the increasing visibility of hardware hackers that Chris Anderson termed a "new industrial revolution" of *makers* (2012). There have been sexual aspects to mods (modifications) throughout gaming history, yet these instances of "pornographic hacking" (Sihvonen 2011, 178–84) have rarely been viewed as serious critical contributions to countergaming as an art form or as a political practice. While Lauteria (2012) conceptualizes pornographic hacking as a strategy of "queer modding as resistance," some have compared sexual artist mods to crude vandalism, while others, including artists themselves, draw sharp distinctions between mods that address a male audience and "erotic" or "educational" instances of pornographic hacking for female consumers.

Anxieties about pornographic hacking reflect cultural shifts within the video games industry and its fandom. As video game studies is increasingly respected by the academy, and gaming companies take on bigger budgets, bigger crews, and more revenue than Hollywood films, video games face pressure to shed the aura of pornography they inherited from their history as arcade machines, placed alongside peep shows and other forms of public entertainment inaccessible to those confined to the domestic sphere. Game culture's uneasy relationship with feminism has also made games' historical association with pornography and other forms of "male entertainment" increasingly problematic. Because game consoles were marketed and consumed as "boy toys" in the 1990s, many of this generation's "girl gamers" have painful memories of controllers and Game Boys being snatched away by proprietary brothers, cousins, and playmates. Women who work in or critique the contemporary games industry have been repeatedly targeted in online bullying and sexual harassment campaigns, with the culture war between feminists and angry video game nerds reaching a peak in 2014's Gamergate controversy. In this context, a tendency to conflate feminism with antipornography critiques of gaming is an understandable response to many feminists' experiences of gamic violation and sexual harassment.

Many aspiring feminists have been quick to throw pornography and sexual representation out of games entirely and to view any links made between video games and sexuality, particularly masculine sexuality, with suspicion. However, if we are to have a truly feminist video game studies, we must learn to understand sexual representation as a source of feminist critique, and we must challenge the preconception of pornographic representation as uncritical and antifeminist. By focusing on countergaming's sexual humor—its "porn parodies"—I hope to show how pornographic and erotic artist mods engage in feminist critiques of the video game industry and dominant games culture, from Joydick's hard-core porn parody of hard-core gaming to the playfulness of Heather Kelley's erotic games.

Though films of the porn parody genre like *The Sex Files* (Sam Hain 2009) and *Batman XXX* (Axel Braun 2010) consistently win top honors at the annual Adult Video News Awards ("the Oscars of porn"), the phrase "porn parody" is redundant. Hard-core pornography in the United States has been full of humor since the earliest silent "stags," watched illicitly by mostly-male groups in smoke-filled rooms. Constance Penley (1997) writes that porn's particular brand of humor is "bawdiness, humorously lewd and obscene language and situations . . . really bad jokes, ranging from terrible puns to every sort of dirty joke" (94). Drawing upon a set of texts ranging from the earliest silent stag films to 1990s humor and pornography from *Beavis and Butthead* to *John Wayne Bobbitt Uncut*, Penley argues

> Given the enormous success of the feminist antiporn movement . . . it may be difficult to recognize that the tone of pornography—when one actually looks at it—is closer to *Hee Haw* than Nazi death camp fantasies. Also difficult to recognize because it so goes against the contemporary typification of porn as something *done to* women, is that the joke is usually on the man. (95)

Focusing on the humor in pornography draws critical attention away from pornography's visual style, allowing for an understanding of porn within its narrative and reception contexts. By reading pornography within a larger cultural context of bad jokes and male homosocial viewing practices, Penley is able to recognize the substantial theme of sexual anxiety and frustration with dominant masculinity in pornography (106–7). Because countergaming's porn parodies spring from a small culture of dedicated hobbyists, independent designers, and artists, it is easy to take them out of context, viewing them as oddballs or commercial designs gone wrong. However, taken as part of a larger cultural conversation about the promises and perils of "hard-core" gaming, hard-core hacker projects emerge as satiric and irreverent jokes at the expense of gaming and some of its fans.

Joydick critiques the simultaneous futurism and nostalgia of gaming culture. Sexual human-computer interaction has long been associated with the world of the future in technofantasies like Howard Rheingold's 1991 *Virtual Reality*, which coined the term *teledildonics*, or remote networked sex with a computer or human partner (345). However, Joydick is also a modification of the Atari Flashback console—a product designed to trade on gamer nostalgia for a time when games' graphics, mechanics, and potentially politics could be perceived as "simpler." Its creators' assertion that the link between the penis, maleness, masculinity, and the ideal gamer is "quite clear" further associates the project with a kind of backward-looking conservatism. Yet the device also demonstrates some of the limits of these fantasies of human-computer sex and of a perfectly phallocentric gaming past.

Atari Flashback may harken to a simpler time, but Joydick makes masturbation anything but simple. By asking prospective users to imagine synchronizing their masturbation with the patterns of a computer game, Joydick demonstrates how console manufacturers' promises to provide intuitive and natural interfaces have often masked the bodily measurement and surveillance tactics of these products. Media scholars have debated the merits of traditional and bodily game interfaces. While some games theorists (Shinkle 2008) argue that bodily interfaces are an effective alternative to the traditional game controller's regime of gestural precision, control, and restraint, others (Parisi 2009; Gazzard 2013; Lipkin 2013) argue that bodily interfaces teach users to make more of their bodies legible to their game consoles.

The commercial success of 2000s bodily interfaces allowed them to produce a "paradigm shift," retraining gamers in a new set of "bodily techniques" for game control (Parisi 2009, 113), as well as "a fear over grammars of (undesirable) bodily action being added to one's gestural language" (Parisi 2009, 120). Joydick asks users to imagine the bodily interface taken to what they posit as its natural conclusion, in which even the user's genitals are incorporated into the gestural language of a computer game. The use of a blue silicone dick to demonstrate Joydick in its marketing materials may be an unintentional effect of censorship practices in mainstream media excluding the representation of the erect penis. Nevertheless, this silicone dick demonstrates that Joydick is not a cisgender male-only product, and its humorous expression of anxieties about phallic sexuality and gaming culture applies even to gamers who do not identify as male or who do not have a long enough flesh dick to work with.[1] Because the project consists simply of a strap to be wrapped around the base of a phallic object, and a ring to be worn on the gamer's finger, Joydick can be used with a variety of dicks, made from a variety of materials. The idea of using a strap-on as an Atari controller suggested by these advertising materials equates the gaming controller with a wider variety of dicks, implying that gaming's phallic power fantasies can be taken up by a variety of users, regardless of anatomy or gender identity.

Joydick is a hard-core joke on hard-core gaming culture. Like hard-core pornography, Joydick addresses anxieties by and about heterosexual cis men through anxious humor at the expense of gaming culture's tastemakers: console manufacturers and obsessive "hard-core" gamers. In a video demonstrating Joydick, a user struggles to masturbate while gaming and loses the game, prompting an intertitle to appear: "Now, even if you lose the game, you can be a winner in life" (Weinstein 2009). If the dick-measuring contest of hard-core gaming were played with real dicks, would users be able to win the game, adapting the familiar and often solitary routine of masturbation to the measurement and surveillance of their game console, or would they have to be satisfied to be "winners at life" instead? When the skillful use of joysticks becomes the measure of masculinity and phallic power in a virtual space, isn't the joystick more like the strap-on than the penis? Is this what gaming culture has come to in the era of the bodily or "natural" interface? Joydick seems to join together video gaming and phallic sexuality, yet it also points to their incompatibility and to the unnaturalness of "natural" bodily interfaces. Joydick's status as a challenge—to the politics of alternative controller design, to the image of masculinity and phallic sexuality in gaming culture, and to the boundaries of its audience—makes its anxious humor and gender-bending particularly resonant.

The erotics of touchscreens and the work of Heather Kelley

Created by a team of students and staff led by Heather Kelley and software engineer Meg Richards at Carnegie Mellon University's School of Art, "Touchable Tent" (Figure 8.2) reimagines the hard, flat touchscreen as soft,

FIGURE 8.2 *Top: the Touchable Tent and Kinect's redirected eye. Bottom: a hand touches the tent from below.*

flexible, and enveloping, designed to be used while lying down with the tent overhead (Kelley 2011b). Touchable Tent uses the scanning abilities of Kinect to detect changes not in the body of the user but in a flexible surface that surrounds the user. Thus while Kinect inspired fear of surveillance in many users (Petruska and Vanderhoef 2014), Touchable Tent cocoons them in a space safe from Kinect's view. Instead of becoming the sole object of Kinect's surveillance, users manipulate and interact with a surveilled object, their movements detected insofar as they touch the tent. Touchable Tent does not openly lampoon Kinect as Joydick does the bodily interface and Atari Flashback. Rather than dismissing Kinect's scanning technology, Touchable Tent redirects its gaze, demonstrating how clever users can reconceive problematic mass-market technologies.

While Joydick represents a hard-core challenge to hard-core gaming, the work of Heather Kelley—an award-winning independent game and interface designer named one of the "five most powerful women in gaming" in 2013 and one of the "most influential women in technology" in 2011—challenges hard-core games culture through the "erotic," a category of representation that feminists often define in opposition to the hard-core through appeals to female sexual subjectivity and empowerment. Kelley has explored the erotics of the touchscreen as a bodily interface, imagining ways that users might become more intimate with their touchscreen devices, and with touchscreens themselves, expanding their sexualities in the process.

What is erotic about Touchable Tent? Though the project certainly provides a relaxing and intimate atmosphere reminiscent of a bedroom, the links between Touchable Tent and the concept of the erotic may not be immediately obvious. Yet, Touchable Tent is a physical representation of eroticism in digital art as conceived by feminist film theory, taking up Laura Marks' (2002) statements on the erotics of "haptic visuality." Because visual representation is commonly associated with the sexual objectification of women's bodies through the male gaze, feminist media theorists have often searched for the erotic in the other senses, including sound and touch. Laura Marks termed the objectifying mode of looking implied by the male gaze in classical Hollywood cinema "optical visuality," and theorized a form of haptic visuality in digital and video art that "tends to rest on the surface of its object rather than to plunge into depth" (8). Like the scanning eye of Kinect, optical visuality analyzes an object from a distance, breaking it down to understand it (Marks 2002, xvi). However, "haptic images invite the viewer to dissolve his or her subjectivity in the close and bodily contact with the image" (13), becoming enveloped as users are in the flexible touchscreen of Touchable Tent. Haptic visuals are ultimately visual in Marks's work: the oscillation between the sensation of touch and the primarily audiovisual appeal of video art creates the simultaneous closeness and distance that Marks theorizes. Touchable Tent takes this conception of video haptics to a new level, asking prospective users to imagine haptic aesthetics as physically touchable and touchscreens as enveloping, safe, and soft.

Touchable Tent can also be seen as part of a larger trend exploring the erotics of touchscreens in Kelley's work. Kelley (also known as moboid) became one of the world's leading designers of women-centered erotic games in 2005, when her game design concept for the Nintendo DS "Lapis" won the Sex in Games Design Challenge at the Montréal International Games Summit. Lapis, which Kelley described as a "magical pet adventure and stealthy primer on female sexuality," made extensive use of the DS's mic and touchpad, asking gamers to stroke or tap the touchpad and hum or blow into the DS's microphone to please a cartoon blue bunny, who floats into the air to show her pleasure (Ruberg 2006). The bunny's desires shift throughout the game, requiring gamers to remain flexible and try a variety of strategies to bring the bunny to her "happy place." Kelley imagined that Lapis might open up space for more gamers to think about sexuality, arguing,

> the people I was reaching with this app were not the ones who were already comfortable with their sexualities and with graphic depictions of women's bodies—those people already have things they can look at and things they can use and things they can do. I was more interested in reaching people who maybe were less comfortable with the really overtly graphic representations but would be able to benefit from improved sexuality in their lives. (Pozo and Kelley 2013)

A later project by Kelley's interaction design startup, Perfect Plum, aimed to improve users' sex lives by expanding upon the small buttons and preprogrammed patterns of traditional vibrator interfaces. "Body Heat," designed with Damien Di Fede and Amanda Williams and produced for OhMiBod's series of sound-controlled vibrators, eventually became the first version of the OhMiBod Remote App in 2011 (Kelley 2011a). The app consisted of a simple black screen with the written instruction to "touch me," and what Kelley called an "abstract very beautiful kind of visualization interface" on the iPhone touchscreen (Game Careers 2011). Touches produced pink, blue, and purple glowing fingerprints on the screen that translated to vibration intensities and speeds. The visualization's fingerprint aesthetics, reminiscent of heat maps or topographies, visualized the act of touching rather than the body parts being touched: "So nothing pornographic, but just very intuitive and beautiful way to control the speed and intensity of the vibrator it is attached to," Kelley noted (Game Careers 2011).

While Kelley's projects reconfigure existing gaming technologies to give them new capabilities, Kelley would most likely not call Touchable Tent or Lapis a "hacker project." "I'm not hacking," she said in an interview. "I'm simply making content [for a device] that uses its capabilities in a way that doesn't get used all that often. Maybe that is the definition, but I'm not hacking. *I'm not taking it apart and reimagining it and putting it back together*" (Pozo and Kelley, emphasis mine). Kelley's disidentification with the concept of hacking as penetrative—"taking it apart . . . and putting it back together"—allows her to reconceive a male-dominated realm full of contradictory associations with violent destruction and construction. Rather than calling herself a "hacker," Kelley identifies with the Situationist concept of *détournement* (Debord and Wolman 1956), a movement to challenge institutional art, academia, and what Guy Debord termed the "society of the spectacle" through playful disruption (Ko 2008). In a contemporary tech culture where terms that imply violent revolution are often used to describe the launch of new companies, as in Tech Crunch's international series of "Disrupt" events showcasing new startups, claims that technology will promote transgressive social change become increasingly difficult to assess. Kelley's return to the concept of *détournement*—playful repurposing of existing cultural artifacts rather than designing dubiously disruptive new ones—marks a departure from hacking's more penetrative and corporate connotations.

Kelley's touch-based *détournements* of existing media interfaces use touch and embodiment to empower users in ways the original technologies did not. Lapis repurposes the cute aesthetics, touchscreen, and mic of the DS to provide a safe space for sex education, while Body Heat repurposes the iPhone's touchscreen as a sophisticated, highly customizable vibrator interface. That Kelley frames this type of intervention not as a violent destruction of Kinect ("hacking") but as a sly discovery of the device's inherent, though underutilized, capabilities speaks to the complexity of the position alternative game designers often take with regard to games and systems of which they are also often fans. Kelley's emphasis on the playful and nonpenetrative aspects of her work disidentifies with hard-core projects like Joydick even as it uses some of the same strategies of playful redesign and sexual critique.

Kelley models a common discourse of the erotic, consistently describing her designs in opposition to pornography as a way of emphasizing her feminist intent. Nevertheless, Kelley's project of empowering consumers through sexual discovery and technology allies with what Jane Juffer (1998) has called *domesticated pornography*. Because "visual pornography is regularly demonized as a threat to the home, regulated quite heavily, and contrasted to the legally and aesthetically legitimated genre of erotica," sexual representation that is designed to be consumed in the domestic sphere tends to identify with the term "erotica," while distancing itself from "pornography," even as these categories remain similar in many ways (Juffer 1998, 7). Juffer argues that the popular stereotype of women enjoying literary erotica more than audiovisual pornography may be due to the fact that women have "greater access to the means of production and consumption" of literary erotica (5). Because they continue to exclude women from porn production and consumption, however, discourses characterizing pornography as a threat do not protect women; they simply guarantee women will remain "victims within the domestic sphere" (Juffer 1998, 9). Upholding the pornography/erotica distinction helps exclude women from viewing audiovisual pornography even as it marginalizes women's erotic production as insufficiently transgressive (Juffer 1998, 2). Moreover, the pornography/erotica binary tends to reinscribe the gender binary and reinforce the heteronormative fantasy that men's and women's sexualities are distinct and complimentary. Rather than viewing Kelley's erotic game design in opposition to Joydick's hard-core porn parody, therefore, I argue that these works represent two allied strategies of pornographic hacking as countergaming.

Arse Elektronika has provided an important space for diverse forms of pornographic hacking as countergaming to coexist. Joydick appeared at the conference in 2009, and in 2014, conference organizer Johannes Grenzfurthner reminisced warmly about the project. Heather Kelley and Kyle Machulis of *Slashdong* have been frequent presenters from games fandom, while many others in sex education and technology scholarship, including Violet Blue, Annalee Newitz, Carol Queen, and Susie Bright, have appeared there since the conference was founded in 2007. Writing in 2010, Feona Attwood describes Arse Elektronika as part of the culture of the "new porn professionals," a group at the intersection of increasing popular interest in sex work and the casualization of online labor who "focused on [attracting] a young, sophisticated, media-savvy audience previously neglected by mainstream porn producers" beginning in the mid-2000s (88). The many presenters at Arse Elektronika, from University professors to self-made writers and experts to porn production companies, "represent some of the many new ways of 'working sex' and demonstrate highly reflexive forms of professionalism in new sites of knowledge production" (98). According to Attwood, describing the new porn professionals is difficult "because they complicate the idea both of 'porn' and of 'professional' . . . [they are] frequently young, white, American women making an often precarious living working with sex in a variety of media" (89). Arse Elektronika's mixture of entertainment and knowledge production is typical of a variety of semiprofessional venues in which new porn professionals showcase their work, including conferences, trade shows, websites, blogs, popular press, and social media. In these spaces, distinctions between the erotic and the pornographic break down, as a diverse group of feminist porn producers, erotica producers, technology fans and developers, and sex educators share the common goal of promoting sex-positive tech culture.

Independent game design and alternative sexual futures

In 2006, Alexander Galloway wrote that "countergaming is an unrealized project," arguing independent gaming had not yet become a movement because countergames were not yet focused on gameplay (126). Since this famous critique of artist mods, independent game production has dramatically expanded. This "rise of the videogame zinesters" (Anthropy 2012) answers

Galloway's call for a true countergaming movement with a wave of fun and irreverent independent game design by amateurs, professionals, and Attwood's "new professionals." Unlike the hardware hacks discussed here, however, many independent small games are chiefly focused on the modification of game software. A notable exception is Anna Anthropy's game installation *Duck Duck Poison*, created for the launch party for *Rise of the Videogame Zinesters* at Babycastles in Brooklyn, NY. This game's specialized controllers, designed by hackers at Babycastles for the party, were bras, with embedded buttons, that gamers wore over their clothing. The game's graphics, designed by Egypt Urnash, are reminiscent of hard-core casual games on sites like hornygamer.com, and the game asks users to imagine themselves as part of a team of busty barely-clothed spies who have been captured by an evil mistress (see Figure 8.3). As images from the installation show, the game's bra controllers had players of various gender presentations pressing button-nipples on their newly-minted breasts or on the bra controllers of other players. Anthropy designed the game to encourage this dynamic. When explaining the game at Babycastles, Anthropy announced, "You can press other peoples' nipples if you want. It's not as if you have to play by the rules" (Lipinski 2012). Anthropy's bra controllers are thus intended not to ask players to conform to a complex set of game rules or control techniques but to open up a space for gamers to play with gender, sexuality, and power relations. *Duck Duck Poison* combines the cheekiness and gender-bending of Joydick with a Kelley-style *détournement* of hard-core casual games. Andrews (2006) argues the breast is the central visual signifier of American soft-core film (14), and *Duck Duck Poison*'s kinky breast-centered narrative might be called a soft-core porn parody of hard-core gaming.

In the rush to ensure video games' feminist future, we must not lose the value of pornography as a critical strategy. Suspicion around

FIGURE 8.3 *Left: the game screen of* Duck Duck Poison. *Right: gamers wearing Anthropy's bra controllers.*

sexual representation in games and the sexuality of game controllers is understandable, as human-computer sexuality and sexuality in video games are often associated with violence against women and dystopian futures in mainstream media representations. Current controversies about the gender, racial, and sexual politics of the video game industry and video game culture have furthermore devolved into sexual harassment and threats of violence against individual critics and game designers. As we push back against the problems of game culture, we must not lose sight of the critical power of sexual representation, particularly in hardware mods that envision alternative relationships between gamers' bodies and game systems. As sexual hardware hacks, countergaming's porn parodies use a variety of hard-core, soft-core, and erotic strategies to critique hard-core games culture and explore new sexual futures through gamer embodiment.

Note

1 cis refers to gender identity where individuals' experiences of their own gender match the sex they were assigned at birth.

References

Anderson, Chris. 2012. *Makers: The New Industrial Revolution*. Kindle edn. New York: Crown Business.

Andrews, David. 2006. *Soft in the Middle: The Contemporary Softcore Feature in its Contexts*. Columbus: The Ohio State University Press.

Anthropy, Anna. 2012. *Rise of the Videogame Zinesters: How Freaks, Normals, Amateurs, Artists, Dreamers, Drop-Outs, Queers, Housewives, and People Like You Are Taking Back an Artform*. Kindle edn. New York: Seven Stories Press.

Attwood, Feona. 2010. "'Younger, Paler, Decidedly Less Straight': The New Porn Professionals." In *Porn.com*, edited by Feona Attwood, 88–104. New York: Peter Lang.

Batman XXX: A Porn Parody. 2010. Directed by Axel Braun. 2010. Los Angeles, CA, Vivid Entertainment. DVD.

Debord, Guy and Gil J. Wolman. 2006. "A User's Guide to Détournement." In *Situationist International Anthology*, translated by Ken Knabb (Bureau of Public Secrets). http://bopsecrets.org/SI/detourn.htm.

Galloway, Alexander R. 2006. "Countergaming." In *Gaming: Essays on Algorithmic Culture*, edited by Alexander R. Galloway, 107–26. Minneapolis: University of Minnesota Press.

COUNTERGAMING'S PORN PARODIES, HARD-CORE AND SOFT   145

Game Careers. 2011. "Women in Tech: Heather Kelley, Founder and Principal at Perfect Plum Talks to Game Careers." YouTube, September 12. youtube.com/watch?v=g-pSLpCc2Rk.

Gazzard, Alison. 2013. "Standing in the Way of Control: Relationships between Gestural Interfaces and Game Spaces." In *CTRL-ALT-PLAY: Essays on Control in Video Gaming*, edited by Matthew Wysocki, 121–32. Jefferson, NC: McFarland.

Juffer, Jane. 1998. *At Home with Pornography: Women, Sex, and Everyday Life.* New York: New York University Press.

Kelley, Heather. 2011a. "OhMiBod Remote App." *Perfect Plum*, November 11. http://perfectplum.com/portfolio/ohmibod-remote/.

Kelley, Heather. 2011b. "Touchable Tent Prototype Aurora." *Perfect Plum*, December 29. http://perfectplum.com/portfolio/touchable-tent/.

Kipnis, Laura. 1999. *Bound and Gagged: Pornography and the Politics of Fantasy in America.* Durham: Duke University Press.

Ko, Christie. 2008. "Politics of Play: Situationism, Détournement, and Anti-Art." In *FORUM* 2. http://forumjournal.org/article/view/599/884.

Lauteria, Evan W. 2012. "Ga(y)mer Theory: Queer Modding as Resistance." *Reconstruction* 12 (2). http://reconstruction.eserver.org/Issues/122/Lauteria_Evan.shtml.

Lipinski, Jed. 2012. "Video-Game Designer Anna Anthropy Describes the Life of a Radical, Queer, Transgender Gamer." *Capital*, April 10. http://capitalnewyork.com/article/culture/2012/04/5665874/video-game-designer-anna-anthropy-describes-life-radical-queer-trans.

Lipkin, Nadav. 2013. "Controller Controls: Haptics, Ergon, Teloi and the Production of Affect in the Video Game Text." In *CTRL-ALT-PLAY: Essays on Control in Video Gaming*, edited by Matthew Wysocki, 34–45. Jefferson, NC: McFarland.

Marks, Laura U. 2002. *Touch: Sensuous Theory and Multisensory Media*, Minneapolis: University of Minnesota Press.

McWhertor, Michael. 2009. "The Joydick Lets Players Play with Themselves to Play." *Kotaku*, February 9. http://kotaku.com/5150129/the-joydick-lets-players-play-with-themselves-to-play.

Nosedef. 2009. "The JoyDick—Play Atari with Your . . . (SFW)." YouTube, October 5. youtube.com/watch?v=puj8m3EJHZE.

Parisi, David. 2009. "Game Interfaces as Bodily Techniques." In *Handbook of Research on Effective Electronic Gaming in Education*, edited by Richard E. Ferdig, 111–26. Hershey: Information Science Reference.

Penley, Constance. 1997. "Crackers and Whackers: The White Trashing of Porn." In *White Trash: Race and Class in America*, edited by Matt Wray and Annalee Newitz, 89–112. New York: Routledge.

Petruska, Karen and John Vanderhoef. 2014. "TV that Watches You: Data Collection and the Connected Living Room." *Spectator* 34 (2): 33–42.

Pozo, Diana and Heather Kelley. 2013. "Visualizing Data for Pleasure: Heather Kelley on Game Design, Sexuality, and User Interfaces." *Media Fields Journal* 6: Data/Space. http://mediafieldsjournal.squarespace.com/visualizing-data-for-pleasure/.

Rheingold, Howard. 1991. "Teledildonics and Beyond." In *Virtual Reality: The Revolutionary Technology of Computer-Generated Artificial Worlds—and How*

It Promises and Threatens to Transform Business and Society, edited by Howard Rheingold, 345–77. New York: Summit Books.

Ruberg, Bonnie. 2006. "The Challenge of Sex: The Sex in Games Design Challenge." *Gamasutra*, January 16. http://gamedevelopment.com/view/feature/130924/the_challenge_of_sex_the_sex_in_.php.

The Sex Files: A Dark XXX Parody. 2009. Directed by Sam Hain. 2009. Los Angeles, CA, New Sensations. DVD.

Shinkle, Eugénie. 2008. "Video Games, Emotion, and the Six Senses." *Media Culture & Society* 30: 907–15.

Sihvonen, Tanja. 2011. *Players Unleashed!: Modding the Sims and the Culture of Gaming*. Amsterdam: Amsterdam University Press.

Weinstein, Noah. 2009. "Joydick." YouTube, February 6. youtube.com/watch?v=8JORtc2gAsY&eurl.

Weinstein, Noah and Randy Sarafan. 2011. "The Joydick." In *Of Intercourse and Intracourse: Sexuality, Biomodification, and the Techno-Social Sphere*, edited by Johannes Grenzfurthner, Guenther Friesinger, and Daniel Fabry, 136–49. Vienna: RE/SEARCH.

Game cited

Anthropy, Anna. 2012. *Duck Duck Poison*. Antropy, Anna.

9

Sexual favors: Using casual sex as currency within video games

Casey Hart (Stephen F. Austin State University, USA)

As a storytelling vehicle, video games possess an interactive dynamic unique to the medium. Whereas other forms of media such as books, magazines, television, and movies present consumers with a picture of a world they may vicariously visit through the eyes and mind of the protagonist, they do not allow the user to actively participate. Concerning elements such as sex and violence, even first-person stories create space between the protagonist and the audience. On the other hand, video games, particularly modern video games, bring the consumer into the stories by allowing them to make decisions that affect the story progression and the gaming experience. This connects the gamer to the experience and makes them responsible for the actions of their character rather than simply being an observer. From this perspective, video games are a unique genre of modern media and should receive special attention from scholars.

This chapter examines depictions of sex in video games in the context of its use as a commodity within the game dynamic. The study examines three popular video game franchises featuring sex-related dynamics that treat sex as a currency to be traded for various rewards rather than as the reward itself.

Video games as mass media

While once considered the domain of children and a fairly niche demographic of adult males, video games have risen to unprecedented popularity. A series of reports from 2013 compiled by the Entertainment Software Association and the Entertainment Software Rating Board estimated that 58 percent of Americans, representing 67 percent of US households, regularly play some form of computer/video game(s). That number is split almost evenly between males (55 percent) and females (45 percent). Additionally, the report found that the highest percentage of regular gamers were not under 18 but rather over 36 years of age. This represents either a drastic shift in gaming demographics or, at the very least, a disparity between preconceived notions of gamer culture and reality.

It is clear that there are more individuals playing video games than ever before, but the true significance of video games begins to become apparent when one considers that in 2009 the video game industry generated an estimated $10.5 billion in revenue (Entertainment Software Association 2010). To place this in context, in the same year, domestic US motion-picture ticket sales grossed $10.6 billion (Nash Information Services 2013). In 2012, *Call of Duty: Black Ops II* made history by generating over $800 million in revenue in its first five days and more than a billion dollars after fifteen days. These figures were trumped in 2013 with the release of *Grand Theft Auto V*, which accomplished the same feat of generating over a billion dollars in just under three days. By comparison, in a given month, the global music industry generates an average of less than $1.4 billion in record and song sales (Bleeker 2013a, b). With more people playing video games than ever before, including females and older consumers (Wohn 2011), and the video game industry generating revenues that compete with traditional media industries, it is clear that scholars cannot ignore the potential impact of this medium.

Sex in video games

The preponderance of research dealing with video games has focused on the form, function, and social impact of violence and sex in the medium. While high-profile social events like the Columbine and Sandy Hook school shootings have made many question the long-term impact of exposure to violent imagery in video games (Dill and Dill 1998; Vorderer and Bryant 2006; Weber, Ritterfeld, and Kostygina 2006), similar discussions regarding sexual content have occurred infrequently. Sexuality in video games, and more specifically sex itself as a video game element, only gained high-profile public attention in cases like the 2005 *Grand Theft Auto: San Andreas* "Hot Coffee" sex scandal (Downs and Smith 2010).

Sexual content in video games has been around almost as long as the medium itself. For example, the primary game dynamic in the 1982 Mystique game *Custer's Revenge* featured a pixelated naked cavalryman with a protruding phallus dodging arrows in order to have sex with a naked Native American woman. Over the years, numerous other games have included blatant or implied sexual content or sexualized gender representations. Currently, sexuality in video games has become fairly ubiquitous with many characters, particularly female characters, depicted in hypersexualized contexts and with unrealistic body features (Downs and Smith 2010; Smith 2006). Characters like *Tomb Raider*'s Lara Croft and *Street Fighter*'s Chun Li are examples of how video games have "hypersexualized" (Heintz-Knowles and Henderson 2001) females through increased bust, leg, hip, and butt sizes. Each of these is also an example of how female power has been fetishized. These characters may be protagonists or otherwise physically powerful characters, but their power is made subsequent to their sexual appeal (Downs and Smith 2010). Thus, a dynamic is created in which the female character is made a sex object in both form *and* function.

The use of sexual content in video games may be an attempt to gain the attention of the *adult* males that now dominate the gaming culture (Downs and Smith 2010), yet the real threat is not simply that sexual content exists but that it is ubiquitous and trivial within video games. Repetitive depictions or references to sex create a schema, or social script, that is repeated both within individual games and across the medium as a whole. These limited and repeated depictions of sex, sexuality, and females as casual and objectified may lead to troubling social consequences.

Social cognitive theory and perception of acceptable sexual context

Recent studies examining the role and impact of sexual content in video games have utilized the theoretical framework of social cognitive theory (Bandura 2009). The theory argues that individuals learn how their social worlds operate by observing others. Under this framework, many studies have examined concepts including video games' impact on the socialization of gender roles (Dill and Dill 1998; Wohn 2011), gender stereotyping and priming (Yao, Mahood, and Linz 2010), hypersexualization of the female and male form

(Downs and Smith 2010; Fox and Bailenson 2009; Lee, Peng, and Park 2009), and the impact of sexual content over time on the perceptions of acceptable sexual behavior (Dill and Dill 1998). These studies have argued that video games provide an arena in which normative concepts of positive and negative social actions may be tested and re-enforced.

Bandura's (2009) social cognitive theory, and particularly his concept of observational learning, intersects powerfully with the medium of video games, since their interactive and immersive nature provides a virtual environment within which the process may occur. In the first phase of this process, the observer must pay attention to a particular script (Calvert and Huston 1987), either because it is of intrinsic interest or importance to the observer or because it is made important by external forces like peer pressure or social expectations. After the observer is paying attention to a particular social script, retention of the mediated message occurs as he or she enters a process of restructuring. During this process, a receiver takes the content of a message and restructures the information to conform to symbolically preconstructed and approved social schema (Bandura 2009; Calvert and Huston 1987). At this point, stereotyping can occur as consumers shuffle information into categories that produce the least cognitive dissonance. Once elements of the script are restructured, individuals test them to see if they are socially tolerable and rewarded (Bandura 2009; Lando and Donnerstein 1978; Paik and Comstock 1994). If a script is observed, restructured, and then reinforced through acceptance or reward, this inevitably leads to overall adoption of the script and consequent behavioral changes.

The particular power of observational learning with regard to video games lies in the fact that the first three phases of the process can be controlled and orchestrated by the dynamics of the game itself. Games establish what scripts the player must pay attention to and what is important in order to progress through the story. Additionally, games reward players for following these scripts. Finally, many games provide repetitive exposure to these scripts and an arena in which the player may test the efficacy of the message. In this way, games create an environment in which the scripts are placed in positions of importance, repeated, and then reinforced through reward.

Research questions

This chapter focuses on the use of sex as a commodified element of game dynamics. The study operates from the theoretical perspective that while using sex as a reward for accomplishing game objectives may lead to the devaluing of sex and sexual partners, this is exacerbated when games use sex as a means to another end rather than an end unto itself. In order to explore how video games may do this and what social scripts are perpetuated through this process, two research questions have been used to examine three highly successful game franchises.

RQ1:   What video game dynamics are used to objectify and commodify sex and sexuality?

RQ2:   What dynamic does the commodifying of sex in video games create between the in-game participants?

The first question focuses on what elements within the games themselves prompt players to take part in objectifying sexual acts. This can include missions, story elements, achievements, or other game dynamics that give players options or opportunities for their characters to have sex. Sex can be either explicit or implied. The second question explores what dynamics are created between the sex partners as a result of the game elements that lead to in-game sex. By using these two questions as a basis for analysis, this study examines how sex itself is framed, but also the messages being propagated regarding treatment of sexual partners.

Methodology

This chapter contains a textual analysis of the form, function, and impact of sex in three highly successful and very popular video game franchises. These franchises include BioWare's *Mass Effect*, Microsoft Game Studio's *Fable*, and Rockstar Games' *Grand Theft Auto*. These franchises were chosen for analysis because they are highly successful, have several titles each, and feature a game dynamic in which sex is used as a means to some other end. In the cases of the *Mass Effect* and *Grand Theft Auto* franchises, the sex dynamics within the games have gained prominent media attention. *Fable,* on the other hand, was chosen because its game dynamic with regard to sex is both nuanced and complex. Finally, each franchise was chosen because, at the time of writing, a new installment had either been recently released (*Grand Theft Auto V*) or scheduled for release in the near future (*Mass Effect IV* and *Fable Legends*).

The examination will occur under the framework of Hall's idea of dominant and negotiated textual meaning (Hall 1980). Within this framework, Hall argues that any mediated text may have numerous possible readings. The preferred interpretation of the text is referred to as the dominant reading. An alternative reading that takes into account social context, cultural abstracts, and hegemonic codes is referred to as the negotiated reading. While the dominant reading is usually limited in scope to the message medium, the negotiated reading recognizes that communication does not occur within a vacuum and that a matrix of meaning is created with the examined text interrelating with other information and social tropes.

Analysis

While quite different in storyline, the three video game franchises examined in this chapter have many similarities regarding the dynamics of gameplay and structure. These similarities are particularly marked in how sexual elements function and are framed. Each of the three franchises provides clear motivation or rewards for the player to pursue sexual encounters, and each allows the player a certain degree of perceived freedom in how they pursue sex. This choice, however, can be viewed as specious, since it is the predetermined game dynamics that provide the player with choices, interactions, and outcomes. Since in most cases the sexual partners are predetermined and have no agency in the situation, this creates a relational dynamic in which they are interchangeable and unimportant and are simply a means by which the player may live out fantasies or achieve some goal. The following sections illustrate elements of motivation and reward, false-choice, and objectification of sexual partners.

Mass Effect

The *Mass Effect* franchise of games follows the adventures of Commander Shepard and the crew of the Normandy as they face an enigmatic alien race bent on the systematic destruction of all sentient life in the universe. It is a large, space-based saga in which the player's choices have lasting effects on how the story unfolds, even between games. The games themselves have been highly successful, with over ten million units sold worldwide (D'Angelo 2012).

With regard to what game dynamics exist within the *Mass Effect* games governing the form, function, and depiction of sex, each game in the franchise begins by allowing the player to choose a male or female character. While this choice may be viewed from a dominant perspective as an attempt to provide players with an avatar that is customized and representative, the only significant differences in gameplay extending from this choice relate to the nature of sex the player wishes to pursue. Players may pursue a *romantic* relationship with a variety of characters, each climaxing in a cutscene showing the involved characters having sex. When players achieve sexual interaction with another character, they are rewarded with an achievement trophy called "Paramour." This trophy is usually visible online to other players and increases the player's gamerscore, which in turn affects their rank online. Compared to the other games analyzed in this chapter, this motivation is much less significant to the game itself. Still, it illustrates that players are rewarded for simply having sex, regardless of their partner. Thus, in addition to vicariously experiencing sex within the game, players are encouraged to pursue sex as a means by which to achieve some other goal. This reduces sex from an intimate experience and transforms it into a means to another end where partners are interchangeable.

Regarding the dynamic of false-choice, while strictly speaking the option for both heterosexual and homosexual relationships has been available, the choices and results for male and female characters are significantly different. Examining the simple dynamic of sexual availability within the *Mass Effect* games reveals a predominantly heterocentric agenda. Video games can be viewed as vehicles within which players can live out fantasies. Thus, the options given to players within the dynamics of the game reveal what fantasies and experiences are endorsed therein. While the *Mass Effect* franchise does include both male and female relationship arcs and limited homosexual relationship tracks, and the options for both heterosexual and homosexual relationships increased through the franchise's three releases, the options are not congruent. Out of the twenty-two potential relationship combinations, thirteen are heterosexual in nature. The dynamic of false-choice becomes evident when one considers that while male Shepard characters can pursue one of nine possible heterosexual relationships or two possible homosexual relationships, female Shepard characters may pursue four heterosexual relationships or seven homosexual relationships. To expand on this, in twenty of the twenty-two relationship arcs, which culminate in sexual cutscenes, players are shown women in positions of sexual availability either individually or as part of a lesbian couple. From this perspective, in 90 percent of the sexual cutscenes, players are exposed to scenarios that could be sexually agreeable to heterosexual males. Furthermore, from a negotiated perspective, it could be argued that representing the strong female "Shepard" character predominantly with homosexual interests, *Mass Effect* endorses a troubling schema in which powerful women are either lesbians or fetishized sex objects.

These dynamics of motivating players to pursue sex and then offering them intrinsically biased and heterosexual, male-centric options create scenarios in which females are commodified and reduced to objects that are interchangeable vehicles by which male players may live out sexual fantasies. This fetishized dynamic becomes even more apparent when considering the hypersexualized body type and clothing of most of the female characters (Downs and Smith 2010; Fox and Bailenson 2009; Lee, Peng, and Park 2009) and considering that in several cases pursuing a sexual relationship involves convincing a female character to act against her best interest. For example, one alien female character has a reduced immune system, and pursuing a relationship with her involves convincing her to ignore the possible dangers that intercourse could pose to her health. Even after sex, she admits she is sick with a variety of illnesses, but "it was all worth it." This form of sexual deprecation objectifies women by removing their agency in favor of becoming sexual objects regardless of the cost to themselves (Nussbaum 1995).

Fable

Similar to *Mass Effect*, the *Fable* franchise is an action/adventure series featuring game dynamics in which player choices have rippling effects throughout the story. The *Fable* games have been met with global popularity since the release of the namesake title in 2004. The most recent installment, *Fable 3*, was released in North America, Europe, and Japan and sold almost five million units globally.

While *Mass Effect* features science-fiction elements, *Fable* is fantasy-based. Instead of lasers and telepathy, *Fable* games feature swords and magic. The stories follow the life of a character simply referred to as "Hero." This gender-neutral moniker allows players to choose a male or female avatar, which the majority of nonplayable characters (NPCs) interact with in a similar manner. The major difference in how male and female NPCs interact with the player is within the realm of sexuality. The *Fable* games have always allowed players to get married to and have sex with various NPCs, who fawn over their sexiness. While a dominant perspective on this dynamic may be at ease with the fact that players are generally required to marry their partners before sex occurs, a more in-depth examination shows the same objectifying dynamic identified in *Mass Effect*.

While some of the *Fable* games make marriage either a predetermined part of the unfolding story or a mission, there are numerous other ways the franchise entices or rewards players for a myriad of sexual activities and relationship deviations. *Fable II* offers the player achievement trophies (identical to those in *Mass Effect*) for various sexual encounters. These include the "Swinger" achievement for enticing more than one villager to come back to your house for an orgy and the "Paramour" achievement for having sex or watching another player have sex (voyeurism) twenty-five times. *Fable III* reimagined the sexual reward dynamic by offering players "Legendary Weapons" that could only be brought to full strength by committing sexual or intrinsically objectifying acts. This included having sex numerous times with numerous men or women (Love Sword, Swinging Sword, and Ice Maiden), participating in orgies (Swinging Sword, Perforator, and Tee Killer Shooter), marrying numerous people (Mirian's Mutilator), and even killing your spouses (Tenderizer and Skorm's Justice). Each of these weapons is among the most powerful and effective in the games, but each also requires players to pursue sex with numerous spouses (heterosexual or homosexual) or frequent prostitutes.

The pursuit of sex/intimate relationships in the *Fable* games leads to the false-choice. As previously stated, NPCs in the *Fable* franchise will react similarly, if not identically, to either a male or female player, and there are similar numbers of potential sexual partners. Unlike the *Mass Effect* games, which feature defined and limited characters that the player may pursue in a somewhat more complex relationship, *Fable* opts for giving the player the choice of almost any NPC in the game. The game dynamics, however, reduce the process of pursuing a sexual partner to the point of triviality. Apart from visiting brothels, players seeking sexual encounters find a villager whose sexual preference is compatible with their avatar's sex. They converse with the NPC, go on a date, buy a gift for the villager, kiss them, marry them, then have sex. The whole process can take ten minutes or less. Once an NPC is brought to the level of sex partner (or "spouse"), they will remain available for the players to use as they desire. Players may also have numerous spouses in various cities throughout the game. While from one perspective this provides the player with a great deal of freedom and choice within the game, the truth is all NPC characters are pursued and used in much the same way. Thus, the choice is truly a fallacy, and the sex partners become completely interchangeable and inconsequential.

This reduction of characters to simple tools for upgrading weapons and attaining achievements creates a dynamic within the game in which relationships are self-focused, and partners and spouses are easily attained, used, and disregarded with no lasting consequences or implications. In fact, while a player can divorce a spouse who will then take a portion of the player's money and possessions, it is much easier to simply kill the spouse and pay a somewhat reduced cost if caught. This is, by definition, objectification of sex and sexual partners. By creating this dynamic, *Fable* endorses a schema in which sex should be easy, quick, and completely self-focused and carry no lasting implications. Furthermore, the dynamic supports the notion that sexual partners are willing and happy to be used until they are of no further use or interest and then may be dismissed with little or no consequences.

Grand Theft Auto

As mentioned earlier in this chapter, the *Grand Theft Auto* (*GTA*) franchise has had tremendous success over the years. Since *GTA III*, installments in the franchise have broken numerous sales records, with the latest earning over a billion dollars in less than three days (Bleeker 2013a, b). *GTA* has also been at the center of a significant amount of public controversy over the years. This includes the aforementioned *GTA: San Andreas* "Hot Coffee" scandal centered on the ability of players to download patches (i.e., content created to add material to the original code of a game or program) that would show the main character having sex. The original game would allow players to have sex but would only play audio of grunts and moans to indicate intercourse was occurring.

Though the "Hot Coffee" scandal featured one of the more denotatively obvious examples of explicit sex in the franchise, examples of objectification and commodification of sex in the *GTA* franchise are obvious and ubiquitous in every game. Apart from the fact that the games feature constant, overt sexual messages on billboards, television commercials, and radio ads during the game, they also feature numerous game dynamics relating to sex that reduce the act itself and the roles of those involved to objects and objectives. Perhaps the most well-known of these dynamics involves the presence of prostitutes within the games. Within the *GTA* franchise of games, prostitutes may be hired and utilized by the player. When using prostitutes, a player's health increases as their money decreases. Though in each game there are other ways in which to regain health, the prostitute game dynamic is always present. As an example of the motivational dynamic, this means that sex becomes one of many ways to regain health in the game. Utilizing prostitutes, however, carries an additional appeal as the player has the ability to kill the woman after sex to regain the money that was spent on the service. This commodifies sex as a means to an end, objectifies females as sex objects with no agency, and creates a dynamic in which the player may abuse or kill the female and be rewarded for it.

Beyond the prostitute dynamic, all installments of the franchise from *GTA: San Andreas* to the most recent release have featured "dating" minigames. These elements feature the player taking women on various dates with the goal of convincing them to have sex. In most cases this means having the main character wear the right clothing, drive the right car, and take the female to various locations that she asks to go. Ultimately, this process is simplistic and trivial. While the game does limit the choices of relationships the player may pursue, the actual process of "dating" is fairly uniform and repetitive.

In most cases, there is little actual reward for the player in pursuing these relationships other than sex itself, and one woman is generally as preferable as any other.

This illustrates the dynamic of false-choice within *GTA*. The games themselves represent a hypermasculine, heterocentric worldview. Even though main characters like Niko, the protagonist of *GTA IV*, may express shame at using prostitutes or other characters for meaningless sex, the motivations and rewards for players doing so still exist. Compared to the *Mass Effect* and *Fable* franchises, *GTA* is much more open and from a dominant perspective features much more freedom in gameplay. From a negotiated perspective, however, the games are incredibly repetitive and feature uniform dynamics and messages regarding the role, form, and significance (or lack of significance) of sex. As main characters are always males, sexual partners are always female, and those females can generally be used, abused, and/or killed with no lasting repercussions to the main character or storyline, the role of sex and sexuality remains fairly constant regardless of player choices.

Discussion

According to Bandura's concept of observational learning, an individual learns how to appropriately interact with their world by observing their environment, testing their observations, and then reproducing those observed social dynamics. This process involves individuals paying attention to social interaction that is of importance to them, internalizing that social behavior by restructuring it based on preconceived social norms, testing it for social acceptance, and then modifying their behavior accordingly. Video games provide a unique form of observational learning in that they present the player with a world in which any social behavior can be acceptable and encouraged based on game dynamics. Furthermore, video games not only have the potential to show any behavior as acceptable but also to provide an environment within which the player may test the behavior and repeat it, free of lasting consequences. Essentially, this means that games provide a facsimile of reality, detached from the subsequent consequences present therein. With regard to sex, game developers can provide players with games that allow any form of sexual fantasy play but detach sex from traditional ideas of intimacy, monogamy, or any consequence or hindrance that might be present in reality. The real issue, then, becomes one of simplistic representations of sex and sexual relationships, either through game dynamics or system limitations.

This, paired with a detachment of sex from any lasting repercussions or responsibilities, propagates a trope in which sex involves only the immediate needs and desires of the individual, with little consideration for one's partner or the future impact of one's actions.

In returning to the first question used to explore the use of sex as a commodified game dynamic, video games like the ones examined here use two major dynamics to frame sex and sexuality. The first of these dynamics is providing players some motivation to pursue sex. This often takes the form of some reward, other than sex itself, for pursuing sex in the game. This includes making sex part of a mission central to the game, offering upgrades or enhancements for sexual acts, or providing players with trophies or "achievements" that are visible to other players. The second dynamic is false-choice. False-choice refers to the illusion of control provided within games as a product of the game dynamics. While players believe they have choices in how to pursue sex or relationships within games, the game dynamics limit these choices and their outcomes. Additionally, the dynamic of false-choice becomes more problematic when one considers that most video games featuring sexual elements frame sex in an intrinsically male, heterosexual perspective. This means that even if a player has a variety of choices, most lead to outcomes that primarily support the same dominant social agenda.

The second question explored what effect these identified dynamics might have on the representation of sexual partners and relationships within video games. In the three game franchises examined in this chapter, the dynamics of motivation and reward and of false-choice led to a significant limiting of the role and agency of sexual partners. This was particularly significant in the depictions of females and homosexual males. In most cases, females ultimately were interchangeable sex partners who could be used to accomplish some objective and then dispatched or disregarded with no lasting consequences. Homosexual males played similar roles when present but were almost nonexistent within the franchises examined. This represents a strong adherence to the hypersexual, hypermasculine worldview discussed earlier in this chapter.

The three franchises examined in this chapter have sold millions of copies around the world over many years. This means that literally hundreds of millions of individuals have been exposed to the game dynamics upon which these games operate and the subsequent messages created by their use. The presence of objectifying content in video games and the commodification and devaluing of sex and sexual partners through triviality should be cause for concern to media-literate consumers and scholars.

References

Bandura, Albert. 2009. "Social Cognitive Theory of Mass Communication." In *Media Effects: Advances in Theory and Research*, edited by Jennings Bryant and Mary Beth Oliver, 94–124. New York: Routledge.

Bleeker, Eric. 2013a. "Can 'Call of Duty: Ghosts' Challenge 'GTA 5's Billion Dollar Sales Record?" ATVI, November 5. http://www.fool.com/investing/general/2013/11/05/can-call-of-duty-ghosts-challenge-gta-5s-billion-d.aspx.

Bleeker, Eric. 2013b. "GTA 5 Sales Hit $1 Billion, Will Outsell Entire Global Music Industry." TTWO, September 28. http://www.fool.com/investing/general/2013/09/28/gta-5-sales-hit-1-billion.aspx.

Calvert, Sandra L., and Aletha C. Huston. 1987. "Television and Children's Gender Schemata." *New Directions for Child and Adolescent Development* 38: 75–88.

D'Angelo, William. 2012. "Mass Effect: A Sales History." VGChartz, April 17. http://www.vgchartz.com/article/250066/mass-effect-a-sales-history/.

Dill, Karen, and Jody Dill. 1998. "Video Game Violence: A Review of the Empirical Literature." *Aggression and Violent Behavior* 3 (4): 407–28.

Downs, Edward, and Stacy L. Smith. 2010. "Keeping Abreast of Hypersexuality: A Video Game Character Content Analysis." *Sex Roles* 62: 721–33.

Entertainment Software Association. 2010. "Essential Facts about the Computer and Video Game Industry: 2010." ESA. http://www.theesa.com/facts/pdfs/esa_essential_facts_2010.pdf.

Entertainment Software Association. 2013. "Essential Facts about the Computer and Video Game Industry." 2013 Sales, Demographics, and Usage Data. ESA. http://www.theesa.com/facts/pdfs/ESA_EF_2013.pdf.

ESRB: Entertainment Software Rating Board. 2010. "Video Game Industry Statistics." Entertainment Software Rating Board. http://www.esrb.org/about/video-game-industry-statistics.jsp.

Fox, Jesse, and Jeremy N. Bailenson. 2009. "Virtual Virgins and Vamps: The Effects of Exposure to Female Characters' Sexualized Appearance and Gaze in an Immersive Virtual Environment." *Sex Roles* 61: 147–57.

Hall, Stuart. 1980. "Encoding/Decoding." In *Culture, Media, Language: Working Papers in Cultural Studies, 1972–79*, edited by Stuart Hall, Dorothy Hobson, Andrew Lowe, and Paul Willis, 128–38. London: Hutchinson.

Heintz-Knowles, Katharine R., and Jennifer Henderson. 2001. *Fair Play?: Violence, Gender and Race in Video Games*. Oakland: Children Now.

Lando, Harry, and Edward Donnerstein. 1978. "The Effects of a Model's Success or Failure on Subsequent Aggressive Behavior." *Journal of Research in Personality* 12 (2): 225–34.

Lee, Kwan Min, Wei Peng, and Namkee Park. 2009. "Effects of Computer/Video Games and Beyond." In *Media Effects: Advances in Theory and Research*, edited by Jennings Bryant and Mary Beth Oliver, 551–66. New York: Routledge.

Nash Information Services. 2013. "Domestic Theatrical Market Summary for 2009." The Numbers. http://www.the-numbers.com/market/2009/summary.

Nussbaum, Martha C. 1995. "Objecticaton." *Philosophy & Public Affairs* Autumn 24 (4): 249–91.

Paik, Haejung, and George Comstock. 1994. "The Effects of Television Violence on Antisocial Behavior: A Meta-Analysis." *Communication Research* 21 (4): 516–46.

Smith, Stacy L. 2006. "Perps, Pimps, and Provocative Clothing: Examining Negative Content Patterns in Video Games." In *Playing Video Games: Motives, Responses, and Consequences*, edited by Peter Vorderer and Jennings Bryant, 57–75. Mahwah: Lawrence Erlbaum.

Vorderer, Peter, and Jennings Bryant. 2006. *Playing Computer Games: Motives, Responses, and Consequences*. Mahwah: Lawrence Erlbaum.

Weber, Rene, Ute Ritterfeld, and Anna Kostygina. 2006. "Aggression and Violence as Effects of Playing Violent Video Games?" In *Playing Video Games: Motives, Responses, and Consequences*, edited by Peter Vorderer and Jennings Bryant, 347–61. Mahwah: Lawrence Erlbaum.

Wohn, Donghee Y. 2011. "Gender and Race Representation in Casual Games." *Sex Roles* 65: 198–207.

Yao, Mike Z., Chad Mahood, and Daniel Linz. 2010. "Sexual Priming, Gender Stereotyping, and Likelihood to Sexually Harass: Examining the Cognitive Effects of Playing a Sexually-Explicit Video Game." *Sex Roles* 62: 77–88.

Games cited

Big Blue Box. 2004. *Fable*. Microsoft Game Studios.

BioWare. 2007. *Mass Effect*. Microsoft Game Studios.

Capcom. 1987. *Street Fighter*. Capcom.

Core Design. 1996. *Tomb Raider*. Eidos Interactive.

DMA Design. 2001. *Grand Theft Auto III*. Rockstar Games.

Lionhead Studios. 2010. *Fable III*. Microsoft Game Studios.

Mystique. 1982. *Custer's Revenge*. Mystique.

Rockstar North. 2004. *Grand Theft Auto: San Andreas*. Rockstar Games.

Rockstar North. 2008. *Grand Theft Auto IV*. Rockstar Games.

Rockstar North. 2013. *Grand Theft Auto V*. Rockstar Games.

Treyarch. 2012. *Call of Duty: Black Ops II*. Activision.

10

"Embraced eternity lately?": Mislabeling and subversion of sexuality labels through the *Mass Effect* trilogy

Summer Glassie (Old Dominion University, USA)

Video games and video game culture are intricately linked with themes of sex, sexuality, and gender, from Mario attempting to save his damsel in distress to the overtly masculine tones of first-person shooters like *Halo* to the buxom cast of *Dead or Alive: Xtreme Beach Volleyball*. Seen as a masculine industry, the long-time trend for video games had been to display capable, heterosexual male leads who either charge in to save the world and the girl or find themselves in male-dominated situations, like war, where romance is absent. In those same games, strong female characters were also a possibility, but their physical appearances were (and still are, in many cases) more feminized and idealistic than realistic, softening the strength they were projecting. Kline, Dyer-Witheford, and de Peuter describe the presence of female characters in mainstream games: "In most games, either females are invisible (hence invalidated) or they appear in a limited set of stereotypical roles, ranging from passive 'prize' to evil threat—what Buchanan calls the 'virgin' or 'vixen' syndrome" (2003, 257). While these stereotypical, gendered depictions in video games are prevalent, there are also growing trends of strong, independent female heroes (Lightning from *Final Fantasy 13*) and weaker, uncertain male heroes (Jude from *Tales of Xillia*) helping to shape new explorations of gender.

Despite these changes to gendered stereotypes, alternatives to sex and sexuality are very rarely explored as heterosexuality still dominates the industry, with homosexuality and bisexuality often marginalized or altogether absent. Two of BioWare's best-selling video game series, *Dragon Age* and *Mass Effect*, are some exceptions, as they allow players, with customizable avatars, to explore heterosexual and homosexual relationships. While this option has garnered positive and negative feedback from both players and critics, BioWare takes this exploration of sexuality one step further to a cross-species level in the spacefaring trilogy of *Mass Effect*. Many of the potential love interests in the trilogy are of different species, but most of them adhere to the traditional heterosexuality that is required for reproduction. The creators, though, have incorporated a fairly controversial element, and one of great interest, with the introduction of the Asari and their unusual culture and mating habits. As an "all-female" humanoid species not bound to the traditional forms of mating, in that they reproduce through a form of telepathic parthenogenesis, the design of the Asari collapses boundaries of sex and sexuality. The Asari are a species rendered as Other, even in comparison to the various beings populating the gameworld. Characters recognize and struggle against prejudice and limited understanding of Asari customs, culture, and practices. These gameworld features allow for a space where awareness and exploration of sexualities outside of the heterosexual binary can take place. The developers, however, struggle with the representation of such beings as they reinforce verbal and visual gendered markings so as to make the Asari familiar and attractive to players.

Crafting a space for sexualities that are alternative to the heterosexual binary is nothing new in the science fiction genre, where fears and desires can be projected onto alien bodies since there is no definite model upon which to ground any norms. The alien body becomes a safe space or, as Hollinger describes it, a "zone of possibilities" (1999). Hollinger draws upon Jagose's concept of the queer as a "zone of possibilities," as it is "both an exclusive and an excessive space . . . inhabited by all that is *not* heteronormative, 'the point of convergence for a potentially infinite number of non-normative subject positions'" (33). Hollinger states, "At its most inclusive, it can incorporate heterosexuality, but a heterosexuality stripped of its conventional privileges: no gendered or sexed identities in this utopian space are compulsory, or universal, or natural; and, none, certainly, are invisible" (33). This zone of possibilities that Hollinger puts forth can be seen in depictions of the alien body in terms of sex and sexuality in both positive and negative manners, ranging anywhere from the parthenogenetic alien queens in the *Aliens* franchise to Octavia Butler's story, "Bloodchild." Thibodeau (2012) discusses the changes that have occurred in representations of the alien body as more traditional, masculine science fiction narratives have given way to marginalized voices: "While alien bodies have often represented feared 'otherness,' they offer feminist science fiction a rich site for the re-imagining of gender, sexuality, and identity within narratives that challenge the heteronormative implications of 'progress' built into space exploration narratives" (263). While it is often feminist and queer science fiction writers and theorists who carve out space to explore "re-imagining[s] of gender, sexuality, and identity," it is interesting to see BioWare, a highly successful video game studio in a masculine-oriented industry, create a design for a species that does not adhere to stereotypical representations of sexual orientations, reproductive processes, and gender identities. By introducing a species such as the Asari, the developers complicate the unconscious way players approach and respond to characters they label as male or female based on appearance and other markings associated with gender, though the developers often undermine their own attempt.

Hollinger's utopian space and the feminist challenges to heteronormativity that Thibodeau explores in her work are not entirely possible in a mainstream video game since developers are trying to appeal to a wide audience of all different ages and backgrounds, though the Asari design pushes at those boundaries even as it exists within them. Alien designs that diverge too far from the human physique and intelligence may be a novelty and a source of interest, but they have yet to be presented to players as potential love interests, which is a central component of play in *Mass Effect*. In the game, players may choose to customize their own version of the human Commander Shepard as they are given the choice between male and female, and may choose from a selection of physical characteristics and an even more limited selection of character background stories. The customizable Shepard may broaden the targeted audience to be more inclusive of female gamers, but there is still the lingering trend of "introducing sex to games in the form of shapely heroines," with BioWare also including male characters representative of idealized masculinity (Kline, Dyer-Witheford, and de Peuter 2003, 264).

All of the potential love interests, then, have physiques that closely resemble the human body or are human themselves. The few exceptions, at first glance, are the characters of Garrus (a Turian) and Thane (a Drell), both of whom can be considered more unusual in their appearances, and Tali'Zorah vas Neema (a Quarian), whose appearance remains a mystery for much of the trilogy, but all three are also bipedal and, as hinted through romance scenes, are capable of engaging in conventional, human sexual intercourse. The characters of Mordin (a Salarian) and the two playable Krogan characters, Urdnot Wrex and Grunt, are not romance options as their species' designs are not portrayed as compatible lovers or mates with human companions, and they are themselves not interested in a relationship with a human beyond as comrades. These different alien species are not presented as willing to engage in a homosexual relationship, though most of them are willing (some with more hesitation than others) to engage in a cross-species relationship. While there are a number of human characters—for example Steve Cortez, Kelly Chambers, Diana Allers, and Samantha Traynor—offered as potential same-sex partners for Shepard, these characters are not romance options until *Mass Effect 2* or *3*. Only Kaidan Alenko, among human same-sex romantic partners, participates in the player's squad at any time, providing he was not sacrificed in the first game, making most same-sex partners marginal to the player's overall experiences within the game. It is the Asari, then, who are the only species willing to cross all boundaries of sex, sexuality, and interspecies relationships throughout the entirety of the series, but even they fit within the image of sexualized, humanoid females. Despite having tentacles instead of hair and having blue skin, the Asari are considered attractive to all sentient species in the gameworld. This attraction to the Asari by the different species is exemplified during an extraneous moment in *Mass Effect 2* between a Salarian, a Turian, and a human at a bachelor party when each of the three males discusses how the Asari look most like his species:

> Salarian: I can understand why I might find Asari attractive, but how can they be attractive to humans too? They look just like Salarians!
>
> Human: What? They look exactly like us! I'm not seeing the Salarian thing at all. At all.
>
> Turian: You're both wrong. Asari look just like blue Turians. Look at the head-fringe!
>
> Human: Wait, you don't think they're like, mind-controlling us to see them as attractive, do you?

For the player and the player's main character, who are both human, the physiques of the Asari are identical to curvy female humans, complete with breasts, and their facial features most closely resemble humans. Whether the human's explanation about possible Asari mind-control is true or not, the developer's design of the Asari is just as much to show why characters would be attracted to this species as it is to make players themselves comfortable with their Commander Shepard potentially wooing the three Asari romance options.

Even though the Asari's appearance fits into conventional ideas of what is attractive and sexually engaging, the underlying design of the Asari is a "point of convergence" from that which is nonheteronormative. As a species of all "females," their society has no dichotomies based on sex, with every individual moving through the three stages of Maiden, Matron, and Matriarch, regardless of which career path and lifestyle choices she makes. The Asari are not bound to gendered stereotypes of what work they may do, with members of the species serving as commandos, fleet captains, courtesans, ambassadors, Justicars, and shopkeepers, and the Asari are the main species shown in-game performing as strippers. By being the first species not only to reach the Citadel, which acts as the center of galactic politics, economics, and culture, but also the first to make contact with other species, the Asari hold a high position as mediators. This is especially true of their Matriarch on the Council, who is a revered voice and adds the influence of a matriarchy to galactic affairs. However, what truly separates them from all other species in the game, and what makes their design a zone of possibilities, is that they are not restrictive in their sexuality. Because the Asari procreate through telepathic parthenogenesis, which the in-game Codex describes as a mind-melding with a mate and tapping into that mate's genetic code by unifying their nervous systems, they are not limited to procreating with a male or even a humanoid (*Mass Effect*). So long as the being is sentient, that being is a potential mate for an Asari. This freedom of sexuality ruptures traditional *human* ideas of sex and sexuality that do not apply to the Asari and yet are applied anyway by in-game characters, players, and, at times, even the developers.

The resulting ruptures in understanding, linked with the Asari's biology operating outside of conventionality, emerge in how other species judge the Asari within the labels of mother-virgin-whore—labels that are based on human reproductive processes and societal norms. Dr. Liara T'Soni, one of the two Asari characters on the player's team and a potential love interest, mentions this limitation in perception by others, stating, "Although we seek to understand other species, it seems few of them seek to understand us. The galaxy is filled with rumors and misinformation about my people" (*Mass Effect 1*). Liara then becomes the voice of Asari culture in her interactions with the player's Shepard and his/her other companions, attempting to decouple the "rumors and misinformation" with which the player comes into contact. The rumors and misinformation in-game reflect the kind of resistance that mainstream society has to people who are marginalized in their alternative sexes and sexual identities. This trend of resistance to such alternatives underlies even science fiction, a genre that thrives on pushing against the limitations of mankind. Hollinger argues, "On the whole, science fiction is an overwhelmingly *straight* discourse, not least because of the covert yet almost completely totalizing ideological hold heterosexuality has on our culture's ability to imagine itself otherwise" (198). For a mainstream video game firmly entrenched in science fiction and themes of war and exploration, traditionally seen as masculine endeavors, *Mass Effect* acknowledges that heterosexuality does have this "ideological hold" on its players and its own industry by including comments about the Asari that can be lewd, confused, and outright offensive. However, through the character of Liara, the developers offer the players a chance to understand how very different the Asari are from the information circulating the gameworld outside of the Codex and how far they exist outside of the players' and characters' comprehension when viewing the species through the lens of human heteronormativity.

As Liara tries to explain about her species, she openly acknowledges that the vocabulary she is using is limited to human concepts: "Mating is not quite the proper term. Not as you understand it," "I know my father— if you want to use that term," and "'Male' and 'female' have no real meaning for us" (*Mass Effect 1*). Liara grounds her use of human language in the fact that Shepard (and the player) would have an easier time understanding familiar concepts, even when she knows these concepts can never truly encompass her species. After speaking with Liara, the labels of mother-virgin-whore become openly problematic as questions are raised: Can a being that does not require physical contact to procreate be considered a whore? Or even a virgin? Can an Asari who has procreated without having sexual intercourse still be considered a virgin while an Asari who has engaged in such intercourse be a nonvirgin? And, if "male" and "female" are terms that have no meaning for the Asari, can we still use the pronoun "she" because the physique resembles a human female, or must a new pronoun be created that is more neutral? Can they be labeled as mothers if they are not necessarily "female?" This last question becomes even more problematic when the player finds out that Liara is the offspring of two Asari and is given a chance in the third game to meet her "father," Matriarch Aethyta. For the Asari, the "mother" is the being who gives birth, and the "father" is the being who gives the other half of the offspring's genetic code, though all Asari offspring are Asari. Liara's father mentions that she also had children with a Hanar, which is a species that looks like a floating, speaking jellyfish. The only real language we have that could convey the experience of a being who is capable of physically fulfilling the reproductive roles of both "mother" and "father" at will and without being asexual is that of the biological term "hermaphrodite" and the social term of "intersex," with the latter term having a history of also referring to homosexuals (Preves 2001, 523). Further, neither appropriately applies to a monogendered species, as both use normative "male" and "female" as their reference points. Describing the Asari, given these limitations, proves difficult, and even now, as I am struggling to try to communicate the conflict of language, I must fall back on the familiar concepts of "mother" and "father"; "she" and "her."

This struggle with language to define and describe the Asari is inherent within the game itself, as seen most sharply in the dialogue of Asari characters and within the game Codex, both of which are naturally represented as experts in regards to the Asari. While much of the dialogue with Liara shows awareness of the problems that accompany placing human labels upon that which lies outside of human experience, the developers create an underlying issue with how gamers perceive the Asari. Liara describes her species as "monogendered" but, again, mentions that "'Male' and 'female' have no real meaning for us" (*Mass Effect 1*). Oftentimes, the word "gender" is used to describe whether someone is male or female when it is meant, specifically, to describe the expectations placed on a person as masculine or feminine according to social norms. Players may not be aware of the difference between the terms "gender" and "sex," but with the Asari possessing a female physique and being called "monogendered" by both Liara and the Codex (which states that, "Although the Asari have one gender, they are not asexual"), players filter their Shepards' interactions with Liara and other Asari as if they were dealing with human females. This filter is intensified by information dispensed by the Codex that is often at odds with Liara's explanations, most especially when it declares the Asari an "all-female race." There is tension then between the game's formal delivery of information about this particular species and the informal way an individual presents herself to the players, with discrepancies threaded throughout the gameworld. The Asari characters who are bystanders to the player's actions— random civilians, shopkeepers, bartenders—constantly refer to themselves and other members of their species within the scope of human concepts, such as calling themselves "daughters" and using gendered pronouns. Even Liara's own "father" makes lascivious comments about her former lover and Liara's "mother," Matriarch Benezia, in regards to her "rack . . . even before she hit the Matriarch stage" (*Mass Effect 3*). The emphasis on the breasts is a human preoccupation, and without further information as to the function of the Asari breasts in regards to childrearing, the comment seems little more than the developers establishing Liara's "father" as masculine, which in turn gives her the appearance of being a lesbian. Comments concerning breasts occur again with Liara's "father" when she uses the phrase "about as useful as tits on a Hanar," separating the Hanar from humanoid beings and rendering them as unattractive as lovers and mates to a human, despite the Asari having a history of mating with this jellyfish species (*Mass Effect 3*). This distinction between Asari and Hanar draws further attention to the physique of the Asari and the fact that they have all the right parts for acceptable sexual relationships with the player's avatar. The masculinized comments from Matriarch Aethyta about breasts and her previous relationship with Matriarch Benezia encourage players to conceptualize the relationship as lesbian, with Aethyta being butch and Benezia being the feminine partner, rather than seeing it as a relationship between two beings who cannot be defined against a heterosexual dichotomy.

Another major way that the developers firmly represent the Asari as "females," despite not being female, is in the naming of the life stages of the Asari after titles given to women—Maiden, Matron, and Matriarch (*Mass Effect 1*). It would be difficult for a player to not consider a character female when that character is constantly introduced as a Matriarch, alluded to as a Matron, or identified as being young enough to be classified as a Maiden. This becomes more difficult when faced with the Asari's physical femininity and the Codex containing fairly stereotypical, gendered descriptions of the Asari's three life stages, even though the titles Matron and Matriarch assume positions of power within a society, something that the Asari can and often do achieve. While the Codex outlines the average ages of an Asari entering into the Matron stage and later the Matriarch stage, it also includes statements about roles Asari tend to adopt as well as what could cause exceptions to those average ages:

> The Matron stage of life begins around the age of 350, though it can be triggered earlier if the individual melds frequently. This period is marked by a desire to settle in one area and raise children, [while] [t]he Matriarch stage begins around 700, or earlier if the individual melds rarely. Matriarchs become active in their community as sages and counselors, dispensing wisdom from centuries of experience. (*Mass Effect*)

At first glance, the information looks standard for an outlining of the lifespan of a species. However, the early triggering of the Matron stage—the stage associated with childrearing—for an individual melding "frequently" as opposed to the early triggering of the Matriarch stage—the stage associated with positions of power within the community—for an individual melding "rarely" subtly conjures the dichotomy of stay-at-home mom versus career woman. The idea that the Matriarch stage can be entered early if the individual consciously abstains from or has no desire to engage too frequently in meldings is resonant with the stereotypical depictions of a woman who "sacrifices" the building of sexually intimate relationships in order to advance her career. Opposed to this depiction is that of a woman who frequently engages in sexual (or, in the case of the Asari, melding) experiences and is focused more on having children. This dichotomy is deepened with the idea that the Matron stage is marked not only by a desire to raise children but also to settle in one area—a kind of nesting period. Despite the concept of the Asari that Liara presents to players of a species that operates outside of true human understanding, BioWare developers undermine their own attempts at having Asari design push at boundaries because of the inconsistent manner in which they portray Asari biology and culture.

The inconsistency with which the Asari are portrayed in their physical design and the Codex's information allow players to push Liara and her species into the category of female, where most of the players then filter all of their experiences with the Asari. By looking through forums, blog posts, and videos of gameplay and cutscenes of players' interactions with Liara and the two other Asari romance options, it can be seen just how players' responses have a tendency to mirror that of in-game species. Gamers often consider Liara a lesbian or as bisexual because she is attracted to and will engage in a relationship with Shepard regardless of the character's sex. There are videos on sites like YouTube from players with titles like "Liara Lesbian Sex Scene" and "Femshep Full Lesbian Romance" and even polls on the official BioWare forums that ask questions like, "Do you think of Liara as a lesbian romance option for Femshep?" While there are players who raise questions as to whether or not Liara can be considered a "woman" or a "girl," the majority of the answers seem to correspond to Liara's female appearance rather than the biological and societal differences Liara's dialogue had put forth in the first game ("Forum: *Mass Effect 3*"). There is also players' response to the "whore" label placed on the Asari, as they debate about what role the Asari play in the overall universe of *Mass Effect*, considering them "sluts" and "whores of the universe" and focusing on the fact that the Asari are the only species really seen as strippers in the game ("*Mass Effect 2*: Asari"). The mislabeling of the Asari's sex and sexuality detracts from the understanding of the Asari as a whole because more attention is given to the "looseness" of their preferences for mates and the gendered stereotypes of these characters, instead of the idea that the Asari are more interested in their partners as both individual beings and for the qualities their species possess.

For those gamers who deride the Asari as "whore of the universe," they are ignoring Liara's own explanations of how members of her species choose to mind-meld with other beings, which take on mystical overtones. When Commander Shepard initially approaches Liara as a potential romance option in the first game, Liara is quick to reassure him/her that she is "familiar with the legend of Asari promiscuity," seeking to clarify the importance of the act of melding as a union. She states, "When one of my people joins with an individual from another species, it is a very deep and spiritual exchange. We do not enter lightly into a union." Because the Asari unify their nervous systems with the individuals with whom they are melding, the process includes a mental coalescing of the two beings. "Thoughts and senses merge, identities intertwine, memories and emotions weave themselves together becoming entangled in a single, rapturous whole" (*Mass Effect 1*). Liara's description of melding goes far beyond the boundaries of a one-night stand or even casual sex, if the act can even be considered sex, as partners give and receive the innermost sanctums of their beings. With the Asari individual tapping into thoughts and memories, and allowing the mate to gain reciprocal entrance to her mind in return, the union goes deeper than what most humans would consider a fully developed, healthy relationship.

While it is possible for an Asari individual to have multiple partners over the course of her long life (their life expectancy ranges to about a thousand years or so), her experiences would still not make her a whore because melding does not always equate to human understandings and practice of sex. As well, the labels placed on Asari as sluts and whores of the universe is simply in reaction to the lack of boundaries for the Asari's preferences of mates, which extend beyond the scope of conventional understandings about sexuality and, therefore, human labels. The most essential aspect of melding is not in the act itself, though, but in the function of the act, which is procreation. By Liara's account, "[Melding] is the lifeblood of my species, the way we evolve and grow as a society" (*Mass Effect 1*). The Asari mate with other species not to "get around" the universe sexually but to continually add to their genetic code. While it is possible for two Asari to mate and produce offspring, there is the risk that their child may be born as something known as an Ardat Yakshi, which is a sterile Asari who will unintentionally kill any being she takes as a lover (*Mass Effect*). For every victim, the Ardat Yakshi grows stronger, as seen in the second game with the homicidal character of Morinth, which causes the Ardat Yakshi to be considered a danger to her people and to anyone with whom she comes into contact. The union with other species, then, is to limit the possibility of Ardat Yakshi and to "share the most basic elements of [other species'] individual and racial identities" that can be used to strengthen the Asari society as a whole (*Mass Effect 1*). The negative comments about the promiscuity of the Asari stem from only looking at sex as recreational rather than as functional. The Asari are a species that do not need to find mates outside of their own kind but do so to improve themselves and pass on the best genetic code they can to their offspring.

While the openness of the Asari to procreating with members of other species without a thought to the biological sex and gender of their mates is a source of contention for both in-game characters and players, the design of the Asari allows for them to be a zone of possibilities to explore sexual identities and relationships of marginalized people outside of the game. By creating a species whose sex and sexuality collapse the heterosexual binary, despite those same characters being portrayed within the sphere of conventional gender markings and language of the heterosexual dichotomy, BioWare developers are pressing at the boundaries of their own industry and the heteronormative foundation of traditional science fiction. It is very rare for a gender variant person to appear in a video game, especially as a character with whom the player's avatar can engage in a sexual relationship. Liara, as a nonnormatively sexed and gendered body, becomes a vehicle through which players can come into contact with and begin to understand a being whose biology and culture are not fully compatible with traditional concepts and language and one who demands to be seen as a person rather than as some monster or foreign oddity. Pearson (2009) notes that

> Heteronormativity presupposes that only heterosexuality is normal and assumes a very limited, hegemonic definition of heterosexuality that works in concert with equally essentialized notions of sex and gender (and of the inherent, "natural" match between biological sex and gender role). Thus heteronormativity has multiple effects: it dismisses as "abnormal" or "perverted" those who do not fit its gender norms, including transsexuals, intersex people, tomboys, "sissies," and effeminate men; and it severely regulates and disciplines the bodies and behaviors of heterosexually identified people. (303)

This pervasiveness of heteronormativity and, according to Hollinger, the ideological hold it has on our culture may be used to understand why the developers were so insistent upon placing a femaleness on the Asari and why players react as they do to a fictional species that clashes with their internalized notions of how sex and sexuality operate in our world, even when those notions exclude people who exist in our very society. The gameworld of *Mass Effect* is a kind of playground in which players can experiment with subversions to this heteronormativity, engaging in a relationship with a character whose physiology and culture encourage relationships based on the qualities of the being instead of worrying about what is socially acceptable.

There may be resistance and scorn directed by some players at the design of the Asari, as seen in game forums and blog posts ("Forum: *Mass Effect 3*" 2012; "*Mass Effect 2*: Asari" 2010), but Liara's role as a representative within Shepard's team and for the players does much in an attempt to alleviate the bias with which her species is received. It may seem as if BioWare was ultimately unsuccessful at creating and implementing a truly revolutionary species design, but the developers actually created a controversy that stirred discourse within groups of players, bringing to the surface issues of gender, sexual identities (even, unintentionally, going so far as to include intersexuality), heterosexual biases, and conflicts with limitations of language. These discussions occur in forums ("About Homesexuality [sic] in ME, and What BioWare Said" on the website *GameFAQs* 2010), entries on personal blogs ("Mass Effect Fail: the Stuff BioWare Didn't Get Right (Part 2)" 2011), and articles on gamer-oriented websites ("The Sex Class in BioWare Worlds"

2014). *Mass Effect* introduced a main character through which nonnormative gender, sex, and sexuality could be explored beyond the limits of language. The Asari, by being Other in terms of being alien, are a safe space for BioWare developers to edge out into a realm beyond heteronormativity, while Asari femaleness softens the alienation players may feel during interactions with the fictional species. Even if players do not understand Liara, she can still be classified as something familiar. For an industry based upon masculinity, the product of a successful video game company giving voice to marginalized Others and raising issues with how mainstream society approaches and deals with those Others is a progressive step in regard to who can be included in video games and what roles they may take.

References

"About Homesexuality in ME, and What BioWare Said." 2010. *GameFAQs*. http://www.gamefaqs.com/boards/944907-mass-effect-2/53444309?page=4.

Davis, Sara. 2014. "The Sex Class in BioWare Worlds." *The Ontological Geek*, 2014. http://ontologicalgeek.com/the-sex-class-in-BioWare-worlds/.

"Forum: *Mass Effect 3*: Poll: Do you think of Liara as a lesbian romance option for Femshep?" 2012. *BioWare Social Network*. http://forum.BioWare.com/topic/384460-poll-do-you-think-of-liara-as-a-lesbian-romance-option-for-femshep/.

Hollinger, Veronica. 1999. "(Re)reading Queerly: Science Fiction, Feminism, and the Defamiliarization of Gender." *Science Fiction Studies* 26 (1): 23–40. http://www.jstor.org/stable/4240749.

Kline, Stephen, Nick Dyer-Witheford, and Greig de Peuter. 2003. *Digital Play: The Interaction of Technology, Culture, and Marketing*. Montreal: McGill-Queen's University Press.

"*Mass Effect 2*: Asari, I Don't Get It, Are They Perfect?" 2010. *GameFAQs*. http://www.gamefaqs.com/boards/944907-mass-effect-2/53582600.

"Mass Effect Fail: The Stuff BioWare Didn't Get Right (Part 2)." 2011. *Go Make Me a Sandwich: A (Mostly) Humorous Look at How Not to Sell Games to Women*. http://gomakemeasandwich.wordpress.com/2011/05/05/mass-effect-fail-the-stuff-BioWare-didnt-get-right-part-2/.

Pearson, Wendy Gay. 2009. "Queer Theory." In *The Routledge Companion to Science Fiction*, edited by Mark Bould, Andrew M. Butler, Adam Roberts, and Sherryl Vint, 298–307. London: Routledge.

Preves, Sharon E. 2001. "Sexing the Intersexed: An Analysis of Sociocultural Responses to Intersexuality." *Signs: Journal of Women in Culture and Society* 27 (2): 523–56. http://www.jstor.org/stable/3175791.

Thibodeau, Amanda. 2012. "Alien Bodies and a Queer Future: Sexual Revision in Octavia Butler's 'Bloodchild' and James Tiptree, Jr.'s 'With Delicate Mad Hands.'" *Science Fiction Studies* 39 (2): 262–82. http://www.jstor.org/stable/10.5621/sciefictstud.39.2.0262.

Games cited

BioWare..2009. *Dragon Age*. Electronic Arts.

BioWare. 2007. *Mass Effect*. Microsoft Game Studios.

BioWare. 2010. *Mass Effect 2*. Microsoft Game Studios.

BioWare. 2012. *Mass Effect 3*. Microsoft Game Studios.

Namco Tales Studio. 2011. *Tales of Xillia*. Namco Bandai Games.

Nintendo. 1983. *Mario Bros.* Nintendo.

Square Enix. 2009. *Final Fantasy 13*. Square Enix.

Team Ninja. 2003. *Dead or Alive: Extreme Beach Volleyball*. Tecmo.

PART THREE

Systems/spaces of sexual (im)possibilities

11

Playing for intimacy: Love, lust, and desire in the pursuit of embodied design

Aaron Trammell (Rutgers University, USA) and Emma Leigh Waldron (University of California, Davis, USA)

Imagine a game with no conflict. Can you? Would it be fun, interesting, shallow, or boring? Frederick Berg Olsen's *The Lady and Otto* (2005) is one such game. In this "Nordic larp," players are told to act the parts of either the Lady or Otto (who have practically identical roles) as they are prompted with a scene. Example scenes include "Otto is in the bathroom, the lock has jammed," and "Lady is climbing into bed. Otto can't sleep." Players then feel their way around the scene until they reach a point of conflict; at this point, a referee intervenes with a whistle. They must then stop and attempt the scene again, this time avoiding the conflict. Play continues like this for about two hours, and while the game may not be a particularly fun one, it certainly makes a point about the centrality of conflict to narrative. Surely interesting games and narratives alike incorporate conflict on some level, but why do game mechanics focus specifically on the simulation of violent and misogynist conflict, in particular? This essay is about the new subjectivities produced by games that deviate from the military-entertainment complex which fundamentally permeates our culture of play. How can we design games to challenge the violent and misogynist status quo of the industry, and what new cultures might emerge when we do?

The video game industry has been heavily critiqued for its overtly military motifs. And although there has been a considerable backlash against media effects approaches that essentialize this phenomenon by assuming that players of violent games will reproduce violence elsewhere in their lives, there have recently been several other approaches that recognize the ways in which violent games are, instead, by-products of the military-industrial complex (Dyer-Witheford and de Peuter 2009; Crogan 2011). If game design is left to the machinations of industry, then it is only violence that will be reproduced through games. The endless reproduction of military and consumer motifs within the market is, according to Stiegler (2014), a symptom of a social system that has begun to consume itself.

To paraphrase Swedish game designer Emma Wieslander's (2004a) provocative question, why do we produce games in which our avatars are far more likely to experience violence and even death than love and physical intimacy? There is hope, however. As Stiegler proposes, therapeutic techniques can be developed to promote healthy economies of discourse and desire,[1] and in this way they can promote processes of individuation that do not result in the ceaseless repetition of banality. For this reason, we argue that it is important to explore game mechanics that have been developed through communities that are not fundamentally linked to mass-market commercial industries. If games are to produce environments of care for players, game mechanics must be sought in new spaces entirely.

Specifically, we are interested in mechanics that have been cultivated by thoughtful designers with an interest in activism and social resistance. This paper considers three specific sex mechanics devised for use in Nordic larp[2]—an avant-garde school of live-action role-playing game design—as a key site of inquiry because of their historical positionality as a response to Weislander's challenge in that they were designed specifically to respond to the apparent lack of sex techniques in gaming (Stenros 2013). These techniques include face-to-face narrative disclosure, an arm-touching technique known as *ars amandi*, and visual simulation using phallic props. This chapter will explore the scope of experimental methods of sexual embodiment in Nordic larp communities in order to create a framework that reads the game mechanics of sex as a set of bodily techniques with concrete design implications. The techniques described here evoke new potentials of individuation and provoke dialogue among and between participants.

Critiques of violence

Game studies scholars have always been troubled by the promiscuity of violence in video games. One need only gaze at the bestselling games of 2013 to observe how intimately related the two are. In a list (Fiscal Times 2013) of 2013's top ten bestselling games, eight of the ten games employ mechanics that require the player to engage in direct combat, use guns for killing or self-defense, or command digital others to brawl to the death. Seven of these eight are sequels to other games as well. Just as these games epitomize the industrial replication of violence, they also epitomize the degree to which violence is linked to industrial processes that excel at replicating themselves. To turn on a console is to flirt with violent media, and to flirt with violent media is to be subject to the production of violence itself.

Reactions to this play have taken many forms in the history of game studies. Some moments (Anderson, Gentile, and Buckley 2007) emphasize how violent video games produce violent behaviors within children, yet other critics argue to the contrary. Games do not produce violent players, scholars like Jenkins (2014) claim. Rather, players have the agency to interpret games however they like and in doing so resist replicating problematic narrative tropes. Recent work in critical game studies offers a middle-ground approach that rethinks the polemics of these viewpoints. It is perhaps best synthesized by Crogan (2011): "[Media studies and video games researchers] throw the baby out with the bathwater, avoiding the question concerning technoculture's relation to war and the military that computer games pose so insistently beyond the media effects debate, which itself is unable to articulate it adequately in these terms." The production of electronic games is fundamentally adjacent to the production of military power. It is this sense of feedback that must be untangled if we are to recognize the political affordances of violent games at all.

The role of commercial video games within the military-entertainment complex is almost universally met with concern by scholars. Halter (2006) argues that games serve as metaphors for the landscape of war. They help to reveal how the practices of war shifted over time. Dyer-Witheford and de Peuter suggest that war relates to the acquisition of capital and point to the ways in which these concepts of empire form the backbone of many video games. Crogan (2011) suggests the military-entertainment complex is so deeply embedded within the heart of computer games that it makes no sense to oppose the two; to speak of computer games is to think through the marriage of entertainment and warfare. Finally, Trammell and Sinnreich (2014) posit that locative games, altered reality games, and gamification are evidence of the ways games transformed from a social metaphor of war to a social instrument of control and coercion.

Video games captivate players within a feedback loop of control. As players input commands, the machine responds by providing players with new situations, inputs, stimuli, and conditions. Crogan (2011) refers to this as the cybernetic aspects of video game systems. Cybernetics, as defined by Edwards (1997), was developed as a language to unify an array of diverse scientific modes. It was a theory of absolute regulation, which promised that the good society would be produced through the merger of bodies, machines, and mathematics. If scientists could ascertain how social configurations worked as social systems, they could be made to run more efficiently through emerging technology. Video games are a peculiar residue of this scientific moment in the mid-twentieth century, but significantly, the feedback systems they produce are devised by software engineers and marketing teams, not social scientists.

Commercial video games are tools of control and coercion, designed to model things that sell, not things that might contribute toward a social good. So it should come as no surprise that violence is so frequently reproduced in games, because violence has always sold when prominently featured in radio, television, film, and art. Because violence is most troubling when it appears in games, given the cybernetics upon which game systems have been modeled, it is important to critique these emergences and recognize how work on violence in games might be considered as supplementary to other related phenomena.

Techniques of care

Stenros offers a catalog of sex mechanics utilized in Nordic larp, moving forward from a quote offered by Wieslander: "In most larps there is, strangely enough, a far higher risk of the character getting killed than making love. It seems that amorous interaction such as lovemaking, cuddling, hugging or just holding hands in a sensual or sexual manner, is quite taboo" (2004). This idea caught fire in the Nordic larp community, as Stenros observes: "The Nordic larp community took this lack as a challenge. Over the years numerous different types of amorous interaction techniques were developed" (2013). His essay, "Amorous Bodies in Play," is an effort to catalog and discuss the differences between some of these sex mechanics. Implicit in this discussion is the idea that violence is poisonous, and therefore its opposite, sensuality, has the possibility to be therapeutic. Here, however, we question whether the two terms should be set in opposition to one another at all, or if violence and sensuality occupy the same problematically visceral category.

It is important to take into account the degree that amorous techniques in role-playing games constitute a sense of care. And, if they do, how could this sensibility translate to video games? It is one thing for two players to kiss one another in a larp; it is arguably another for one *Second Life* avatar to kiss another. Additionally, live-action role-playing games offer a way to understand the design affordances of amorous mechanics within a playspace, and they help us to understand these mechanics.

Care, for Heidegger (2008), can be understood as a set of practices that constitute one's *being* in the world. Heidegger argued that *being* relates to deliberate action or care. This perspective differs from prior ontological maneuvers that can be roughly considered Platonist or Aristotelian. The quality of one's existence depends on the forms of action one takes. Given that techniques, if anything, are culturally transmitted forms of action,[3] the techniques and mechanics that constitute and govern one's actions are, in this sense, directly related to the quality of one's existence and life.

Unlike other media, video games necessitate that players take action within them. As such, they are intimately related to the very essences of the players participating in the game. For Steigler it is important, then, to consider the nature of the technologies we see as essential to our lives. He argues that the techniques and technologies that are produced by the logic of the market tend to be poisonous in nature. For this reason, we believe that the first step in defining a therapeutic ethic of game design must be a critique of the market. Such a critical lens provides practitioners with the intellectual purchase to critique otherwise innocuous products and allows them the tools to design games in a way that deliberately resists the capture of capital.

Finally, the ability of technology to bring people together is, for Steigler, its ultimate potential. Steigler explains that Simondon's idea of individuation must be updated to encompass the potentials of collaborative work. Instead of techniques and technologies working to distinguish one person from another, they can also work to help groups define their own collective identities (Crogan 2010). For instance, the technology of open source computer software allows for a collective sensibility around design that is somewhat free from the demands of the market, whereas proprietary software like Adobe Dreamweaver encourages users to respond to the aesthetics of the market and produces a sense of individuality that is necessarily attached to the product's own affordances. In this way, those who work with open source software may court a sense of collective configurability that ranges far beyond the walled gardens of Adobe.

Amorous techniques in Nordic larp allow a space of care for both the self and others. These techniques coalesce diegetically around ideas of character. Role-playing presupposes a fundamental distinction between player and character. Nordic larp techniques exemplify how expectations of and rituals for enacting care are different for the player and the character. Players are not expected to care for one another in-game, for example, although this sense of care may be taken up by the group or community in structures outside of the narrative of the game. Instead, players play at care for one another during the course of the game by embodying characters that care for one another within the narrative context. Nordic larp designers have addressed this difference in two ways: first, with play techniques that allow characters to seamlessly simulate experiences within the diegesis of the game; and second, with practices external to the gameplay that provide space and guidance for the players to think through, process, and otherwise make sense of their in-game experiences.

As Stenros notes, techniques are developed to provide a means for experiencing something that is either impossible (time travel) or impractical (swordfighting) to simulate. Techniques imposed for practicality reasons arise out of a concern for safety and take for granted a certain disjunction between the in-game experience of the character versus the out-of-game experience of the player. Just as "boffer" (foam-padded) weapons emulate real swords because the latter can seriously harm players, sex also has the potential to negatively affect the player. The attempt to find a correlative "safety" mechanic for simulating sexual encounters, therefore, highlights the similarities between violence and sex. It is a fallacy to stage violence and sexuality in binary opposition given their visceral similarities and subsequent exploitation in the commercial sector. That said, designers greet both forms with different tactics of censorship, and it must be acknowledged that explorations of queer sexuality within games are as rare as explorations of pacifism. Game designers work, instead, to offer intricate technology trees that reinforce the barbarism of unending and total war and often consign to represent sexuality with boobs, chauvinism, objectification, and other common tropes of heteronormative sociality.

While such intervening techniques acknowledge the dissociation between player and character, Nordic larps focus on the hard-core[4] aims to dissolve these boundaries as much as possible. The premium placed on immersion encourages players to experience their characters' journeys as completely as possible. Nordic larp appeals primarily to embodied practices that produce affects within players. The call for sex techniques, therefore, arises from a sensibility that encourages players to aim for affective resonance (known as "bleed")[5] while, somewhat paradoxically, acknowledging that the residue of that bleed is unpredictable and somewhat uncontrollable.

The technicity of sexuality

Several techniques for simulating physically and emotionally intimate experiences have been developed and used in Nordic larp, to varying success. Here, we will represent the spectrum of existing techniques with an analysis of three specific mechanics and the games for which they were developed.

The first technique was developed for a game called *Summer Lovin'* (2014).[6] *Summer Lovin'* tells the story of three sexual encounters between acquaintances at a summer music festival and encourages exploring the awkward (and therefore "realistic") aspects of sex, as opposed to the romanticized versions depicted in most popular media. This involves two players sitting knee-to-knee, holding hands, and maintaining eye contact while verbally describing their characters' actions and feelings, a technique, which Stenros identifies as *establishing the events*. This portion relies on verbalizing and narrating physical encounters, which served the writers' vision to "force people to talk about sex, to verbalize both what actually goes down in a sexual situation and the feelings involved" (Lindahl, Nilsen, and Westerling 2014). Here, the Game Master's responsibility is to keep the players on track with describing with specificity their physical actions *as well as* their internal reactions to what is taking place.

With its emphasis on narrative over embodied practice, this technique may seem to impose the greatest distance between the player and their character. However, the affective resonance of the liveness and unpredictability of the encounter is in no way mitigated, as one interviewed player reported: "The incredible amount of nervous energy was there. Obviously the nudity and physical sensations were not." In this way, *Summer Lovin'* deliberately acknowledges and works to delve into the multiple ways in which sexual encounters affect us, outside of the erotic. While this technique does elicit certain sensations, some players experience frustration when running up against the "translation" issue of the visceral to the cerebral. Another player reports: "I would get all tongue-tied and nervous trying to talk out things that I normally do without talking. I can simultaneously interpret English/French, but not body/description."

Ars amandi, on the other hand, takes up the issue of embodiment by emphasizing the tactile experience of intimate encounters. Developed by larpwright Emma Wieslander (2014) in a deliberate effort to rectify what she saw as an imbalance in larp designs, this technique aims at tapping into physical sensuality while still providing a barrier between the player and sexual arousal. *Ars amandi* involves players touching each other's hands, arms, shoulders, and neck as a way of simulating intimacy. This technique was originally developed for a game called *Mellan Himmel och Hav (Between*

Heaven and Sea) (2003), in which the erogenous zones of the characters in-game *were* the arms. Since then, however, it has been widely adopted and adapted for use in a variety of different games, representing anything from kissing to sexual intercourse, depending on the context (Figtree 2013). In this way, while perhaps not as explicit as *Summer Lovin'*, *ars amandi* focuses on simulating an embodied sense of sensuality for the player. Although other storytelling methods must set the scene of the game, *ars amandi* has the capacity to elicit extremely strong experiences for the player. There are even some reports of relationships having begun out of game due to the technique.

A third technique, known as Phallus Play, also operates symbolically, but is more overtly sexual in content. This technique relies on the use of a phallic prop, such as a dildo, to mime a sexual encounter. Players using this technique remain fully clothed, so the prop is used merely to signify sexual contact, not to enact it physically. This technique, therefore, operates similarly to *ars amandi* in its symbolic representation of physical intimacy, but it is more similar to narrative techniques in its emphasis on creating a vivid and provocative scene for viewers, rather than a sensual experience for players. As organizer Tor Kjetil Edland (2012) reports, "Ars amandi felt more sensual and erotic, while doing a scene with the phallus method felt more like watching a hot sex scene in a movie." One particularly interesting tenet of this technique is that the phallus is intended to represent sexual aggression, so it can be used by and with characters of any gender. Outside of in-game practices, the wider context and implications of the techniques must also be taken into consideration, and one major drawback to this technique therefore is the reification of heteronormative phallocentric interaction as "standard."

While the Nordic larp community has made efforts to design techniques that allow for expressing sexual intimacy between two or more partners and allowing for various combinations of genders, it is interesting to note that no formal attention has been paid to the expression of "self-love." Although many designers emphasize that since sex is a natural and common life experience, it must, therefore, play a part in larps that aspire to naturalism, masturbation is prominently missing from these stories. Perhaps it is because such solitary scenes would often take place in private and therefore, arguably, outside the diegesis of the game. The possibility remains that solitary techniques have not been considered because there is no need to establish safety from oneself. If sex techniques are created in an effort to provide players with a mechanism through which to police their personal boundaries, then it stands to reason that a player need not protect herself from her own advances, or at least knows when to back off. The lack of attention to techniques for simulating masturbation points to the fact that techniques for sex exist as a safety measure, because sex is not necessarily always a technique of care but rather, as in real life, carries with it the potential for eliciting discomfort at best and trauma at worst. Without a clear vision on the designer's behalf regarding how sex and sexuality will be implemented in games, and without player consent that this manner of play is worth exploring, the deliberate nature of the act is lost. Implementations of sexuality in games run the risk of transforming the sacred into the banal, and as such, they must be considered with care by both designers and players.

Automating sexuality

Because of the ways that feedback has been hard-baked into the design of video games, it has been argued by theorists such as Frasca (2003), Bogost (2010), and Flanagan (2009, 2010) that games can function as excellent persuasive tools. Going a step further, Flanagan (2010) has even argued that games are specifically useful for addressing issues of social justice: "Games are particularly well-suited to supporting educational or activist programs in which the fostering of empathy is a key outcome. This is because games allow players to inhabit the roles and perspectives of other people or groups in a uniquely immersive way." Although games are often able to produce affects of fear, care, concern, or excitement within their players, Flanagan (2010) continues, they are rarely accurate simulations of the phenomenon they aim to model. In this sense, the focus which Nordic larp places on the hard-core and sometimes precise replication of sexual encounters is at odds with Flanagan's (2010) concept of critical play, which utilizes game mechanics in order to produce radical social change as opposed to radical subject experiences.

This tension, between means and ends, is the core problematic for the design of radical video games. If Nordic larp offers a glimpse at how a near-perfect simulation works as a means to produce affects and subjectivities within player groups, then Flanagan's call for an ethic of activism within game design prompts us to question the ultimate aim of these games. The inclusion of sex mechanics is an insufficient justification for an ethic of activism and care in game design. Critical approaches to sex mechanics in games read them as the beginning of one of many important conversations, not an end. In many ways the critical apparatus of the Nordic larp community has been the dialogue produced within the community, not the mechanics of the games. The example of *Kapo* below points to how sex mechanics function as a site of discursivity amongst community members and questions whether this discursivity can be replicated within video games.

Transformative reports

Because the tradition of Nordic larp often produces a wealth of documentation about game events, it is not difficult to locate examples from the community that speak to the ways the implementation of sex through clever game mechanics can yield a radical player experience. It is important, for this reason, to rely upon some of this documentation to consider the use of sex mechanics in Nordic larp and glean some insight as to how it offers transformative potentials for design—be they helpful or harmful.

Player Kalle Grill (2012) addresses the ways in which sex mechanics can prompt a transformative dialogue in his reflections on his experience playing *Kapo*, a larp infamous for its level of gritty intensity. The characters in *Kapo*, a Stanford Prison Experiment-like larp designed to explore power, had been placed in a concentration camp in present-day Copenhagen. Conditions in the camp were brutal, and characters experienced torture, humiliation, starvation, sleep deprivation, beatings, and, of course, rapes. Kapo employed the *ars amandi* technique, and Grill goes into extensive detail about the various ways it occurred throughout the game (both positively and negatively). Grill acknowledges the ways in which simulating sex can have a much deeper effect on the player than violence because

> the physical circumstances differ. Player and character share bodies and sexuality is strongly connected to the body.
>
> Though whether we are sexually attracted or not of course depends on many other factors, when there is attraction it is both strongly felt in the body and directed at another body. Hostility, in contrast, is more in the mind and is directed at personalities and perhaps social roles, not so much at bodies (89).

Grill goes on to discuss how this bodily confusion establishes something very different in rape scenarios than in other violent scenarios because, although the violent aspect of it remains almost fully within the diegesis of the game, the sexual attraction is pervasive and potentially even pleasurable to the player.

Grill asserts that there is social merit to this type of experiment, stating

> I think it is good that we can experience rape from the inside of a rapist by larping. We can do so, of course, only to the extent that we can experience anything by larping. It is not the real thing, but it gives us an experience much richer than any other art form and so it can provide valuable teachings about who we are and could be under other circumstances. In the case of non-consensual sex, it can teach us something about our too many depraved fellow human beings who actually rape and abuse (90).

Although Grill suggests that there is potential for positive societal transformation due to larp experiences such as this, *Kapo* also exemplifies how sex in and of itself is not necessarily the antithesis of violence, precisely *because* these simulated experiences can affect players in such lasting and significant ways. This is also why additional safety techniques surrounding the use of sex simulation techniques, such as the use of safe words like "cut" and "brake," have been developed and continue to be hotly debated.

For a particularly powerful example of the ways in which game experiences can bleed into players' lives outside of the game, we could again look to *Mellan himmel och hav*, the game for which Emma Wieslander developed her *ars amandi* technique. Many of the participants in this game were so strongly affected by their in-game experiences that they took up new intimate relationships in the real world, even after the game had ended. Some players broke up with their former partners, and others were influenced to explore new sexual orientations and polyamorous relationship models. Such lasting effects have the power to be both positive (encouraging open-mindedness and progressive social change) and negative (in their tendency to be somewhat insularly focused), as noted by two voices from the community:

> The participants were suddenly thrown into situations where they had physical contact with people they would normally, for one reason or another, never touch. As a consequence, very many of the participants were smitten with a poly-sexual analysis of human relations—and they took it into practise, because they had experienced that these ideas functioned. A big number of break-ups, amorous adventures, and attempts to establish new norms followed among the players. Heterosexuality and monogamy were undermined among the participants to the benefit of polygamy and a general questioning of gender. (Gerge and Widing 2006)

Gerge and Widing go on to describe how the people who participated in *Mellan himmel och hav* felt an almost "cultish" bond, and some had the tendency to judge or ostracize members of the community who had not shared in the experience and therefore did not share the same values and beliefs borne of embodied play.

Dialogue in meatspace

Perhaps what Nordic larp does best in its approach to sex (and violence)—and what video games could benefit from incorporating as well—is acknowledging how much the fictional experiences within games can affect "real" life and deliberately implementing systems for effectively coping with this. For example, both the narrative description technique and Phallus Play incorporate the use of "inner monologues." In these monologues, characters describe not only their actions, but also how they are feeling and how they hope the scene will play out. Although this is not a required element of *ars amandi*, it is an extremely common element of all Nordic larp. This metatechnique encourages reflexivity about the game and helps create an environment in which the consequences of one's actions carry a substantial weight.

While inner monologues are done in-character, Nordic larp also provides a structure for players to "debrief" after a game's conclusion. These sessions are often facilitated by game organizers and involve solitary reflection, discussion with a partner or in a small group, or even roundtable conversations with the entire cast. Debriefing is an essential element of Nordic larp where players recount their in-game experiences and share how those scenes made them feel. Processing scenes that involved sex and intimacy, therefore, often play a prominent part in debriefing.

Intimate video play

Immersion, though not always a point of discussion in video game design, is a topical subject in conversations regarding theater and larp (White, Harviainen, and Care Boss 2012). Still, as video games become more immersive, it becomes easier to imagine the ways they might work to model complex modes of sexuality. Though the hard-core and realistic simulations of the Nordic larp community are in some ways an extreme lens through which the embodiment of sex in games can be viewed, such a viewpoint is a necessary one to consider given aspirations of realism and immersion considered central to the marketing of many mass-market video games.

Sex mechanics in games should not be considered in opposition to violence. Instead they have much in common with the principles of violent game design insofar as they are related to the production of affect within players. Though violent game mechanics and sexual game mechanics have been designed to evoke feelings, they are seldom devised in a way that produces dialogue. What would it mean for a computer to prompt player reflection after a steamy encounter in a game like *Leisure Suit Larry*? Can a sense of dialogue be provoked within the auspices of a computer game, or is the game instead a one-way discussion between designer and player?

A true sense of discourse may be conspicuously absent from computer games, given that it is limited to the imaginations of the writers who must attend to all potentials of the dialogue when programming the game. This apparent drawback, however, can also be a strength. Techniques like "cut" and "break" have been implemented in Nordic larp as a way for players to mitigate the effects of an emotionally harmful or difficult situation. Unfortunately, players facing these difficult situations often report feeling uncomfortable with having to break up the diegetic action of other players participating in the scene. In a single-player computer game, however, "cut" and "break" can be implemented almost flawlessly, and uncomfortable players can end a scene, without a sense of social pressure, whenever they like. What is absent remains a second person with whom to discuss the scene afterward.

Perhaps massively multiplayer online role-playing games (MMORPGs) are the space where these various perspectives ultimately converge. While game designers have structural control over many elements of the MMORPG environment, players also host discussions with one another in these worlds. In these games, moderators could take the time to encourage debrief sessions during moments of the visceral. After the excitement of the raid, players could gather to discuss their feelings; characters with in-game relationships could meet in preprogrammed spaces that offer moderators who are trained to counsel during moments of stress. Even in computer games like *Mass Effect*, where sex and sexuality play a well-fleshed-out narrative role, companies should consider offering online counseling as an option to players after dramatic moments.

The suggestion that intimacy should be implemented alongside mechanics that facilitate counseling is surely a daunting one for designers hoping to produce safe, thoughtful games. And, just as sex can be implemented poorly in games, discourse can also be poorly facilitated by inexperienced counselors or worse, automation. As techniques and technologies of sex allow for more embodiment, it is important that they are facilitated in a deliberate fashion between caring partners. Sadly, it is more likely that we will see a vibrating wiimote implemented as the special "touch of love" ability of a corseted villainess before it is included in the arsenal of MMORPG players seeking to get to know each other in a more caring way. This is the precise logic of the market that developers must resist: instead of reducing sexuality to the logic of marketing, they should design games with mechanics that allow interested and caring players to interact with one another in a way that is more than the ceaseless repetition of violence. This, however, is unlikely, as visceral embodied modes of interaction open the door to a litany of legal problems that invariably reinforce the idea that we, as a society, should make war and not love.

Intimacy in games has the potential to allow us to imagine games as emotive spaces of self-betterment. But, without discourse, this space of growth can easily turn poisonous, producing effects of carnality akin to the barbarism of video game violence. Ultimately, because discourse is so integral to the transformative and critical aspects of all Nordic larp, it is this space of dialogue that needs encouragement alongside all sex mechanics in games. Just as the violence in games is problematic only insofar as it is produced without critique or conscience, so is sexuality. We will inevitably feel intimacy in new and profound ways as games continue to be developed, and it is important for developers to consider the ways that players can be urged to reflect upon these experiences.

Notes

1 Bernard Stiegler draws on Derrida's work in *Plato's Pharmacy* to define technologies and techniques as either poisonous or therapeutic. This distinction follows from Plato's dialogue in *The Phaedrus* wherein medicines are defined with both terms: therapeutic when they are used to cure ailments and poisonous when abused or administered improperly. The metaphor is invoked in *The Phaedrus* as a way to critique language, rhetoric, and therefore truth as these modes of knowledge can be understood as techniques and technologies, which can either help or harm a population. We have adapted this language here in order to consider games as techniques of play with a set of both therapeutic and poisonous potentials that must be critically addressed.

2 "Larp" as a term is derived from the abbreviated form of "live-action role-play" and is used in this paper as a way to define all games of this genre. Nordic larps are generally designed with the intent of using games as a means of exploring deeper social issues and questions about human experience, as opposed to creating an escapist fantasy in which to play out the traditional "hack and slash" hero's journey. For example, Wieslander developed the *ars amandi* technique for the game *Mellan Himmel Och Hav* (*Between Heaven and Sea*), which created a fantasy world in which to explore new ways of assigning and expressing gender and relationships. More recently, the games *Summer Lovin'* and *Just A Little Lovin'* developed new techniques to suit their unique purposes. *Summer Lovin'*, which utilizes a descriptive technique, was designed with the intention of encouraging people to feel comfortable talking about sex, and *Just A Little Lovin'*, which employs the use of prop dildos, is an emotionally intense game about the AIDS pandemic in New York in the 1980s. For more examples and definitions of Nordic larp please see *The Nordic Larp Wiki* (nordiclarp.org/wiki/).

3 Technique, drawn from the Greek word τέχνη (techne) meaning craftsmanship, craft, or art, implies an approach toward production that emphasizes the cultural, shared, and embodied aspects of the act. This definition has been expanded to specifically delineate many embodied practices of shared cultural behaviors by Marcel Mauss in his essay "Techniques of the Body." Importantly, bodily techniques are learned cultural behaviors, even techniques as common as walking, washing, and jumping.

4 Hard-core as in its musical equivalent "hardcore music," which lays claim to an authenticity that is produced by pushing boundaries and doing things to the extreme. In one famous instance, players of the Nordic larp System Danmark, who took the roles of street people, allowed other players to urinate on them in accordance with the dogma of the game's diegesis. Although such play was forbidden in the game, a culture of support for hard-core behavior helped to justify and encourage this form of player action.

5 "Bleed" is a specific term used by the Nordic larp community referring to the experience of fictional, in-game, character experiences "bleeding out" into the player's day-to-day life, or, alternatively, the player's personal background "bleeding in" and affecting their in-game character. For more on bleed, see Lizzie Stark's (2012a, b) essay "Nordic Larp for Noobs" and Sarah Lynne Bowman's (2013) presentation "Bleed: How Emotions Affect Role-Playing Experiences".

6 *Summer Lovin'*, though closely related to Nordic larp, particularly in its emphasis on using gameplay to explore emotions, is technically a Jeepform game. Jeepform games combine elements of narrative tabletop games with live-action role-playing but are less concerned with naturalistic immersion. For more on Jeepform see Lizzie Stark's (2012a, b) primer, "Jeepform for Noobs" and the Jeepform website, jeepen.org.

References

Anderson, Craig, Douglas Gentile, and Katherine Buckley. 2007. *Violent Video Game Effects on Children and Adolescents: Theory, Research, and Public Policy*. Oxford: Oxford University Press.

Anonymous. 2013. "The 10 Bestselling Videogames of 2013." *Fiscal Times*. http://www.thefiscaltimes.com/Media/Slideshow/2013/12/13/10-Bestselling-Video-Games-2013.

Bogost, Ian. 2010. *Persuasive Games: The Expressive Power of Video Games*. Cambridge, MA: MIT Press.

Bowman, Sarah Lynne. 2013. "Bleed: How Emotions Affect Role-Playing Experiences—Sarah Lynne Bowman." April 18. http://www.youtube.com/watch?v=AtjeFU4mxw4&noredirect=1.

Crogan, Patrick. 2010. "Knowledge, Care and Trans-Individuation: An Interview with Bernard Stiegler." *Cultural Politics* 6 (2): 157–70.

Crogan, Patrick. 2011. *Gameplay Mode: War, Simulation, and Technoculture*. Minneapolis: University of Minnesota Press.

Dyer-Witheford, Nick, and Grieg de Peuter. 2009. *Games of Empire: Global Capitalism and Video Games*. Minneapolis: University of Minnesota Press.

Edland, Tor Kjetil. 2012. "The Power of Repetition." In *The Book of Just a Little Lovin'* (2013 Denmark run), edited by Casper Groneman and Claus Raasted, 30–7. Copenhagen: Rollespilsakademiet.

Edwards, Paul. 1997. *The Closed World: Computers and the Politics of Discourse in Cold War America*. Cambridge, MA: MIT Press.

Figtree. 2013. "Soren Lyng Ebbehoj: Touching, Body, Language, Physicality, and Feelings in Nordic Larps." http://www.youtube.com/watch?v=fK_aXriW1DM.

Flanagan, Mary. 2009. *Critical Play: Radical Game Design*. Cambridge, MA: MIT Press.

Flanagan, Mary. 2010. "Creating Critical Play." In *Artists Re: Thinking Games*, edited by Ruth Catlow, Marc Garrett, and Corrado Morgana, 49–53. Liverpool: Liverpool University Press.

Frasca, Gonzolo. 2003. "Simulation versus Narrative: Introduction to Ludology." In *The Video Game Theory Reader*, edited by Mark Wolf and Bernard Perron, 221–37. New York: Routeledge.

Gerge, Tova, and Gabriel Widing. 2006. "The Character, the Player, and Their Shared Body." In *Role, Play, Art*, edited by Thorbiörn Fritzon and Tobias Wrigstad, 47–56. Stockholm: Föreningen Knutpunkt. http://jeepen.org/kpbook/kp-book-2006.pdf.

Grill, Kalle. 2012. "Ars amandi in Kapo." *The Book of Kapo: Documenting a Larp Project About Dehumanization and Life in Camps*, edited by Claus Raasted, 82–90. Copenhagen: Rollespilsakademiet.

Halter, Ed. 2006. *From Sun Tzu to XBOX: War and Video Games*. New York: Thunder's Mouth Press.

Heidegger, Martin. 2008. *Being and Time*. Harper Perennial Modern Classics. London: HarperCollins.

Jenkins, Henry. 2014. "Reality Bytes: Eight Myths about Video Games Debunked." *PBS: The Video Game Revolution*. http://www.pbs.org/kcts/videogamerevolution/impact/myths.html.

Lindahl, Trine Lise, Elin Nilsen, and Anna Westerling. 2014. *Summer Lovin'*. http://jeepen.org/games/summerlovin/.

Stark, Lizzie. 2012a. "Jeepform for Noobs." Lizzie Stark. http://lizziestark.com/2012/09/17/jeepform-for-noobs/.

Stark, Lizzie. 2012b. "Nordic Larp for Noobs." Lizzie Stark. http://lizziestark.com/2012/08/08/nordic-larp-for-noobs/.

Steigler, Bernard. 2014. "The Disaffected Individual in the Process of Psychic and Collective Individuation." *Ars Industrialis*. http://arsindustrialis.org/disaffected-individual-process-psychic-and-collective-disindividuation.

Stenros, Jakko. 2013. "Amorous Bodies in Play. Sexuality in Nordic Live Action Role-Playing Games." In *Screw the System—Explorations of Spaces, Games and Politics Through Sexuality and Technology*, edited by Johannes Grenzfurthner, Günther Friesinger, and Daniel Fabry. Arse Elektronika Anthology #4. RE/Search & Monochrom.

Trammell, Aaron and Aram Sinnreich. 2014. "Visualizing Game Studies: Materiality and Sociality from Chessboard to Circuit Board." *Journal of Games Criticism* 1 (1). http://gamescriticism.org/articles/trammellsinnreich-1-1.

White, William J., J. Tuomas Harviainen, and Emily Care Boss. 2012. "Role Communities, Cultures of Play and the Discourse of Immersion." In *Immersive Gameplay: Essays on Participatory Media and Role-Playing*, edited by Evan Torner and William White, 71–86. Jefferson: McFarland.

Wieslander, Emma. 2004a. "Positive Power Drama." *Beyond Role and Play*, edited by Markus Montola and Jaakko Stenros, 235–42. Helsinki: Ropecon.

Wieslander, Emma. 2004b. "Rules of Engagement." *Beyond Role and Play*, edited by Markus Montola and Jaakko Stenros, 181–86. Helsinki: Ropecon.

Games cited

Berner, Anders et al. 2011. *Kapo*.

BioWare. 2007. *Mass Effect*. Microsoft Game Studios.

Linden Research. 2003. *Second Life*. Linden Lab.

Nilsen, Elin. 2012. *Summer Lovin'*. Larp Factory.

Olsen, Frederik. 2005. *The Lady and Otto*. http://jeepen.org/games/ladyotto/
    lady_and_otto.pdf.

Sierra Entertainment. 1987. *Leisure Suit Larry*. Sierra Entertainment.

Wieslander, Emma. 2003. *Mellan Himmel och Hav*.

12

It's not just the coffee that's hot: Modding sexual content in video games

Matthew Wysocki (Flagler College, USA)

In the mid-eighties, Cantor and Cantor (1986) studied how soap opera audience members impact and influence the stories that producers develop. This "active" audience can propose content by getting their opinions and ideas in front of these producers through fanzines, for example. While they do not directly write shows, their suggestions have at times been incorporated into media product. Similar to these fans are the gamers who mod (modify) games, altering the game in a variety of ways, primarily through changing the appearance of characters, adding levels, or activating cheats. While much of this modding is done to increase the play aspects of gaming, some individuals instead code in content of a more adult nature, including nude codes and animated sexual encounters. The most notorious example of this is the "Hot Coffee" minigame that was buried in the code of *Grand Theft Auto: San Andreas*, but other popular targets include *Skyrim*, *Oblivion*, *The Sims*, and even, surprisingly, *Minecraft*. By participating with their products of consumption in such a way, ultimately, the gamers responsible for these mods are going beyond being audience to being creator of their own media that they consume.

Games are seen as inherently interactive, a term that has seen quite a bit of debate regarding how to conceptualize it (Aarseth 1997; Wolf 2000; Manovich 2001). Lopes (2001), however, provides us with a sense of what interactivity means with regard to gaming because he considers games a "paradigm" of what he calls "strong interactivity." For Lopes what "is engaging in a good game is that the course of the game depends on the players' choices. Their choosing some moves over others is part of what makes each playing of a game unique. Games are 'strongly interactive' because their users' inputs help determine the subsequent state of play" (68). This separates them from weakly interactive media where all that is determined is what media will be accessed or the order of access of said media. Strong interaction results from user action. This chapter seeks to further develop our understanding of the practices and activities of the game modding community, specifically focusing on the interactive nature of modding, especially in the intersection of games and sexual content. It also looks at how these modders ultimately function as producers and expanders of the media content that they also consume, helping to recontextualize the concept of interactivity beyond the idea of user input into the state of play. And part of the focus is to attempt to determine the nature of this modded sexual content. That is, does it serve as the addition of sensual/erotic adult content into gaming or does it primarily consist of prurient and juvenile embellishments?

Interactivity and audience impact

Cantor (1987) interviewed producers in an attempt to determine what part the audience played in the creation of content. Those interviewed had two notions of the audience they were writing for. Some wrote for themselves, believing that if they liked it, so would a mass audience. The rest wrote believing that if it appealed to them, it would not appeal to an audience. In both cases, they had a poor idea of what the audience actually liked and wanted.

But it is the work she did with James M. Cantor (1986) on soap operas that provides a base for what this project seeks to develop. Their research determined that some audience members do have impact and influence on the stories that producers create. They claim that the "interested viewers who communicate their opinions through letter writing or fan magazines and through face-to-face contacts are very important even though they may be a small minority" (223). These audience members can even go so far as to influence content. The reason for this influence is because they are active and get their opinions and ideas in front of these producers. "These viewers are powerful because writers and producers most often keep them in mind when initiating themes or continuing a relatively conservative view of the social world" (223). They further determine that when a show is in trouble in the ratings, these audience members' influence wanes greatly. Both of these articles conclude that there are limitations to what an audience can do, no matter how active they might be; shows were written for obtaining demographics.

The idea of interactivity in video games, or media in general, is not a new one. Crawford (1984) argues that games have four crucial indexes, one of which is interaction. Media allow different levels of dynamism for representing reality. Games are the most fascinating, in his opinion, because they

> allow the audience to explore [reality's] nooks and crannies to let them generate causes and observe effects. Thus, the highest and most complete form of representation is interactive representation. Games provide this interactive element, and it is a crucial factor in their appeal.

The gameplayer is free to explore the various causes and effects that a game provides. This can lead to the player exhausting all the potential outcomes that the game delivers.

But here interaction is seen as a social or interpersonal component. Games are interactive because a player can interact with an opponent—either another player or the illusionary opponent provided by the computer. The interactivity is a element of competition. A player is not creating something new with the media but rather is limited to the options available in the programming of the game and is reacting accordingly, but relatively freely, based on rules.

Continuing from this point that Cantor and Cantor get us to, we further explore mod creators by focusing on the field of active audience research. Specifically, uses and gratifications theory seeks to determine what people do with media. This theory works from two assumptions. Rubin (1993) spells these out as "First, media audiences are variably active communicators. Second, to explain effects we must first understand audience motivation and behavior" (98). These basic ideas are built off other premises:

(a) Communication behavior such as media use is typically goal-directed or motivated . . . .
(b) People select and use communication sources and messages to satisfy felt needs and desires . . . .
(c) Social and psychological factors mediate communication behavior . . . .
(d) Media compete with other forms of communication for selection, attention, and use . . . .
(e) People are usually more influential than media in media-person relationships (98).

The crucial elements of this list for this work are the first two: that media use is goal-directed and that people use media to satisfy felt needs and desires. These two have the greatest impact on the media use being studied here.

A number of factors expound upon the idea of audience activity. These involve audience activity as "selectivity." Here, activity is judged by how much audience members choose to pay attention to what they are watching, as well as perception and retention. "Utilitarianism" posits that audience members rationally choose their use as it satisfies clear needs and motives. "Intentionality" refers to when audience members apply cognitive structures to consume and remember information. "Involvement" deals with both affective mental arousal and parasocial interaction. Lastly, "imperviousness to influence" refers to the ability of audience members to resist the messages directed at them by the media (Biocca 1988). But these theories and ideas refer to audience activity while actually engaged with media consumption. Furthermore, they seek to explain and define the audience's mental and psychological activity. They ponder whether the audience becomes involved on an intellectual level or whether they are just oblivious consumers.

Mods, labor, and resistance

Mods are programs or alterations of source codes created to modify video games. While not all mods are for computer games, a majority of them are, both due to the greater ease of accessing source codes on computers as opposed to consoles and due to the subsequent ease of sharing these codes over the Internet. Mods are created by what could be termed the general public, to differentiate them from video game employees working for the benefit of their company. Sihvonen (2011) explains that "modding can be defined in one simple and straightforward sentence: it is the activity of creating and adding of custom-created content, mods, short for modifications, by players to existing (commercial) computer games" (37). Nieborg (2005) asserts that modders must have "noncommercial" motives, and therefore mods must be provided for free to other gamers. This distinguishes them from commercial products that might be built on existing game engines but are sold as commercial products. In some instances, games have game engines that make it easier for players to alter game content (Ondrejka 2006), while others make it easy for players to call up and access their source code. They have become increasingly popular over the years, with Au (2002) even going so far as to claim that "player-created additions to computer games aren't a hobby anymore—they're the lifeblood of the industry" in his article announcing the launch of Steam in 2002.

Furthermore, mods are traditionally delineated into two main forms: partial and total conversions. Partial conversions, where the addition is "supplementary," involve minor changes to the actual game structure. These include things like creating new maps, costumes, or characters or altering the objectives of the game (like changing a death-match game into protect-the-flag style game). Total conversions significantly alter the structure and look of the game, creating in essence an entirely new game. They involve complete replacement of the original artistic elements of the game and possibly altering the gameplay as well. These are much less common than partial conversions due to both the amount of time and effort involved and the potential copyright issues that might arise from using a proprietary game engine with new content. In her study of modding in *The Sims*, Sihvonen argues that perhaps it is better to consider these divisions as either "game-provided" or "user-extended," depending on whether they result from aspects inherent in the game code or player practices, though even then she recognizes this division is not a strict one (89). Within these types, she then conceptualizes four modding categories: interpretation, configuration, reworking, and redirection. Interpretation and configuration both involve modding within the framework of altering the game-provided code, though in fact merely playing the game can be read as an act of interpretation. Configuration requires the creation of new elements for the game but within the framework of what the game code already allows. Reworking and redirection entail higher-level alteration. Reworking has to do with "altering the game's aesthetics and mechanics, usually by adding new gameplay elements" (89). And redirection deals with creating external objects such as screen shots and gameplay videos.

For a number of researchers (Sotamaa 2005, 2010), the focus on modding is its connections to ideas of production and consumption similar to Cantor and Cantor's interactive audience. Kline, Dyer-Witherfor and de Peuter (2003), for example, point out how modding can "'close the loop' between corporation and customer [by] reinscribing the consumer into the production process" (57). The concept here is that support for the practice of modding makes for more loyal customers, encouraging their devotion to one's company and its products. Postigo (2007) goes so far as to identify modders as "fan-programmers" building off Jenkins' (2002) idea of "convergence" between fans and game producers. Nieborg further supports this idea that modding is "stimulated, institutionalized and becomes a collaborative instead of a participatory culture" and, because of the nature of most modders' agreement to follow end using license agreements (EULAs), results in a "commodified" culture. EULAs spell out what modders can and cannot do from a legal perspective when coding games. Since most modders follow these restrictions in order to potentially gain recognition (if not employment) from the game developers, they work with the interests of the manufacturers.

Nieborg and van der Graaf (2008) determine that total conversion modding in the Valve community goes so far as to be read as an extension of the game industry itself. These modders are "emulating the first party developers' risk-averse, capital-intensive mode of production and within [this] proprietary context, total conversion modding has become a 'proprietary experience' as modders anticipate the developers' act of reappropriation and subsequent commodification" (192). Game modders' work is undertaken and completed with the same methods and outcomes as the very companies whose work they seek to mod. As a result, they feel that most modders are not likely to create mods that have the possibility of not finding favor with an audience and therefore focus on conversions most likely to find favor of promotion by the companies whose products they are altering.

But this avoids realizing the potential of what modders could accomplish with their time and efforts. Kücklich (2005) speaks to the potential of modders to create a new form of labor that can transcend traditional boundaries of ownership. The possibilities exist that "modders are . . . in a unique position to challenge the ways we think about the relationship between work and leisure in the post-industrial age, and to explore new modes of non-alienated labour. Modding could emerge . . . as a cultural practice that extends beyond the confines of digital games." Since this labor is conceptualized as a leisure or play activity, Kücklich christens this hybrid of work and play as "playbour." Similar to this, Lauteria (2012) recognizes "the political relevance of modding as a means of resistance to the gamified global capitalism of Empire" (4). Overall, he determines that what "mods have the capacity to do politically is create new spaces for resistant play" (23).

Modders are dedicated audiences interested in using their energy to alter their objects of consumption and even create additional content for their own and others' utilization. In doing so, they add value to works that have been produced for them. What modding entails involves audience activity separate from using a media product in its intended manner (i.e., playing the game as programmed). It is crucial to consider how this has impacted upon subsequent usage and consumption of the media product. The goal of the following analysis is to look at what type of involvement an audience has with a chosen media form *after* their initial consumption of that media; what they have developed for the game that goes beyond the expected playing of the game; the point when the audience goes from being active consumer to interactive cocreator. So what is of interest here is what happens when a player goes further and wants to create content for an already existing commercial media product, especially when that content is of a sexual nature.

The mods

The most well-known, and perhaps most infamous, sexual content mod is the Hot Coffee mod. Technically speaking, the Hot Coffee code was actually a piece of fossilized content discovered by Patrick Wildenborg for *Grand Theft Auto: San Andreas*. Pallant (2013) defines fossilized content as "code which, during the development process, has become redundant, but which is more convenient to leave *in* rather than remove (134)." CJ, the main character in *GTA: SA*, was capable of "dating" various women in the game. Successful dates led to him being invited inside "for coffee." During actual gameplay, this interaction was only heard and not seen. The rewards for achieving this were benefits like extra vehicles or not losing weapons when hospitalized due to one girlfriend being a nurse. As mentioned, a gamer searching through the game files found this leftover code and created a mod that allowed players to access it. The Hot Coffee mod replaces the audio content with a minigame (Figure 12.1) that allows the player to enter the girlfriend's bedroom and control the character's actions during sex. In order to earn the rewards offered by the game, the player was required to please whichever girlfriend was being romanced at the time.

The discovery of this code and the mod to access it ended up being a public relations black eye for game developer Rockstar Games. The company initially attempted to claim that the Hot Coffee mod actually was the result of programming the content into the game, but subsequent hacking of the console versions revealed that they too contained the content in question. Subsequently the game was re-rated as Adult Only 18+ in the United States, and Rockstar was forced to remove the content altogether on future versions in order to earn back its Mature rating. The company also released a

FIGURE 12.1 *Hot Coffee Mod.* Grand Theft Auto: San Andreas, *Rockstar North.*

subsequent patch for the game that blocked access to the minigame even if the Hot Coffee mod was installed on a user's computer.

The desire to uncover and share this content speaks to the drive of some modders to create adult content. Even a game as notorious for its adult content as *Grand Theft Auto* was not considered frank enough with its depictions of sex, so modders and players wanted more. It was merely convenient that *GTA: SA* made this process so easy by leaving in content of this nature that the programmers decided was too explicit to include in the final released version.

Nudes and skins

From a coding perspective, the easiest type of adult content to mod consists of nude skins. These primarily involve overlaying the visual presentation of characters in a game with a partially or totally naked one, or going into the code to remove clothing from characters and then overlaying naked art code (Figure 12.2). Practically every computer game that features female characters or avatars has had someone make nude skins for them, though popular subjects include *The Sims*, *The Elder Scrolls* series, the *Dragon Age* series, the *Fallout* series (Figure 12.3), the *Grand Theft Auto* series, *World of Warcraft*, and, not surprisingly, Lara Croft (Figure 12.4). It also comes as no surprise that several of these games are among the most common for this type of modding, considering that they are also among the most common for mods of a nonsexual nature. In fact, *Skyrim*, and several other games, comes with a prepackaged "Creation Kit" that allows for ease in mod creation. *Skyrim* provides aggregation of their mods on the Steam Workshop and Skyrim Nexus, among other sites.

FIGURE 12.2 Dragon Age 2 *nude skin from nakedskins.com.* Dragon Age 2, *BioWare.*

FIGURE 12.3 *Fallout nude skin from nudepatch.net.* Fallout 3, *Bethesda Game Studios.*

FIGURE 12.4 *Lara Croft nude skin from nudepatch.net.* Tomb Raider: Underworld, *Crystal Dynamics.*

Nude patches are not the only types of adult skins being made; a certain amount of fetishistic mods exist. Chief among these are the creation of bondage clothing overlays, but other types of nontraditional desires are also available. One example would be "Sporty Sexy Sweat" created by Skyrim Nexus Mods user Xs2reality who describes the mod as a "specular texture mod which will enable [a] sweaty wet body for your favorite female character. Your character will have a sexy glistening wet skin which will enhance the realism, sexiness and all the fine details of the skin" (Figure 12.5). Browsing these sites, it quickly becomes obvious, though, that a vast amount of the content created by modders is of female nude skins, whether human or not. The vast majority of it reinforces a male gaze, and it would prove quite easy to argue a heteronormative reading of this type of content, especially since most nude patches in essence merely overlay a visual element with no actual in-play benefits, literally creating content that exists for its "to-be-looked-at-ness" (Mulvey 1975) status. Most of what is to be looked at is nubile female bodies. Admittedly, most mods are merely mapping over the already existing in-game characters, thereby revealing the traditional stereotypical gender portrayals of most existing female video game characters, but some modders also create content that allows for altering these avatars, usually with the intent of accentuating female physical attributes. This is not to say that there are no male nude skins; there are just far fewer examples. The games that are most likely to have these patches are *The Sims*, *Fallout* (*3* and *New Vegas*), and *The Elder Scrolls*; *Skyrim* is the game with by far the largest amount of nude male skins (Figure 12.6), and this particular example is also notable for having content of a much more blatant and hard-core sexual nature.

FIGURE 12.5 *"Sporty Sexy Sweat" mod.* The Elder Scrolls V: Skyrim, *Bethesda Game Studios.*

FIGURE 12.6 Skyrim *male nudes*. The Elder Scrolls V: Skyrim, *Bethesda Game Studios*.

These types of mods are so commonplace that a number of websites have been created as clearinghouses for this type of content, including nudepatch. net, nudemods.org, nakedskins.com, and nudemod.com. In addition to providing downloads or links to downloads for this type of content, some of the sites also offer instructions to players for how to create their own to share with other players. The creator/host of nudepatch.net claimed their motivation was a desire to give players something they have always wanted since the start of computer games:

> With the advent of computer games new art named briefly as a nude patch was born. To change textures and skins of heroes of game, transforming the boring dressed heroines into naked beauties, to change registration wall-paper in game for a pornographic skin, or to think out new erotic clothes for the characters.
>
> I think each player, at least time in the life dreamt to play nude Blood Rayne, to see naked Alyx from Half Life, to run about on forgotten vaults in search of ancient treasures playing for exposed Lara Croft from Tombraider. All it became possible thanks to naked patches on nudepatch.net
>
> This site the largest base of naked patches in the world! We have collected the best patches for the most popular computer games which you can quickly download from our site. In the list our popular nude mods are such monsters of the computer game industry as sims 3 (nudity patch)

> For downloading modes also are accessible to little-known games, such as Sillent Hill, Vampire: The Masquerade—Bloodlines, Singles and thousand others Are selected creations of the best artists of nude patches, you can add the patch, if something has been passed . . . readme or additional credits if will contact us, please [sic throughout]. ("About Nude Patch")

While it may be debatable that "each player" has dreamed of transforming their avatars into naked beauties, there is a demand here, and one these sites are willing to meet—either by laboring to create content or doing the work necessary to provide access to it. The individuals involved in these mods want to see naked avatars, and this is not being provided by the mainstream commercial game companies. Even a game that comes close to providing nude avatars, like *Saints Row: The Third*, presents its naked characters with heavy pixilation over the more salacious parts of the characters. And it should come as no surprise that modders have created skins that overlay genitals on the *Saints Row* avatars, in effect revealing what is being hidden by putting texture art on top of it.

Sexual encounter mods

The games that have had sexual encounter mods created are some of the same games that are most popular for nude mods in general, with the most common being *The Elder Scrolls* and *Fallout* series because of their highly accessible toolkits. Mods that allow for simulated sexual encounters between characters, however, are more rare than merely doing nude patching because of the larger amount of coding that is required for altering in-game actions. In fact, most mods of these types that are available first do a nude skin patch before adding other content. For a sex mod for *Skyrim*, "Benjamin Metalmaster" posted a video (Figure 12.7) to YouTube (that has since been removed from the site) showing a Khajit character that has agreed to pay a merchant 188 septims if he were also allowed to "fuck you" while using additional dialogue options that led to the encounter taking place in a public market. In the introduction to the video, Benjamin detailed what went in to creating this mod:

> Basically what I have here is to be the only uncensored and original form of the sex mod in *Skyrim*, I think censorship is wrong and sick on all levels. The five mods which have created this mini sex game are Behaviour patcher, Nude Males, Nude Females, Animated Prostitution and Girls of Skyrim. I shall now leave the introduction and show you the video! Watch it before it's banned by the cunts who censor shit [sic].

FIGURE 12.7 Skyrim *sex mod*. The Elder Scrolls V: Skyrim, *Bethesda Game Studios*.

So in order to enable this content in the game, five separate mods must be obtained and enabled in order to activate access to a sexual encounter. The encounter itself, like most sex mods, is not a controllable experience other than choosing positions or camera angles for display. So, unlike the Hot Coffee mod, there are no minigame elements in order to ensure a more favorable response from the other "participant."

The site "World of Adult Mods for Oblivion & Skyrim"[1] catalogs a number of sexual encounter mods available for *The Elder Scrolls*. Most also involve acquiring a number of other mods first in order to enable in-game sex. Depending on the mod, the sexual encounters range in terms of positions and activities, including but not limited to missionary, oral sex, rear-entry positions, etc. They also vary in whether they enable nonheterosexual encounters to occur. Some even go so far as to allow for public encounters that can cause NPCs to become aroused or hostile. Once downloaded and installed, these mods permit such behavior as "traditional" encounters between characters for sexual satisfaction, but they also enable the use of sex to avoid paying various fines or for access to things like rooms in inns. Some also involve enabling a level of "prostitution" where the player's character can gain money in exchange for having sex or for allowing other NPCs to have sex with the main character's NPC companion. In one of the most extreme cases, there is even a mod that allows the main character to offer their companion as a sex object to the various aggressive species of the world in exchange for not engaging in combat.

Essentially, these mods involve a significant amount of effort while doing very little to change the essence of the games they are made for. Storylines do not change; end scenarios are not altered. And while allowing a bear or innkeeper to sexually assault your companion might modify some aspects of gameplay, they are not significant changes in that specific area. So modders undertake this labor to add content they desire to engage in, which they feel is missing from their gaming experience. If the developers will not program it in, they will put in the time to ensure that they get it.

Conclusion

There has been a definite increase in the amount of commercial game releases that offer opportunities for players to explore romance and pursue sex. Yet they traditionally stop short of creating explicit content in order to avoid crossing the rating line from Mature to Adult Only. Simulated sex occurs, but some aspects of clothing or discreet positioning remain. Dialogue occurs, but the language remains suggestive, not frank. Nudity is hinted at but not revealed for male or female avatars. Even *God of War 3*, with its topless women and sex minigame, cuts away to a reaction shot from NPCs. But in much the same way as games explore increasingly complex aspects of modern life like depression and politics, gaming could explore adult content in a realistic and provocative fashion. For example, while not everyone played *Mass Effect* for the romantic and sexual aspects, a lot of fans did get swept up in it. Their reward may have been emotionally fulfilling but not physically stimulating. As graphics and cutscenes become more realistic, so too could representations of adult content. Games *could* be sexy and sexual. While we are seeing an increase in this type of content, it is not given the same level of attention by game developers as, say, an amazingly rendered exploding skull, primarily because of concerns over limiting the audience that would be interested or able to purchase such games. Ultimately, this leaves the interactive audience of modders to explore and create this level of content instead.

There is tremendous opportunity for gamers who wish to consume sexual content here, and it is imperative to question if the reality does meet the potential. So far, the majority of sexual mods reinforce male gaze and juvenile sexual content. Unrealistic, pornographic representations of sex and sexuality abound. But, for these modders and the players who download their work, sexual modifications are what they have chosen to focus their efforts, their "playbour," on. There is desire for content of a more mature nature. The nude skins and sex simulations created by the modding community speak to a desire for games to be mature in ways that go beyond realistic violence. These are activities that do as Kücklich suggests and go beyond the current confines of digital gameplay. Beyond that, unlike other forms of game modding, there is little desire from the game manufacturers to commodify these activities. *Mass Effect* sex simulations will never become the next *Counter Strike*, and Blizzard Entertainment is not going to add Dark Elf nude skins in their next update of *World of Warcraft*. And for most, if not all, games, modding content of a sexual nature is in clear violation somewhere in their EULAs, making this content perhaps not revolutionary, but rebellious. In light of the fact that sexual content still remains a taboo that mainstream developers seem hesitant to explore beyond certain levels, mods of this nature are a space of resistance for the player looking for sex play in their gameplay.

Note

1 Be aware that this site is incredibly buggy and will attempt to open spam and other intrusive content.

References

Aarseth, Espen. 1997. *Cybertext, Perspectives on Ergodic Literature*. Baltimore: Johns Hopkins University Press.

Au, Wagner James. 2002. "Triumph of the Mod." *Salon.com*. http://salon.com/tech/feature/220/04/16/modding/.

Biocca, Frank A. 1988. "Opposing Conceptions of the Audience: The Active and Passive Hemispheres of Mass Communication Theory." *Communication Yearbook* 11: 51–80.

Cantor, Muriel G. 1987. *The Hollywood TV Producer*. New Brunswick: Transaction.

Cantor, Muriel G., and James M. Cantor. 1986. "Audience Composition and Television Content: the Mass Audience revisited". In *Media, Audience and Social Structure*, edited by Sandra J. Ball-Rokeach and Muriel G. Cantor, 214–55. Newbury Park: Sage.

Crawford, Chris. 1984. *The Art of Computer Game Design*. Berkeley: Osborne/McGraw-Hill.

Jenkins, Henry. 2002. "Interactive Audiences?: The 'Collective Intelligence' of Media Fans." In *The New Media Book*, edited by Dan Harries, 157–70. London: British Film Institute.

Kline, Stephen, Nick Dyer-Witherford, and Grieg de Peuter. 2003. *Digital Play: The Interaction of Technology, Culture, and Marketing*. Montreal: McGill-Queen's University Press.

Kücklich, Julian. 2005. "Precarious Playbour: Modders and the Digital Games Industry." *The Fibreculture Journal* 5. http://five.fibreculturejournal.org/fcj-025-precarious-playbour-modders-and-the-digital-games-industry/.

Lauteria, Evan W. 2012. "Ga(y)mer Theory: Queer Modding as Resistance." *Reconstruction: Special Issue: Playing for Keeps: Games and Cultural Resistance* 12 (2). http://reconstruction.eserver.org/Issues/122/Lauteria_Evan.shtml.

Lopes, Dominic M. McIver. 2001. "The Ontology of Interactive Art." *Journal of Aesthetic Education* 35 (4): 65–81.

Manovich, Lev. 2001. *The Language of New Media*. Cambridge, MA: MIT Press.

Mulvey, Laura. 1975. "Visual Pleasure and Narrative Cinema." *Screen* 16 (3): 6–18.
Nieborg, David B. 2005. "Am I Mod or Not?: An Analysis of First Person Shooter Modification Culture." Paper presented at Creative Gamers Seminar—Exploring Participatory Culture in Gaming. Hypermedia Laboratory (University of Tampere). http://gamespace.nl/content/DBNieborg2005_CreativeGamers.pdf.
Nieborg, David B., and Shenja van der Graaf. 2008. "The Mod Industries? The Industrial Logic of Non-Market Game Production." *European Journal of Cultural Studies* 11 (2): 177–95.
nudepatch.net. "About Nude Patch." http://nudepatch.net/about/#.VKiQvCiieGk.
Ondrejka, Cory. 2006. "Escaping the Gilded Cage: User Created Content and Building the Metaverse." In *The State of Play, Law, Games, and Virtual Worlds*, edited by Jack Balkin and Beth Simone Noveck, 158–79. New York: New York University Press.
Pallant, Chris. 2013. "'Now I Know I'm a Lowlife': Controlling Play in *GTA: IV*, *Red Dead Redemption* and *LA Noire*." In *CTRL-ALT-PLAY: Essays on Control in Video Gaming*, edited by Matthew Wysocki, 133–45. Jefferson: McFarland.
Postigo, Hector. 2007. "Of Mods and Modders: Chasing Down the Value of Fan-Based Digital Game Modifications." *Games and Culture* 2 (4): 300–13.
Rubin, Alan M. 1993. "Audience Activity and Media Use." *Communication Monographs* 60 (1): 98–105.
Sihvonen, Tanja. 2011. *Players Unleashed! Modding The Sims and the Culture of Gaming*. Amsterdam: Amsterdam University Press.
Sotamaa, Olli. 2005. "'Have Fun Working with Our Product!': Critical Perspectives on Computer Game Mod Competitions." *Proceedings of DiGRA 2005 Conference: Changing View—Worlds in Play*.
Sotamaa, Olli. 2010. "When the Game Is Not Enough: Motivations and Practices Among Computer Game Modding Culture." *Games and Culture* 5 (3): 239–55.
Wolf, Mark J. P. 2000. *Abstracting Reality: Art, Communication, and Cognition in the Digital Age*. Lanham: University Press of America.
World of Adult Mods for Oblivion & Skyrim. http://elderscrollsadultmods.blogspot.com.

Games cited

Bethesda Game Studios. 2006. *The Elder Scrolls IV: Oblivion*. 2K Games.
Bethesda Game Studios. 2011. *The Elder Scrolls V: Skyrim*. Bethesda Softworks.
Bethesda Game Studios. 2008. *Fallout 3*. Bethesda Softworks.
Bioware. 2011. *Dragon Age 2*. Electronic Arts.
Blizzard Entertainment. 2004. *World of Warcraft*. Blizzard Entertainment.
Crystal Dynamics. 2008. *Tomb Raider: Underworld*. Eidos Interactive.
Mojang. 2011. *Minecraft*. Mojang.
Obsidian Entertainment. 2010. *Fallout: New Vegas*. Bethesda Softworks.
Rockstar North. 2004. *Grand Theft Auto: San Andreas*. Rockstar Games.
SCE Santa Monica Studio. 2010. *God of War 3*. Sony Computer Entertainment.
The Sims Studio. 2009. *The Sims 3*. Electronic Arts.
Volition. 2011. *Saints Row: The Third*. THQ.

13

Death by Scissors:
Gay Fighter Supreme and the
sexuality that isn't sexual

Bridget Kies (University of
Wisconsin-Milwaukee, USA)

"The world's first gay themed video game"—that was how multimedia company Handsome Woman Productions described its upcoming title *Ultimate Gay Fighter* in the fall of 2013. Like Capcom's *Street Fighter* series and the *Mortal Kombat* franchise, *Ultimate Gay Fighter* would be a fighting game, designed for play as a mobile phone app. Following the announcement of the game's future release, the Huffington Post Gay Voices declared Handsome Woman had created a "brilliant subversion of the traditionally masculine world of fighting video games" (Nichols 2013). The *Advocate* declared it a "fabulous twist on the hetero-dominated world of fighting games with a wink and a nudge aimed at LGBT gamers" (Peeples 2013). Game blogs also responded to Handsome Woman's press release and two trailers. Much of the buzz online was praising of the concept for a game that moved LGBT characters to the foreground of gameplay.

The game's release was delayed due to "legal pressure from an unnamed mixed martial arts promotional company" (Farokhmanesh 2014). Though Handsome Woman has never specified who the unnamed company was, the title "Ultimate Gay Fighter" was clearly too similar to the UFC reality television series *Ultimate Fighter*. Given the explicitly LGBT content of the former and the homoeroticism of the latter (which I will discuss later), the correlation seems fitting. Nevertheless, in an official statement explaining the delay,

Handsome Woman asked fans to think of a new title and in April of 2014 selected *Gay Fighter Supreme* (*GFS*) as the new name for the game.

At the time of this writing, the game has still not been released,[1] yet access to actual gameplay has not seemed to interfere with the ability of the media, gamers, and the LGBT community to offer praise and condemnation. While game trailers and press kits often generate buzz long before a title is released, the hype surrounding *GFS* is noteworthy in that it speaks to representations of a minority group still struggling for visibility in gaming. As video games begin to add more player options for a character's sexual identity, *GFS* depicts homosexuality through fighting rather than the romantic cutscene traditionally found in role-playing games. Since there is no downloadable game as yet, *GFS* also demonstrates the power of game trailers to convey ideology apart from the game itself.

In this chapter, I use *GFS* as a case study in how LGBT representation in games has evolved. I examine the relationship between a game's ideology or social commentary and the group it depicts, through *GFS*' emphasis on fighting. Since much of the hype about *GFS* occurred before its release, I also examine the relationship between the gaming community and prerelease media like trailers, which I argue can be understood as texts in their own right. My goal is to demonstrate how the idea behind *GFS* and the comments it has inspired offer a new way to think about LGBT representations in games, regardless of GFS' eventual release and actual gameplay.

Presenting your contenders: Game trailers

Since *GFS* has not yet been released, we can only speculate on how "machine operations" and "operator actions"—the collaboration of game and play—will shape its discursive meaning. It is more fruitful to think of *GFS* at this stage as a series of videos on YouTube (the trailers) and press materials. Its ideology can therefore be derived from this available material, which is static rather than ergodic.

Game trailers exist for the same reason that movie trailers do: to attract interest in something soon to be released. Within video game culture, a number of freestanding videos exist on sites like YouTube: "let's play" games in which players capture their gameplay, often to instruct others; unboxing videos, in which enthusiastic players document the opening of a new game for the first time; and the aforementioned trailers. Each kind of video can be read as its own freestanding text, devoid of any user input, although each clearly refers back to games and gameplay.

Videos about games therefore function as what Gray calls paratexts. Borrowing the term from Genette, Gray explains that paratexts are "not simply add-ons, spinoffs, and also-rans: they create texts, they manage them, and they fill them with meaning" (2010). Paratexts may be *in medias res* texts like "let's play" videos or DVD special features that assume some working knowledge of the text itself, or they may be "entryway" texts that entice audiences to look at something new. Gray uses movie posters and movie trailers as examples of entryway texts; game trailers perform a similar function for video games. A game's trailer can help shape our interest by distilling the game to its essence, since one or two minutes of video content must represent the experience of immersing in the dynamic game world for hours of play. It is due to this distilling and refining that Gray argues paratexts may also be understood as texts in their own right and a "film or program is but one part of the [total] text, the text always being a contingent entity, in the process of forming and transforming or vulnerable to further formation and transformation." Although Gray is not expressly writing about games, the idea that a text continues to transform seems quite applicable to gameplay. No doubt a reading of the trailers for *GFS* will shift once the game is released and we are able to play it.

Although *GFS* currently does not exist in game form, I have argued here for an understanding of its paratexts, including trailers and the press kit, to be read and understood as texts in their own right. Additionally, we have access to user-created paratexts in the form of media commentary, YouTube comments, and blogs. This user-created content is interacting with *GFS* and, though not changing the game itself, is altering interpretations of the game that circulate in society.

We have never been gay/ we have always been gay

Across media, there has historically been a repeated theme of the gay man as pervert or predator (Streitmatter 2009). Until the 2000s—the turning point at which same-sex marriage started to become legal in the United States—many newspaper and magazine articles were devoted to advising straight men on how to avoid the "lustful gaze" of gay men. In fictional content on television and in film, the stereotype of the compulsive gay sex fiend has often been accompanied by images of "funny clowns, flaming queens, fairies, fags and flits" (Raley and Lucas 2006).

Since their inception, video games have depicted characters that flout traditional gender and sex roles. Although video game historians and bloggers seem to disagree on what qualifies as the first gay-identified character, the examples they often cite date back as far as the 1980s. In a blog post highlighting important first moments in the game industry, Cobbett (2011) names *Moonmist* and *Circuit's Edge* as the earliest examples of games with explicitly gay or lesbian characters. Among early examples of gay characters, though, it was "rare to find a nuanced take on sexuality and romance" (Mulcahy 2013). Gay and lesbian characters who did appear in games were "usually minor characters; mostly predatory or lecherous men included for comedic effect." Cobbett notes that even today "gay characters tend to be used more for comedy or eroticism than as regular people."

In addition to being stereotyped as predators, these early examples were often not playable characters. Because games rely upon user input and interactivity, games that do not feature the ability to play a gay or lesbian character—to embody him or her—assume the heterosexuality of the player and reduce the gay character to a spectacle for the gaze. In film theory, Mulvey (1999 [1975]) argues that because film relies upon the act of looking, what we see on screen becomes the object of our gaze. Since many directors and cinematographers have historically been (and continue to be) men, and many of the objects being looked at are women, the act of watching a film becomes an eroticization and fetishization of the female body. Furthermore, narratives of men falling in love with women encourage the camera to eroticize the female body in close-ups and ask the audience to look at female characters with the same erotic desire as the male characters. As Mulvey explains, women on screen function as "an erotic object for the characters within the screen story [their love interest], and as erotic object for the spectator within the auditorium." The early examples of video games that only feature nonplayable LGBT characters inherently make those characters "other" to the player. Mulvey argues that cinema presumes a male audience gazing at female bodies on screen, regardless of who is actually watching films. While video games are somewhat different because of their emphasis on interactivity, Mulvey's argument is useful in thinking about how games with nonplayable LGBT characters presume the heterosexuality of the player, regardless of who is actually playing.

The presumption of the player's heterosexuality does not take into account the number of LGBT-identified gamers, who may feel at odds with gameplay and a gaming industry that does not always consider them. For instance, Pulos (2013) describes how LGBT players of *World of Warcraft* band together in guilds to shield themselves from the "top-down creation of heteronormativity" within the game. When gay characters or cutscenes are featured for a predominantly straight audience, there can be tension between who is playing (gazing) and who is being gazed at. A now famous example is the accidental lesbian kiss that occurred during a demonstration of *The Sims* in 1999. In an article for *The New Yorker*, Simon Parkin (2014a) describes this as the turning point in the popularity of *The Sims*. The game was then tweaked so that romance could result from user-directed actions, which developer Patrick J. Barrett III sees as an exciting moment in gaming history: the ability of players to control characters' actions to lead them to homosexuality (Parkin 2014a). The openly gay Barrett believes that the kiss led to *The Sims'* fast sales because it allowed gay players to see themselves and their lives reflected through gameplay. In an interview on NPR about his article, media reporter Parkin (2014b) calls attention to the fact that gamers are "an overwhelmingly male audience, and a very, very common male fantasy is the lesbian kiss." So the lesbian kiss potentially contributed to sales because it was an attractive feature that enabled straight men to perpetuate the male gaze—here, doubly reinforced through sexism and heterosexism.

More recently, games have begun to include playable characters whose sexuality, gender, and options for activities such as marriage are flexible, though not all attempts have been received with equal praise. BioWare created a designated same-sex world, Makeb, in its massively multiplayer online role-playing game, *Star Wars: The Old Republic*. Rather than simply being a safe space, Makeb also segregated gay characters and players behind a paywall, leading blogger Mary Hamilton (2013) to call it a place where gamers could "pay-to-gay." Activist/artist Anna Anthropy created *The Hunt for the Gay Planet*, an interactive fiction on Twine that parodies the Makeb debacle. The premise of *Hunt* is that the player is journeying through the galaxy to find the mythical planet Lesbionica, where, according to the game's narrative description, she can "feel the heat of a lady's reciprocating gaze without having to feel the burn of a thousand judgemental [sic] stares."

Perhaps the three games to garner the most attention for their LGBT content in recent years are BioWare's 2012 release *Mass Effect 3*, the Fulbright Company's 2013 adventure game *Gone Home,* and Naughty Dog's 2013 release *The Last of Us. Mass Effect 3* features options to play Commander Shepard as male or female, with same-sex romances for both. Similar to the development of *The Sims*, the *Mass Effect* trilogy initially included lesbian romance but ignored gay men; this was changed in the third release. It is possible that the lesbian content of *Mass Effect*, like the kiss in *The Sims*, was intended to titillate heterosexual male players as much as it was intended to evoke a sense of inclusivity among LGBT gamers. For Mulcahy, however, the new sexual and gender flexibility mirrored the game's themes: "Suddenly the narrative opened up to new possibilities, a positive development in a game that is all about choice and consequences." The various configurations of love scenes have been posted numerous times to YouTube and written about on gaming and popular culture blogs. In an interview with *IO9*, *Mass Effect*'s executive producer Casey Hudson describes the inclusion of same-sex romance as a way to fill what the development team began to see as a "conspicuous absence" in representation (Anders 2012). Hudson continues to explain that the goal for BioWare and *Mass Effect* is to "always be inclusive." Since BioWare was also responsible for the misstep with *Star Wars: The Old Republic*, we can see how difficult the goal of "always being inclusive" is—and how much more work needs to be done to achieve it.

Another recent game to receive attention for its LGBT inclusivity is the first-person adventure game *Gone Home*. The player does not directly engage in same-sex romance; instead, gameplay enables the player to discover her young sister's struggle with her sexual identity. Through the perspective of an inquisitive, concerned sister, *Gone Home* is able to address sensitive subjects like a teenager experiencing a sexual awakening and feeling the need to run away in order to be with her new love.

The Last of Us features a secondary character, Bill, whose homosexuality is in the background of the game's narrative (he has lost his partner). Additional downloadable content for the game *Left Behind* includes a cutscene of a kiss shared between a young woman and her female friend, and so the game, like *Gone Home*, deals with teenage sexuality—in both cases, specifically, lesbian identity. The Gay and Lesbian Alliance Against Defamation (GLAAD) responded positively to the LGBT content in *The Last of Us* and called Bill "deeply flawed but a wholly unique gay character" (GLAAD's Entertainment Media Team 2013).

Although this list of recent games featuring LGBT characters and storylines is not exhaustive, it provides a framework for understanding the kinds of representation previously seen in games. LGBT characters may be foregrounded, as in the case of *Mass Effect* and *Left Behind*, or in the background of a game world, as in *Gone Home* and *The Last of Us*. They may be nonplayable secondary characters or playable characters whose sexuality is determined by actions taken within a game. In all these cases, however, identifying a character as LGBT is accomplished through sex and romance: in cutscenes that show same-sex kissing or in the exposition of forbidden or lost lovers. In short, sexual *identity* is conflated with sexual *activity*.

What makes *Gay Fighter Supreme* an interesting example in the development of LGBT representation is that its characters are identified through traits and behaviors other than sexual activity and romance plots. As Sedgwick (1990) notes, other identifying traits, like age and race, are "visible in all but exceptional cases," while homosexuality can only be inferred through clues in speech and behavior unless a person verbally asserts it. *Gay Fighter Supreme* makes the sexual orientation of the characters visible through "stock gestures" that have long been identified with homosexuality (Beaver 1981). In the next section, I will explore how those gestures at once reinforce outside stereotypes and celebrate the community's nonnormativity. Here, however, I would like to emphasize that the predominant way *GFS* characters can be read as LGBT is through their fighting skills. By calling them *gay* fighters, rather than just fighters, the game shows how sexual orientation may comprise part of one's identity beyond one's sexual practices.

Counter to the sex and love in the previous game examples, *GFS* is all about combat, pitting members of the LGBT community against each other. As *GFS* draws upon other fighting games for its look and gameplay, it calls attention to the homoerotic elements in those games. Whether a homoerotic reading of *Mortal Kombat* or *Street Fighter* is intended by game developers or players, sociologists and cultural theorists have long argued that displays of hypermasculine aggression in sports and martial arts often mask same-sex desire not traditionally sanctioned by culture (Pronger 1992; Kaufman 2001). In her study of literature, Sedgwick (1985) finds that because of the time and energy male rivals expend competing with each other, usually for a woman's affection, they become fixated with their competition and each other. That is, their ultimate interest comes to lie in each other. Consalvo (2003) uses Sedgwick's ideas in a reading of the game *Final Fantasy IX* to show how video games enact this male rivalry. Consalvo's argument is that the same-sex desire between rivals depends upon the player's gender and sexual identity, since the player embodies one of those rivals. My point with *GFS* is that because all the characters are gay, the desire that is unspoken in Sedgwick's literary examples and Consalvo's game examples is brought to the surface. In this way, the very idea of a gay fighting game enables us to question the potential for same-sex desire in other nongay fighting games. *GFS* therefore calls attention to how fighting games have been, at least implicitly, invested in latent same-sex desire, long before same-sex relationships were featured in gameplay and cut scenes.

"Campy Entertainment": Gay-on-gay violence

The core mechanic of fighting games is relatively simple: two combatants battle each other, often to the death. A player selects a combatant as avatar and may play against the computer or against another player. The avatar is selected from a cast of characters that each has a special skill. In *Mortal Kombat* and *Street Fighter*, avatars may be buxom women with gymnastic skills or muscular men. In *Gay Fighter Supreme*, the assortment of playable combatants is intended to represent a wide spectrum of the LGBT community. Some characters have real-world referents, while others represent stock types. All feature traits commonly attributed to different LGBT people. For instance, the character Sappho Ethridge [sic] is created from a mash-up of traits stereotypically associated with lesbians, such as having short hair and wearing combat boots, but her name refers to lyric poet Sappho and openly lesbian singer Melissa Etheridge. The fashionista, Ford Jacobs, gets his name from designers Tom Ford and Marc Jacobs, both of whom are openly gay. Other characters, like Gogo Gary and Bardwell, "the king of the leather bars," trade on more general stock types—here, the muscle queen and the leather daddy.

While particular stereotypes may be offensive to some within the LGBT community, it is not the goal of this paper to evaluate their accuracy or appropriateness. Instead, I want to demonstrate that the types used in *Gay Fighter Supreme* are broader than the "funny clowns" and "flaming queens" that commonly represent the LGBT community in other forms of popular entertainment. On television and in film, for instance, contemporary LGBT characters tend to be white and middle-class. While the early gay rights movement emphasized its difference from straight America, the goal among advocacy organizations in the last twenty years has been assimilation. As Becker (2006) describes, in the 1990s "images of angry protesters shouting, 'We're here! We're queer! Get used to it' were replaced by photos of suit-clad gay leaders . . . hobnobbing with the likes of Ted Kennedy." This has translated in entertainment to depictions of gay men who conform to traditional gender norms, avoid overt expressions of sexual desire, and seek marriage and parenthood as life goals. The characters in *GFS*, by contrast, range from effeminate to masculine. For some, gender expression diverges from biological sex. In contrast to the overrepresentation of white men in most media, *GFS* includes player-fighters of different races and ethnicities. Rather than subscribing to the rhetoric of assimilation, *GFS* reifies difference: first, that *gay* fighters are different from (straight) fighters and second, that gay fighters come in a variety of body types, skin colors, and personalities.

According to the game's tagline, however, "the only colors in this rainbow are black and blue" (Handsome Woman Productions 2013). There may be room under the rainbow for different kinds of LGBT people, but they must all love to fight and be willing to fight each other. Emulating *Mortal Kombat*'s "Fatalities," GFS features "gaytalities," wherein the player can execute their opponent with special forces unique to the LGBT community. Sappho Ethridge, for example, can turn her legs into scissors and cut her opponent in two to commit "death by scissors." This particular "gaytality" trades on the lesbian sex act of scissoring. While references to scissoring in popular culture are typical derogatory, or at least, confused—"*how* do they do it?"—here, scissoring enables the lesbian fighter's moment of triumph. This particular gaytality turns the conventional titillation of lesbian sex on its side; the player still watches the scissoring, but it is now a violent, rather than sexual, act. The game's press kit also promises that "rainbows and unicorns are used for gore how fabulous!! [sic]" (Handsome Woman Productions 2013). Each gaytality capitalizes on skills and traits unique to the LGBT community and transforms each into a strength in the battle.

Video games have long been studied for their potential to encourage violence in real life, and while many of these studies are flawed, the fact remains that media and government attention to video games often emphasizes their violent qualities to the exclusion of any other facets (Squire 2002). *GFS* centers on "gay-on-gay" violence. Players participate in violence against a minority group that is often victimized by acts of violence in real life. Since the player's avatar is also a member of that minority group, his or her potential victimhood may be exchanged for power and dominance, something not often achieved in real life (or, for that matter, in other games).

For all the game's possible ideological positions on gay-on-gay violence, Handsome Woman describes it as "campy entertainment" and as "an ironic commentary on how we [the LGBT community] all label and fight each other" (as quoted in Farokhmanesh 2014). This statement might be understood through an examination of camp and its function within the LGBT community. Sontag (1964) describes camp as "good *because* it's awful" and the action of camping as employing "flamboyant mannerisms . . . gestures of duplicity, with a witty meaning for cognoscenti and another, more impersonal, for outsiders." For Sontag, there is a "peculiar affinity and overlap" between camp and what she calls homosexual taste. The many references to LGBT identity in *GFS* may have humorous resonance for LGBT players but may be lost on some straight players. Beaver (1981) similarly argues that camp is the "desire of the subject never to let itself be defined as object by others." The use of stock characters and stereotypes within *GFS* can be read as an attempt to provide power to the LGBT community by letting LGBT players embody "gay fighters" and reclaim stereotypes so often found in other media images. But, Beaver cautions, camp often "exposes more than it protects." In utilizing certain stereotypes for humor, *GFS* still participates in propagating those stereotypes. Its objective—LGBT community members fighting each other to the death—allegorizes divisiveness within the LGBT community and makes those divisions apparent to non-LGBT players.

As the self-described first gay video game, *GFS* sets the tone that gay gameplay is about more than just the sex scenes found in titles like *Mass*

Effect. The gay-on-gay violence may be an alarming depiction of a community that has experienced more than its fair share of real-world violence at the hands of outsiders. Its use of camp provides humor to the game but also reinforces certain stereotypes. And yet, by turning gay identity into a strength through "gaytalities," the game may empower as much as it disempowers.

A love letter to gay brothers and sisters

We could easily argue that it does not matter much what a game developer's intent is; more important is how players play the game, since a game relies upon user input. Galloway (2006) posits that "video games are actions" and without player input remain in an "abstract rule book" or as "static computer code." Wirman (2009) suggests that cocreativity, as defined by Banks (2002), is a better "way to understand the ways in which authorship of a game is shared between paid game developers and the players of a game." Wirman argues that things such as modifications (mods) and fan art are emblematic of games' cocreative possibilities but wants to expand the concept of cocreativity to include gameplay itself. Through gameplay, she contends, players become producers of meaning, which leads her to conclude that "games are better understood as platforms for *experiences* than as *products*" and that they are "only partly predetermined or precoded before the activity of play takes place" (emphasis mine). Following Wirman's arguments, we can see that criticism of *GFS*' stereotyping or its depictions of violence within the LGBT community should not solely be borne by Handsome Woman. What players do with the characters and what ideology players bring to the game equally affect the meanings of *GFS*.

Despite the possibility for player-produced meaning, Phi (2009) argues that the identity of a game's creator can inform the game's meaning or implicit ideology. A survey of games reveals that many, even the ones made by Japanese designers, have a Eurocentric bias. Phi, who studies representations of Asian-Americans, finds this limiting and argues that it is "rare that we [the Asian-American community] are presented with a main character that we can identify with racially." Likewise, it is still uncommon enough for an LGBT person to see himself or herself reflected in a game that the occurrence still warrants attention. Steps forward in representation are sometimes flukes, as in the case of the unplanned lesbian kiss in *The Sims*, and sometimes calculated choices made by development companies to sell more games. *Grand Theft Auto IV*'s add-on *The Ballad of Gay Tony*, for example, was clearly created and released for its potential sales power and not as important social commentary on the part of Rockstar Games. Its title may have enticed LGBT gamers to purchase it, but the player plays as "straight Luis" who works for "gay Tony"—thus perpetuating the gaze at the other (Goldstein 2009).

Handsome Woman Productions was started by Michael Patrick, who is openly gay, specifically to create and release *Gay Fighter Supreme*. The company's mission statement describes its work as "specializing but not limiting to the LGBT community," though to date *GFS* is the only project announced on the company's website. Patrick explains that he intended *GFS* to offer different depictions of the LGBT community, something other than the "sassy best friends, the funny ones, the ones who sing, and the ones who decorate your house" that are often seen in the media (Handsome Woman Productions 2013). He further describes the game as a "love letter" to his "gay brothers and sisters" and declares: "We are warriors." His use of first-person ("we") and his openness about his own sexuality are deliberate choices to work against the discrepancy between creator and player that Phi found in her survey of games. Through its LGBT-themed mission and its founder's sexuality, Handsome Woman strives to assure LGBT players that *GFS* is for them as much as it is about them.

The game also articulates its connection to contemporary social politics through its villains. As explained in the press kit, the League of Oppressive Self-Righteous Zealots (LOSRZ, pronounced "losers") has arranged the fighting competition in order to make the LGBT community destroy itself. Like the contestants, the individuals who make up the LOSRZ range from the specific to the more general. The most obvious, Anne Paylin, is drawn from Sarah Palin (known for being a leader in the uber-conservative Tea Party which the LOSRZ resembles) and conservative commentator Ann Coulter. Another is a bombastic preacher, perhaps alluding to the Westboro Baptist Church or more generally to the "moral majority" and Christianity's longstanding objection to homosexuality.

Traditionally, the basis for homophobic remarks and antigay legislation had to do with sex acts as much as gender role defiance. The sentiment of "we don't want to see that" resulted in sodomy laws and policing of bath houses, in addition to social sanctions for gay men especially (Chauncey 1995). In *GFS*, however, there is no sex—just violence—and so the LOSRZ's hatred of the LGBT characters must be based on the characters' transgressive gender identity (i.e., women who are too tough and men who are too effeminate) or based on LGBT identity itself, regardless of how it is revealed or concealed. The LOSRZ therefore reinforce systemic bullying of the LGBT community simply for being itself. The backstory to the game is that the first LGBT fighting competition winner was abducted and brainwashed by the LOSRZ and now fights for them. The LOSRZ plan to do the same thing to the winner of this year's contest; the player may win or lose to the LOSRZ.

Thus, depending upon the outcome of gameplay, *GFS* has the potential to show an insidious side to the conservative right wing and the triumph of the LGBT community's diversity—or to position LGBT people as pawns for those who hate them. Determining the meaning here is dependent upon gameplay, upon cocreation. Additionally, it is unclear from the game trailer and press kit if the LOSRZ are nonplayable characters or possible avatars. Being able to play as one of the LOSRZ would additionally alter the meaning of the game, since the player would no longer be experiencing combat as an LGBT "warrior" but would instead gaze at the other through the eyes of the ultimate villain: a homophobe.

Conclusion

In spite of the small size and newness of the team behind the game, and the game's delayed release, *Gay Fighter Supreme* has already garnered a variety of responses from the media and the LGBT and gaming communities. Within three months of being posted to YouTube, the game's trailer had nearly two hundred thousand views and hundreds of comments. Those comments range from appreciation of the game as satire to criticism of its use of stereotypes, regardless of the writer's disclosed sexual identity.

More numerous than comments about whether the game is offensive are comments about how the game's design and aesthetics look simplistic, boring, or unappealing. The world seen in the trailers is two-dimensional, with little visual detail in the background, and while it harkens to the visual design of *Mortal Kombat*, it is also a look that seems outdated when compared to the elaborate world design and graphics of contemporary games like *Grand Theft Auto V* and *BioShock Infinite*. That so many comments from the public are focused on aesthetics may indicate that discussions of stereotypes and ideology will be shoved aside once the game is released, if players find it badly designed.

Part of the strategy behind the game's design may be ease of use as a mobile phone app, and part may be attributed to its camp sensibility, the idea that it is "so awful it's good." However, if the game does not sell well or, for that matter, is never released, how useful is it as an example? Can we genuinely look at *GFS* as altering LGBT representations in gaming if no one plays it? I argue that the sheer act of engaging in debate over the game's meaning is what is important when it comes to inciting social change. The idea of the game and the reactions it has provoked have already begun to shift social discourse about representations of the LGBT community in video games.

The game industry has begun to increase its depictions of LGBT characters in many kinds of video games, through things like options for players to enact same-sex romance and secondary character backstories of coming out. This coincides with an increase in visibility in other forms of popular entertainment, like film and television. In these other media, as well as in contemporary politics, there has been a trend toward depicting the LGBT community as similar to straight America, mostly through an emphasis on the goals of marriage and parenthood. Recent video games have likewise allowed for same-sex romance narratives and cutscenes by simply replacing heterosexual interactions with homosexual ones.

There remains, I contend, both the opportunity and the need for video games that offer alternative depictions of LGBT identity. Handsome Woman's *Gay Fighter Supreme* offers a racially and ethnically diverse group of avatars; gameplay emphasizes fighting, rather than love or sex; and its camp humor and social allegory raise questions about the relationship members of the LGBT community have with each other and with straight America. Its premise suggests a new way in which the video game industry might represent LGBT identity: as sexuality that is not sexual.

Note

1   After writing but prior to publication, *Gay Fighter Supreme* was released.

References

Anders, Charlie Jane. 2012. "Why Did BioWare Add a Gay Option to *Mass Effect 3?*" *IO9*, March 5. http://io9.com/5890426/why-did-bioware-add-a-gay-option-to-mass-effect-3.

Banks, John. 2002. "Gamers as Co-Creators: Enlisting the Virtual Audience—A Report from the Net Face." In *Mobilising the Audience*, edited by Mark Balnaves, Tom O'Regan, and Jason Sternberg, 188–212. Brisbane: University of Queensland Press.

Beaver, Harold. 1981. "Homosexual Signs (In Memory of Roland Barthes)." *Critical Inquiry* 8 (1): 99–119.

Becker, Ron. 2006. *Gay TV and Straight America*. New Brunswick, NJ: Rutgers University Press.

Chauncey, George. 1995. *Gay New York: Gender, Urban Culture, and the Making of the Gay Male World, 1890–1940*. New York: Basic Books.

Cobbett, Richard. 2011. "They Did It First." *PC Gamer*, February 20. http://www.pcgamer.com/2011/02/20/they-did-it-first/.

Consalvo, Mia. 2003. "Hot Dates and Fairy-Tale Romances: Studying Sexuality in Video Games." In *Video Game Theory Reader*, edited by Mark J. P. Wolf and Bernard Perron, 171–94. New York: Routledge.
Farokhmanesh, Megan. 2014. "*Ultimate Gay Fighter* to Change Its Name in Response to Legal Tangle." *Polygon*, April 7. http://www.polygon.com/2014/4/7/5590742/ultimate-gay-fighter-to-change-name-in-response-to-legal-tangle.
Galloway, Alexander. 2006. *Gaming: Essays on Algorithmic Culture*. Minneapolis: University of Minnesota Press.
GLAAD's Entertainment Media Team. 2013. "The Most Intriguing LGBT Characters of 2013." GLAAD, December 26. http://www.glaad.org/blog/most-intriguing-new-lgbt-characters-2013.
Goldstein, Hilary. 2009. "*GTA IV: The Ballad of Gay Tony* Review." *IGN*, October 28. http://www.ign.com/articles/2009/10/28/gta-iv-the-ballad-of-gay-tony-review.
Gray, Jonathan. 2010. *Show Sold Separately*. New York: New York University Press.
Hamilton, Mary. 2013. "*Star Wars: The Old Republic*, the Gay Planet, and the Problem of the Straight Male Gaze." *Guardian*, January 25. Games Blog. http://www.theguardian.com/technology/gamesblog/2013/jan/25/star-wars-old-republic-gay-planet.
Handsome Woman Productions. 2013. "The *Ultimate Gay Fighter* Press Kit." http://handsomewomannyc.com/pressKits.html.
Kaufman, Michael. 2001. "The Construction of Masculinity and the Triad of Men's Violence." In *Men's Lives*, edited by Michael S. Kimmel and Michael A. Messner, 13–25. Boston: Allyn and Bacon.
Mulcahy, Terry. 2013. "The Gaying of Video Games." *Slate*, November 12. Outward. http://www.slate.com/blogs/outward/2013/11/12/video_games_embrace_gay_romance_from_the_ballad_of_gay_tony_to_the_last.html.
Mulvey, Laura. 1999. "Visual Pleasure and Narrative Cinema." In *Film Theory and Criticism: Introductory Readings*, edited by Leo Braudy and Marshall Cohen, 833–44. New York: Oxford University Press. Originally published in *Screen* (1975) 16 (3): 6–18.
Nichols, James. 2013. "'Ultimate Gay Fighter' Video Game to Be Released by Handsome Woman Productions." *Huffington Post*, November 25. Huffpost Gay Voices. http://www.huffingtonpost.com/2013/11/25/ultimate-gay-fighter_n_4337688.html.
Parkin, Simon. 2014a. "The Kiss That Changed Video Games." *New Yorker*, June 18. http://www.newyorker.com/tech/elements/the-kiss-that-changed-video-games.
Parkin, Simon. 2014b. *On The Media*. By Bob Garfield. NPR, July 18.
Peeples, Jase. 2013. "WATCH: LGBT Culture Becomes Fierce in Ultimate Gay Fighter Game." *Advocate*, November 25. http://www.advocate.com/arts-entertainment/entertainment-news/2013/11/25/watch-lgbt-culture-becomes-fierce-ultimate-gay.
Phi, Thien-bao Thuc. 2009. "Game Over: Asian Americans and Video Game Representation." *Transformative Works and Cultures* 2. http://dx.doi.org/10.3983/twc.2009.0084.
Pronger, Brian. 1992. *The Arena of Masculinity*. New York: St. Martin's Press.

Pulos, Alex. 2013. "Confronting Heteronormativity in Online Games: A Critical Discourse Analysis of LGBTQ Sexuality in World of Warcraft." *Games and Culture* 8 (2): 77–97.

Raley, Amber B., and Jennifer L. Lucas. 2006. "Stereotype or Success? Prime-Time Television's Portrayals of Gay, Lesbian, and Bisexual Characters." *Journal of Homosexuality* 51 (2): 19–38.

Sedgwick, Eve Kosofsky. 1985. *Between Men: Literature and Male Homosocial Desire*. New York: Columbia University Press.

Sedgwick, Eve Kosofsky. 1990. *Epistemology of the Closet*. Berkeley: University of California Press.

Sontag, Susan. 1964. "Notes on 'Camp.'" *Partisan Review* 31 (4): 515–30.

Squire, Kurt. 2002. "Cultural Framing of Computer/Video Games." *Game Studies* 2 (1). http://www.gamestudies.org/0102/squire/.

Streitmatter, Rodger. 2009. *From "Perverts" to "Fab Five."* New York: Routledge.

Wirman, Hanna. 2009. "On Productivity and Game Fandom." *Transformative Works and Cultures* 3. http://dx.doi.org/10.3983/twc.2009.0145.

Games cited

Anthropy, Anna. 2013. *The Hunt for the Gay Planet*. Anthropy.
Bioware. 2007. *Mass Effect*. Microsoft Game Studios.
Bioware. 2011. *Star Wars: The Old Republic*. Electronic Arts.
Bioware. 2012. *Mass Effect 3*. Electronic Arts.
Blizzard Entertainment. 2004. *World of Warcraft*. Blizzard Entertainment.
Capcom. 1987. *Street Fighter*. Capcom.
Fullbright. 2013. *Gone Home*. Midnight City.
Handsome Woman Productions. 2015. *Ultimate Gay Fighter/Gay Fighter Supreme*. Handsome Woman Productions.
Infocom. 1986. *Moonmist*. Infocom.
Inspired Media Entertainment. 2006. *Left Behind*. Inspired Media Entertainment.
Irrational Games. 2013. *BioShock Infinite*. 2K Games.
Maxis. 2000. *The Sims*. Electronic Arts.
Midway Games. 1992. *Mortal Kombat*. Midway Games.
Naughty Dog. 2013. *The Last of Us*. Sony Computer Entertainment.
Rockstar North. 2008. *Grand Theft Auto IV*. Rockstar Games.
Rockstar North. 2013. *Grand Theft Auto V*. Rockstar Games.
Square. 2000. *Final Fantasy IX*. Square.
Westwood Associates. 1990. *Circuit's Edge*. Infocom.

14

Iterative romance and button-mashing sex: Gameplay design and video games' Nice Guy Syndrome

Nicholas Ware (University of Central Florida, USA)

L ove is a game. Metaphors of play dot the landscape of romance and sexuality in several categories: sexual dynamics ("role-play"), sexual conquest ("scoring"), emotional manipulation ("playing games with my heart"), the rules of attraction ("having game"), or even the single life itself ("playing the field"). Pop music, which addresses love in every metaphor possible, has adopted "love game" to aid in its own discourse of sex and romance. In the last half-dozen years, artists as disparate as Eminem and Lady Gaga have titled songs as such. The popularity of the metaphor comes from its versatility and allowance of liminal space. If love is a game, the stakes are not so high that loss is equivalent to devastation or death. Rather, in a game, loss is a natural part of the learning process. There are rules to be followed. Players use information gained in losing a game to eventually win that game, because rules allow for consistency of experience. Love is a game, and games are simple, fun, and logical. If only it were the case.

The true messiness of love aside, if we accept the popularity of "love is a game," then might video games—the dominant style of game of our modern era—be the best medium through which we as humans can experience representations and simulations of love, romance, and sex? Games allow for a fluidity of identity that other nonplayable media do not. The openness of the medium allows players to experiment with a simulation of love, romance, and sex with low emotional stakes compared to real-world interactions. "When taking gameplay into account . . . sexuality as expressed in [video games] might possibly allow for some 'queer' reading, if the player of the game desires it. That might be the case for some players, if when people engage in play, they put on various 'masks' of identity and experiment with alternate rules (and discard social conventions), if only temporarily" (Consalvo 2003, 191). Players are able to experience—through avatars—romance (among many experiences) from the point of view of characters with different gender and/or sexuality configurations than their own. These experiences can affect players due to what James Paul Gee calls a "reflective identity," a sense that the avatar is both the same as a given player and not the same. This dual consciousness allows for both selfless and selfish feelings in the avatar's actions (Gee 2007). In the case of many Western-style role-playing games such as the *Dragon Age* or *Mass Effect* series, the lead character can be fully customized in gender and race and then can interact with other nonplayable characters whose sexuality—heterosexual, homosexual, or bisexual—is scripted. The potential for good in such interactions seems self-evident; players are able to experiment with enacting different genders and sexualities and through those experiences explore their own feelings or become more open to nonheteronormative sexualities. These experience should be more reflective than, for example, watching a documentary about a LGBTQ (lesbian, gay, bisexual, transgender, or queer) identified teen coming out to his or her parents. While nonplayable media can certainly create empathy or cause the viewer to relate to the subject, they do not demand a reflective identity in the same manner as a game. However, optimism about games as a progressive sexuality learning space is largely based on an assumption of proper representation of nonheteronormative relationships—always a question mark in a games market that seems to cater to heterosexual adolescent males more than any other demographic—and, unfortunately, does not consider the ramifications of gameplay design and strategy in the lessons learned from the sexuality tourism available in video games.

This essay seeks to address those issues through an examination of iterative design (and the iterative gameplay practices such design requires) and its relationship to the social phenomenon known colloquially as "Nice-Guy Syndrome." Iterative design has long been one of the dominant design philosophies applied in the creation of games. The process of iteration— prototype, test, analyze results, prototype again, and continue the cycle until satisfied (Salen and Zimmerman 2004)—had led to games becoming both highly efficient and standardized. Life experiences tend to get reproduced in games using similar mechanics (three-dimensional movement, menu systems) or algorithmic methods (building up "power" in a "meter," toggling switches). Gameplay requires both intentional and physical affordances (Gregersen and Grodal 2009), and, translated through a standardized interface (a controller), the number of possible inputs are limited. Affordances, as explained by the term's originator James J. Gibson, are "what the environment offers the animal," and "implies a complimentarity of the animal and the environment" (Gibson 1979, 56). The concept was further refined by Michael Tomasello into intentional and physical affordances (Tomasello 1999), with intentional affordances being imitative actions with an object without necessarily having firsthand physical knowledge of the results. In the case of virtual environments, an intentional affordance is a player's assumption of action within the game world coupled with a practiced physical action (physical affordance with a controller) that he or she takes. Because there are not many physical actions available on a controller that mimic many of the things an on-screen character might do, players learn very quickly to map actions onto button presses, despite the lack of physical correlation with pushing a button and, for example, jumping. The button press has become the default "take an action" affordance when dealing with virtual space. For example, in a video game involving both wooing women and manipulating devices, the process of making these in-game choices may be based on choosing options from a menu by pressing a button. This similarity often leads not only to similarly designed games, but also to similar gameplay strategies. Players learn to press the "action button" around any suspicious object or select any menu item that was not previously available. Players enculturate these trial-and-error, infinite-continues, explore-every-option modes of game navigation seeking either the specific content they want or, in the name of 100 percent completion, all of the content. This strategy, both of design and play, is true of in-game actions from treasure-seeking to fighting to exploration to romance and sex.

This is a problem, of course. Romance and sexuality are nearly the opposite of a menu-based system or flipping a switch. The same sequence of romantic actions does not lead to the same outcome, even with the same individual. However, in many video games that deal with sex and romance, it does. Sex becomes a "reward" to players for their correct choices. Incorrect choices are hardly deterrents. If players fail to choose a correct option in a dialogue tree, the saved game can be reloaded and new options tried: an iterative process. Games, essentially, have Nice Guy Syndrome. Nice Guy Syndrome is a pop psychology term for subtle misogynistic behavior found in young men where they seem to believe that an accumulation of nice deeds and moments of emotional support for women in their lives entitles them to sex with those women, and that those women are foolish for not offering sex or a relationship to them after they have demonstrated what "nice guys" they are.

The pejorative use of "Nice Guy" and "Nice Guy Syndrome"—almost always capitalized and sometimes written as "Nice Guy™" to denote this specific meaning of the term—appeared online in 2002 as a response to the colloquial phrase "nice guys finish last" (Know Your Meme 2014). It has since been adopted by pop feminism as well as the men's rights movement, though in different ways. The Nice Guy mentality is reinforced in games where romance is designed as a series of actions where "doing the correct thing at the correct time" leads to sex as a reward for those behaviors.

This essay will isolate and explore these types of designs in various games, relate them to scholarship on sex in video games as well as larger cultural tendencies, and offer a path to some design alternatives. By uncovering these problematic gameplay elements and their genesis in design and patriarchal culture, we can avoid reifying these problematic ideologies as well as make games that allow us to play romance with more robust, realistic interactions—and perhaps even play sex as something more than the mashing of buttons or shifting of control sticks.

Iterative design and iterative gameplay creates iterative romance

Iterative design can best be described as "a play-based design process. Emphasizing playtest and prototyping, iterative design is a method in which design decisions are made based on the experience of playing a game while it is in development" (Salen and Zimmerman 2004, 11). The simplest version of iteration, simplified for not just games but nearly any production process, can be expressed by the following instructions:

1   Design Object.

2   Create prototype of Object.

3   Test prototype of Object.

4   If Object can be improved, repeat steps 1 through 3; otherwise, produce final version of Object based on prototype of Object.

This model has been the backbone of the video game industry for a long time. Video games tend to look for particular elements to improve. "It is through iteration that game designers achieve the right balance between challenge, choice, and fun" (Salen 2007, 318). Additionally, game designers tend to favor iterative strategies in game design because "learners can dive in first and learn through critical experimentation, developing hypotheses about how things work and testing out these theories within an iterative framework" (Salen 2007, 319). Iterative design allows the designer the freedom to fail as an important part of the process of succeeding; it is assumed that every version of the game designed until the final version will have some discernible flaw.

Iterative design practices often produce games that themselves offer iterative gameplay. Just as a game designer tunes a game to be increasingly precise through multiple prototypes, many game types require players to tune their gameplay strategies as difficulty escalates through the same set of tasks. For example, the tower defense genre offers new waves (iterations) of enemies with each success. The field of play stays the same, but players must adjust their strategy or object placement to address the increasingly slim odds of victory (Despain 2013, 95). Because the patterns are consistent, players learn effective strategies that are repeatable even if failure occurs—the same placement of defense units should produce the same results, and thus a failure indicates a need for a change. But tower defense is not the only genre that features iterative gameplay and rewards iterative strategies. Platformer games like the *Super Mario* series rarely feature dynamic enemy or obstacle placement. Shoot-em-up games like *Gradius* or *R-Type* (and their current, niche descendants, "bullet hell" games) are all about pattern-learning and player iteration. Almost every mainstream game follows the same philosophy: the more a player plays, the better that player should be able to perform. To compensate for games becoming too easy or boring due to player mastery, designers often employ more precise challenges. There have been some recent attempts to make artificial intelligence (AI) systems that learn player strategies or respond directly to the players' level of success, such as "The Director" that Valve Software utilizes in the *Left 4 Dead* series, which aims to create a more variable and cinematic experience in a first-person shooter (Newell 2008). However, these types of AI systems are innovations and not the standard experience in most game genres.

Game designer Chris Crawford stresses that the iterative quality of interaction is its key feature, even in human interactions like conversation (Crawford 2002, 6). This is also true of gameplay in video games. Because iterative design tends to create iterative gameplay, iterative strategies—trial and error—tend to be the most successful in increasing player performance. Because failure (or suboptimal play) is key in iterative gameplay strategies, failure has become less and less of an impediment to success in video games. The arcade model of pay-per-play financially incentivized a strange tightrope when it came to punishing players. Players needed to be punished enough that they must spend more and more quarters or tokens to proceed, but the penalty could not be so harsh as to turn them off of the play experience.

Ideally, players would see their trial-and-error iterative strategies pay off on subsequent plays and progress steadily, increasing both enjoyment of the game and the game's coin box. However, with the move to home consoles and PCs and the advent of better data storage options, many PC, console, and mobile games are constantly autosaving players' progress. Failure is rarely punished with starting over from the beginning of a level or losing all of one's gold or items. There is a nominal loss of time and progress, but iterative strategies are even more beneficial to players when the penalty of failure is lessened so greatly. Iterative strategies are no longer risk-versus-reward, but rather try-for-reward. Unlimited continues are the norm.

The problem with this model is that the narrative simulations of life present in games tend to become flat gameplay experiences, and the iterative gameplay interactions with those simulations do not adequately represent the gravity or unpredictability those situations would hold if they were encountered in the physical world and not the virtual one. People of every age are at times confused or hurt by their romantic experiences, particularly young people—the target demographic for many games. Dating anxiety is an acknowledged psychological issue and "adolescents' dating anxiety may interfere with their dating experiences" (Glickman and La Greca 2004, 575). If we are to take video games as a cultural object that affects cultural understanding—as we have books, films, and music—it is imperative to demand more nuance and sophistication in the game mechanics that represent these vital cultural experiences. Instead, the flattening of the experience is often present, less in the fictional depiction of relationships between characters than in the interaction of a player with the game. For example, in the Japanese role-playing game *Shin Megami Tensei: Persona 4*, the main character (whose name is customizable but defaults to Yu) is encouraged to create Social Links with nonplayable characters in order to unlock more powerful combat abilities. These Social Links also comprise the bulk of the game's narrative. Yu is a high school student and must budget his time with various members of his high school and surrounding community. Some of these members are young women with whom Yu can become romantically involved. Eventually, once Yu's Social Link with a female character is strong enough, they will become a couple, and the final Social Link results in a very chaste implied sex scene where the female character and Yu are left alone, and the scene fades to black on some romantic moment, fading back in some time later, at which point the female character informs Yu how special the unseen moment—implied to be sex—was for her.

In order to strengthen the Social Links, Yu must spend time with these characters, sometimes for calendar-specific events, and engage in conversations with them. The conversations are very typical for role-playing games. After the female character is given a set amount of dialogue, players select one of a few (usually three) choices of response. Typically, when there are three responses, one is "good," one is "ok," and one is "bad." The effectiveness of players' choices is represented by graphical flourishes that come off the female character's avatar. It should be noted that in *Persona 4* players always benefit from better Social Links and never from lower Social Links. Therefore, there is never any benefit to choosing anything but the "good" dialogue choice. While any player could use a game guide to know ahead of time the results of his or her dialogue choice, an iterative strategy could be (and often is) used to maximize these types of interactions. By playing the scenario, then restarting and choosing other options, players quickly learn the best thing to say and are rewarded with a more powerful character and, eventually, virtual sex between Yu and the female character's avatar.

Problematically, sex is presented as a reward for a series of correct choices. This is a very poor representation of attraction, romance, and sex, which are often unpredictable and in flux. Responses can be tempered by mood, relationship history, or the inflection in a person's voice. Conversation, while it is broadly iterative in nature as Crawford claims, is complicated by such a wide array of contexts that the very simple menu systems of conversation in video games are not adequate to represent the array of possibilities in human emotional exchange. Let us imagine some instructions for a game like *Mass Effect 3*, where menu systems are very common for interaction both with objects and characters:

- Walk your character up to XXXX.
- Press the A button to bring up a menu.
- Choose the correct option. XXXX will be turned on.

In these types of games, XXXX could be a toaster or a human being.

If the goal of a game is to truly encapsulate the human experience in an interactive virtual world, romance needs to be less about menu choices. It need not reward iterative strategies nor flatten romance so that it is analogous to any interaction with any game object. Romance is not trial-and-error without any repercussions for failure. The game of love is far more robust.

Nice Guy Syndrome and button-mashing video game sex

In nearly every video game in which players' characters can engage in sex through a series of choices, video games force players to act as the "Nice

Guy" and reward players accordingly. A "Nice Guy" is a semi-derogatory designation used in Internet discourse (and now in general discourse) to refer to men who have "Nice Guy Syndrome," a term in popular culture that comes from pop psychology. "The Nice Guy Syndrome represents a belief that if Nice Guys are 'good,' they will be loved, get their needs met, and live a problem-free life" (Glover 2001, 5). In contemporary use, the "Nice Guy" refers to men who assume that "good" behavior toward women—listening to their problems, supporting them emotionally, doing favors for them—will eventually pay off with a relationship and/or sex. The type of men referred to often populate message boards dedicated to "Men's Rights," a larger, more blatantly misogynistic and antifeminist subculture mainly residing on the Internet that started as a response to second-wave feminism (Coston and Kimmel 2013). However, most feminists—academic and popular—see Nice Guy Syndrome and Nice Guys as a separate issue to address. Men's Rights and Pick-Up Artist subcultures see Nice Guys as weak-willed men who need to "man up," while pop feminism subcultures see Nice Guys as men who have been misled by patriarchal hegemony into assuming that women should reward their "positive" behavior with romantic and sexual attraction.

The connection that Nice Guy Syndrome has to MRA—Men's Rights Activism—has recently been highlighted in mainstream culture due to Elliot Roger's killing spree near the University of California, Santa Barbara. Roger wrote a 137-page manifesto before beginning his spree that left six dead and thirteen injured. Titled "My Twisted World," it contained blatant misogynistic language and themes and promised a "Day of Retribution" against women (CBS News 2014). In an attempt to distance themselves from the tragedy, MRA members adopted the refrain "not all men," as if to say not all men are murderous, even if they feel the same way Roger did (Baker-Whitelaw 2014). This is, of course, true, but it is also a diversionary tactic to avoid talking about ingrained issues of misogyny.

I bring up the tragedy at Santa Barbara not just to support the idea of Nice Guy Syndrome as a problem that needs to be addressed but also to point to the tendency to address the more superficial and immediate aspects of misogyny/Nice Guy Syndrome as opposed to the root ideology. Since iterative design reinforces a certain kind of player behavior, the stories players help tell through games by enacting that behavior are only one problem. Discussions of underdressed and oversexed female game characters without agency are appropriate. Such discussions are also hardly popular, as testified by the backlash Anita Sarkeesian has seen for her *Tropes vs. Women in Video Games* series, which included death and rape threats and the free sharing of her personal information among those who wish to silence her (Campbell 2014). While the battle Sarkeesian and others fight in order to make the content of video games better—more and better female characters, fewer narrative misogynistic moments—is laudable, the very design process also needs addressing. Iterative design rewards Nice Guy Syndrome.

Nice Guy Syndrome becomes a successful strategy when romance and sex are playable—and not scripted—elements of a game. Players are rewarded for attention and "correct" answers. Nearly the perfect example of this is in the game *Dragon Age: Origins*. *Dragon Age: Origins* should be praised for some of its choices; it is not exclusively heteronormative and features bisexual characters. However, the way gameplay is structured in *Dragon Age: Origins* is very aligned with Nice Guy Syndrome. There are four characters with whom romance is a possibility. Two of these characters are bisexual and two are heterosexual, so regardless of a player-character's chosen gender, three of the four are available in a single playthrough. Romance works off an affinity system called Approval, which is visible on the status screen of any long-term party member, even the ones that are not available for romance. High Approval makes combat interactions with these characters more effective and also unlocks side quests. As power and additional content are meaningful rewards in *Dragon Age: Origins*, this creates demand for players to maximize Approval. As further incentive, with romance characters, certain levels of Approval, which vary by character, open dialogue options to kiss and eventually have sex with that character.

There are three main ways of raising Approval in *Dragon Age: Origins*: (1) choosing in-game actions with which the romantically-available character agrees; (2) choosing correct dialogue responses when in conversation with the romantically-available character; and (3) giving the romantically-available character appropriate gifts. "Appropriate" usually lines up with the character's class and interests; for example, giving the witch character spell books will raise her Approval dramatically. There are things that this Approval system does not consider that are all highly influential in the decision to start relationships or even the decision to have casual sex: characters' personal physical preferences, other characters' pursuits or preexisting relationships, or even strong consequences to "dealbreaker" actions. Gifts, as the primary means of raising Approval, are able to overcome otherwise heinous player choices, such as murder.

Dragon Age: Origins is actually one of the more in-depth games when it comes to romance and sex. Unfortunately, even though the characters players can pursue seem fully drawn through the narrative, with rich interior lives, backstories, personalities, and goals, the process of wooing becomes nothing more than "fill the meter and make your move." This is such a flat, unrealistic way of representing romance in games, but it certainly has its generic history. The dating simulation genre—niche in America but far more popular in

Japan—has long used this gameplay structure as its core mechanic. Players typically choose one among many girls to woo; time plus correct responses plus gifts equals true love. In erotic dating games, this same formula also equals very graphic sex. Romance in these video games is merely a reward for time and attention. This is the thinking of the Nice Guy.

One of the foundational game series in the Japanese dating simulation genre is *Tokimeki Memorial*. While the roots of the genre go back as far as 1984 with *Girl's Garden* (Moss 2011, 1), *Tokimeki Memorial* was the first dating simulation to be a big hit and spawn a large number of sequels and spin-offs. Originally released on the PC Engine in 1994, but rereleased the next year on the PlayStation, *Tokimeki Memorial* made enough of an impact that in 2006 readers of Japanese video game magazine *Famitsu* voted the PlayStation version as the twenty-third greatest game of all time (Edge 2006). Including remakes and spin-offs, there have been more than fifty *Tokimeki Memorial* games released in Japan. The core gameplay of the series consists of scheduling dates, going on dates, and building the main character's stats. The main character has a whole harem of girls to woo, but he must build himself up in such a way that he is attractive to the girl he most wishes to "win" at the end of the game. Game-days can be spent going on dates with the various girls or performing academic and athletic activities around school. The former gives players an opportunity to answer a question that, when correctly answered, will increase the "love meter" with that particular girl. The latter will increase stats that affect how much the love meter might rise or fall with a certain girl. For example, in the PlayStation version of *Tokimeki Memorial*, the stats were Stamina, Humanities, Science, Art, Athletics, Knowledge, Appearance, Perseverance, and Stress. These statistics must meet a certain threshold by the end of the game (three school years of in-world time) for each girl to be properly seduced. Mia Kagami, who's only into really good-looking guys, requires a very high Appearance stat to even meet her, much less win her heart.

Tokimeki Memorial was hugely influential not just in kickstarting the entire dating sim genre in Japan but also in the way its gameplay influenced the love mechanics I've already described in *Persona 4* and *Dragon Age: Origins*. The issue here is not that *Dragon Age: Origins*, *Persona 4*, or *Tokimeki Memorial* specifically are doing romance a disservice. Rather, it is that video games are meant to be won, but romance is not actually something that is "won." The verbiage is wrong. Nice Guy Syndrome treats love like a video game: pick the right choices, do the right things, win the girl. This is iterative strategy in action. Because iterations in design require using the knowledge of what has already been successful in order to design and refine a concept, these systems of play—menus, correct question choices, gifts, and the choice of many possible love partners—are iterated between different games and generations. From *Tokimeki Memorial* in 1995 up to the modern console era, both the mechanics and the strategies to address those mechanics have remained the same. In order to address iterative design, iterate in one's play by attempting something new, seeing reaction, and using reaction to attempt something better and continue doing so until the goal is achieved. In iteratively-designed video games, this strategy is incredibly successful. Sometimes, it should be. But it maps so poorly onto real human emotion and relationships, especially romance and love. Complicated, dynamic, and context-driven feelings and interactions don't translate well into algorithmic gameplay.

Sex, too, faces problems when translated into iterative play. It is rare that sexual intercourse is a playable part of a video game. In the examples of *Shin Megami Tensei: Persona 4* and *Dragon Age: Origins*, the sex is noninteractive and mostly off-screen. However, there are a few examples of intercourse being playable in mainstream games. One example is the infamous "Hot Coffee" mod for *Grand Theft Auto: San Andreas* (*GTA: SA*). The programmers initially included a sex minigame but abandoned it; however, instead of deleting the minigame, they simply made it inaccessible through normal play. An enterprising group of modders discovered the code that initiated the minigame and created a mod for the PC version of *GTA: SA*, and then later the PlayStation 2 and Xbox consoles. Both the nonmodded and modded versions allow the main character, Carl, to date and have sex with up to six female characters. In the unmodded version of the game, the sex is off-screen, though sounds are heard. In the modded version, the sex is interactive, using a timed button press system very similar to *GTA: SA*'s dancing minigame. There is no nudity, but an animation of Carl thrusting toward the girlfriend of choice is seen. Another mainstream game to feature a sex minigame is the *God of War* series. The experience is very similar to *GTA: SA* and features call-and-response button presses as affordances of sexual thrusting. Note that in both of these games, the player-character is a fully realized fictional male, not a customizable character or cipher, like in *Dragon Age: Origins* or many Japanese dating sims, respectively.

These sex minigames represent the true worst of the reductive interactivity of video games. To make it clear, "worst" here is not a moral worst. There should not be an uproar about sex portrayed in video games simply because that sex happens to be casual. Rather, that sex would be reduced to a rote button-pressing minigame and insist on being so phallocentric—the button presses are simply penile thrusts—is worrisome. This flat representation reifies the presumed straight male audience, unsupported by industry demographics. According to the 2014 Entertainment Software Association Essential Facts report, "women aged 18 or older represent a significantly greater portion of

the game-playing population (36%) than boys aged 18 or younger (17%)"
(Entertainment Software Association 2014). These design choices serve an
audience that is unreflective of the majority of the game-playing population,
and that iterative romances and button-mashing sex reduce an interesting and
rich human factor into a shallow and unsatisfying—pun intended—gameplay
mechanic. What, then, are solutions for designing better sex?

Building a better romantic sex game

I believe that strides in better content—the kind of changes that public
discourse around video games currently calls for—are absolutely part of the
solution to creating better romance and sex in games. The efforts of Anita
Sarkeesian and other feminist thinkers and activists in both the game industry
and the broader tech industry are vital and should continue and be supported
by game designers and academics. However, the gap in that discourse—
women need to be more involved in designing games, and women need
to be considered more thoughtfully within games—cannot fully address
the fundamental design principles that support the Nice Guy love and sex
mechanics. A shift away from iteration as the foundational design philosophy
in game design must occur. This does not mean iterative practices in workflow
need to be eliminated entirely. Iteration is still a useful tool for bug fixes and
polish. However, a few adjustments can be made that might not only alleviate
some of the iterative play practices that reinforce patriarchal thinking when
applied to love and romance mechanics but also open up design in a broader
sense. Many of these practices are already being explored and better games
are being created. This should absolutely continue.

The first opportunity to make romance and sex better—and combat Nice Guy
Syndrome through iterative strategies—is to increase the influence of random
number generation (RNG) on design philosophy. Now, naturally, computers
cannot actually create true randoms, because random number generation in
any programming task is based on an algorithm (Salen and Zimmerman 2004,
184). However, embracing RNG to a greater degree with creating gameplay
centered on romance will, without having to necessarily build greater
contextual modifiers into character behavior, more accurately represent the
often-inscrutable variations of relationships. This must be embraced not just
as a variable that a player interacts with but on a fundamental scale of holistic
game experience, down to the chance that love does or does not manifest
as an option. In life, sometimes two people do not meet simply by chance.
Games can represent that using RNG.

If iterative strategies are still present, a way to alleviate Nice Guy Syndrome is to minimize the presentation of algorithmic representations of love. The ability to immediately discern the effectiveness of a particular dialogue choice, gift-giving, or other gameplay action—whether it be through graphical flourish such as in *Persona 4* or meter-checking in *Dragon Age: Origins*—encourages players to treat the in-game relationship like a prize to be won instead of an experience to convey. While there will always be metatexts available for players to use to metagame (FAQs and Walkthroughs), games should try to represent romantic cues less as meters to fill and more as human moments of interaction.

Another solution is to embrace emergent gameplay and collective experience in designing romance mechanics. Essentially, the focus shifts from "gaining love" to "creating contexts" within which love may or may not appear. Abandoning the meter mechanic and instead creating a web of various contextual variables that allow love to happen or not happen—likely through cutscenes—will discourage players from pursuing "love points" and instead will reward them with unique romantic experiences based on the gameplay choices they are already making. Additionally, once procedural generation in design begins to filter from waves of enemies and aesthetics into the narrative elements of games, we may see procedurally generated romance that offers the unpredictability and depth of true romance. Accepting and creating fundamentally new design methodologies and philosophies may bring new sets of issues, but any alternatives to iterative design should be pursued by the industry as possible solutions.

The goal of reforming iterative romance design in video games is not to shame designers but to better represent the very rich and barely realized realm of romance in gaming and drive design forward instead of retracing rote, problematic generic conventions. In addition to reforming gameplay, the industry also needs to realign its focus away from the "core male" demographic. Progress has already been made in this realm, but more can be pursued. Romance is too complicated a ritual to be represented by a meter, and sex too key to human society to be reduced to button presses. While nice guys should win games, Nice Guy strategies should not win hearts in games. Games can, should, and will do better.

References

Baker-Whitelaw, Gavia. 2014. "Why Elliot Rodger Is Being Linked to the Men's Rights Movement." *The Daily Dot*, May 25. http://www.dailydot.com/news/elliot-rodger-mens-rights-activists/.

Campbell, Colin. 2014. "Sarkeesian Driven Out of Home by Online Abuse and Death Threats." *Polygon*, August 27. http://www.polygon.com/2014/8/27/6075679/sarkeesian-driven-out-of-home-by-online-abuse-and-death-threats.

CBS News. 2014. "Timeline of Murder Spree in Isla Vista." May 26. http://www.cbsnews.com/news/timeline-of-murder-spree-in-isla-vista/.

Consalvo, Mia. 2003. "Hot Dates and Fairy-Tale Romance: Studying Sexuality in Video Games." In *The Video Game Theory Reader*, edited by Mark J. P. Wolf and Bernard Perron, 179–94. New York: Routledge.

Coston, Bethany M., and Michael Kimmel. 2013. "White Men as the New Victims: Reverse Discrimination Case and the Men's Rights Movement." *Nevada Law Journal* 13 (2): 368–85.

Crawford, Chris. 2002. *Understanding Interactivity*. San Francisco: No Starch Press.

Despain, Wendy, ed. 2013. *100 Principles of Game Design*. San Francisco: New Riders.

Edge. 2006. "Japan Votes on All Time Top 100." *Edge*, March 3. http://www.edge-online.com/features/japan-votes-all-time-top-100/.

Entertainment Software Association. 2014. *Essential Facts about the Computer and Video Game Industry*. http://www.theesa.com/facts/pdfs/ESA_EF_2014.pdf.

Gee, James Paul. 2007. *What Video Games Have to Teach Us about Learning and Literacy*. New York: Macmillan.

Gibson, James J. 1979. "The Theory of Affordances." In *The People, Place, and Space Reader*, edited by Jen Jack Gieseking, William Mangold, Cindi Katz, Setha Low, and Susan Saegert, 56–60. New York: Routledge.

Glickman, Alissa R., and Annette M. La Greca. 2004. "The Dating Anxiety Scale for Adolescents: Scale Development and Associations with Adolescent Functioning." *Journal of Clinical Child and Adolescent Psychology* 33 (3): 566–78.

Glover, Robert. 2001. *No More Mr. Nice Guy!* eBook. Barnes & Noble Digital.

Gregersen, Andreas and Torben Grodal. 2009. "Embodiment and Interface." In *The Video Game Theory Reader 2*, edited by Mark J. P. Wolf and Bernard Perron, 65–84. New York: Routledge.

Know Your Meme. 2014. "Nice Guys." http://knowyourmeme.com/memes/nice-guys.

Moss, Richard. 2011. "From *SimCity* to *Real Girlfriend*: 20 Years of Sim Games." *Arstechnica*, June 20. http://arstechnica.com/gaming/2011/06/history-of-sim-games-part-1/6/.

Newell, Gabe. 2008. "Game Newell Writes for Edge." *Edge*. http://www.edge-online.com/features/gabe-newell-writes-edge/.

Salen, Katie. 2007. "Gaming Literacies: A Game Design Study in Action." *Journal of Educational Multimedia and Hypermedia* 16 (3): 301–22.

Salen, Katie and Eric Zimmerman. 2004. *Rules of Play: Game Design Fundamentals*. Cambridge, MA: MIT Press.

Tomasello, Michael. 1999. *The Cultural Origins of Human Cognition*. Cambridge, MA: Harvard University Press.

Games cited

Atlus. 2008. *Persona 4*. Atlus.

Bioware. 2009. *Dragon Age: Origins*. Electronic Arts.

Bioware. 2007. *Mass Effect*. Microsoft Game Studios.

Irem. 1987. *R-Type*. Tonka.

Konami. 1985. *Gradius*. Konami.

Konami. 1995. *Tokimeki Memorial: Forever With You*. Konami.

Nintendo EAD. 1985. *Super Mario*. Nintendo.

Rockstar North. 2004. *Grand Theft Auto: San Andreas*. Rockstar Games.

SCE Santa Monica Studio. 2005. *God of War*. Sony Computer Entertainment.

Valve Corporation. 2008. *Left 4 Dead*. Valve Corporation.

15

Climbing the heterosexual maze: *Catherine* and queering spatiality in gaming

Jordan Youngblood (Eastern Connecticut State University, USA)

To play with sexuality in gaming is to experience it spatially. And an examination of queer sexuality in games must take into account what kind of movements, actions, and paths are provided for the player to explore, specifically focusing on the digital body's deployment within gamespace and how such spaces shape sexual performativity. In order to queer game space, this chapter draws upon the work done by Sara Ahmed in her 2006 book *Queer Phenomenology*, particularly in her complicating of the term "sexual orientation" and how objects are situated within space to determine sexual and gendered performances. However, as Ahmed's concepts focus repeatedly on the *physical* body, they—like Butler's (1993) ideas of how bodies come to matter in physical spaces—must be adapted and reconsidered in light of avatars and digital environments. I place Ahmed in conversation with spatial analyses of games from Aarseth (2007), Ash (2010), and Walz (2010), with an emphasis on how each discusses the nature of environments to define the actions available, denied, encouraged, and discouraged to those bodies inside them. Ahmed (2006) notes in her introduction that "orientations shape not only how we inhabit space, but how we apprehend this world of shared inhabitance" (3). In exploring how games turn the societal mandates of object choice, desire, and reproduction into explorable environments, we can see they offer a decidedly unique means of comprehending how we come to desire objects: the timetables we are given to desire them, the paths we are forced to take to reach them, and the deviant paths deliberately left out of play. *Catherine*, by Japanese game developer Atlus (2011), is a specific example of queering orientation within gamespace: specifically, the task of climbing a series of block-based mazes directly echoes the sexual relationships and expectations experienced by the avatar within the game's narrative.

Determining theoretical "Directions": On gamespace

The usefulness of queer theory for discussing gamespace finds its origins in "queer" itself: the word is drawn from the Indo-European root *terkw-*, meaning to turn, bend, or twist. As Ahmed notes, "queer is, after all, a spatial term, which then gets translated into a sexual term, a term for a twisted sexuality that does not follow a straight line, a sexuality that is bent and crooked" (67). This "turn" to the spatial drives *Queer Phenomenology*, where Ahmed focuses upon the ways in which bodies are directed spatially toward "straight" lines of desire and what it might mean to be queerly "disoriented" within an environment. In a similar fashion to Butler, Ahmed finds these straight lines determined by repetitive social pressures that construct not only the body they "press" against, but also the life it is required to live; as she writes, "the social pressure to follow a certain course, to live a certain kind of life, and even to reproduce that life can feel like a physical 'press' on the surface of the body, which creates its own impressions. We are pressed into lines, just as lines are the accumulation of such moments of pressure" (17). The language of physical contact repeats throughout, with Ahmed often evoking the idea of bodies touching, grasping, or contacting one another due to accumulating pressures.

The effect of this pressure leads to the question of *actions*, particularly in terms of what can and cannot be accessed spatially. Expanding on Butler's ideas of performativity and identity, Ahmed notes that "the normative can be considered an effect of the repetition of bodily actions over time, which produces what we can call the bodily horizon, a space for action, which puts some objects and not others in reach" (66). Ahmed's concept of the bodily horizon as a "space for action" eventually returns to the central idea of "orientation," as the seemingly "natural" habit of straight behavior is shown to be a series of governing principles that demand adherence; thus, "we can reconsider how one 'becomes straight' by reflecting on how an orientation, as a direction (taken) towards objects and others, is made compulsory. In other words, subjects are required to 'tend toward' some objects and not others as a condition of familial as well as social love" (85). To become disoriented, then, is to go "offline," so to speak—to desire objects typically left out of reach, or to direct one's life along paths that do not lead to reproducing either other human beings or normative social values.

Ahmed's move to a spatial understanding of queerness is particularly apt for gaming, given the medium's focus upon developing environments for players to explore and inhabit. Aarseth goes so far as to claim that "the defining element in computer games is spatiality" (44), arguing that games are, at their core, driven by the need to represent and negotiate digital spaces. Aarseth puts forth the idea of games as "allegories of space: they pretend to portray space in ever more realistic ways but rely on their deviation from reality in order to make the illusion playable" (47). For Aarseth, the question of spatiality in gaming is not whether or not games realistically represent spaces, but rather in how digital spaces are a direct reflection of the various rules and algorithms encoded into the game—a "reductive operation leading to a representation of space that is not in itself spatial, but symbolic and rule-based" (45).

This turn from viewing gamespace as a one-to-one reflection of literal geography to a mapping of encoded possibilities once again shifts the question to that of action and choice. Ash expands upon Aarseth's spatial emphasis by utilizing Caillois's (2003) concept of teleplasty, meaning to mold or form at a distance. Ash argues that games fall under the categories of teleplastic technologies, which determine the potentials and possibilities for human action, movement, and sense: "In this sense, technologies do not only preempt what one can do and the ways in which one can do it; technology itself acts to pre-empt possibilities for sense by shaping the user's 'phenomenal field' (their capacity to sense space and time, and entities within that space-time)" (415). This concept of the "phenomenal field," when combined with what Zimmerman and Salen (2003) deem the "space of possibility" within games—that is, the actions, meanings, and relations that can spring forth from a set of defined rules and structures (67)—brings us back toward Ahmed's idea of the "bodily horizon" as a space for action. Certain game spaces, in essence, make even more explicit the edges and limits of that bodily horizon, utilizing the avatar as an "allegory"—to use Aarseth's term—for the ways in which bodies are orientated. As Walz notes in his analysis of games as echoing architectural spaces,

> The designedness of an environment—or an object or another player—is not only a question of design culture, but also of how the potential playground is embedded into a certain culture of norms, values, and other

more everyday behavioral scripts. In that, the designedness dimension of our play-space also reminds us of the cultural dimension of play—of how a space is always embedded into contexts. (87)

As with the question of the body, this is not to read space in games as a purely restrictive construction; Ash views the teleplastic nature of games as both limiting *and* opening possibilities, where "environments and interfaces can imbue users with a new range of capacities with which to sense space and time, and to orientate themselves" (415). In fact, Ash argues, the effect of being confined within the game world can alter the player's perspective of how she is oriented in the "natural" world, as "the user can enter into a disinhibiting ring (the tightly controlled set of possibilities and actions designed into the game), without having to give up their 'open' relation with the world (the capacity to reflect upon entities in the game from a theoretical perspective)" (422). Ahmed, drawing on Diprose (2002), similarly claims that "the world described by phenomenology is an 'interworld,' or an 'open circuit' between the perceiving body and its world" (54). Let us then consider how the experience of a player controlling a surrogate body through a digital world *extends* this interworld further, as the relationship of player and game brings forth moments where the avatar is oriented in space—causing the player to reflect on her own orientation. For a queer understanding of gamespace, this consideration must take into account not only moments of being explicitly directed toward (or away from) sexual choices but also the way in which even seemingly benign objects—like a climbable pile of interconnected boxes—can impact orientation.

"If you don't want to die, you've gotta climb": *Catherine* and compulsory heterosexuality

Gallagher (2012), in an essay on the actual lack of sex in modern gaming, posits that, rather than designing a way to simply recreate intercourse in games,

> designers might be able to concentrate on creating mechanics capable both of providing a satisfying play experience and of conveying, allegorizing, or commenting upon the nature of characters' sexual relationships. Atlus' *Catherine*, in which the hero's sexual anxieties are conveyed through fiendish block puzzles, arguably constitutes a move in this direction. (412)

While Gallagher stops his discussion of *Catherine* here, I want to pick up where he left off, particularly in his invocation of spatial allegory. I position *Catherine* as an allegorical experience of playing compulsory heterosexuality, where the various block puzzles of the game represent not only our protagonist's sexual anxieties but also the societal structures determining those anxieties: designing lines toward objects of desire like a wife and child, threatening elimination of nonreproductive lines and objects, and finally forcing the player to question the extent to which she chooses one path or another. While the game's narrative declares "there is no wrong way to climb the tower," playing *Catherine* quickly reveals the contradictions at the heart of that claim, both in gamespace *and* in "real" space.

The game's plot revolves around Vincent Brooks, a 32-year-old systems engineer in a long-term relationship with a woman named Katherine. Having dated Vincent for five years without any suggestion of marriage, Katherine begins to openly question their relationship. Shortly after this conversation, Vincent begins to have nightmares of a large tower of falling blocks, which he must ascend as quickly as possible to ensure he does not fall and die (as dying in the nightmare leads to death in the real world). He soon discovers that others suffer these nightmares, as a group of local men begin to be found dead in their beds. A common thread emerges: they have either cheated on their partners or failed to make any sort of significant commitment to them. Vincent, already "guilty" of the second, soon finds himself guilty of the first by getting involved with a younger, buxom blonde woman, named—of course— *C*atherine, after meeting her at the local bar. Caught between Katherine and Catherine while also surviving the nightly trials in his sleep, Vincent begins to crack, weaving a set of lies to placate both women while hiding their existence from one another. Eventually, it is revealed that Catherine is not human at all but a succubus visible only to Vincent, an extension of his nightmares sent to tempt him away from Katherine and into a different lifestyle. This leads to the game's ending, where, depending on the choices made by the player in the game, Vincent eventually ends the nightmares and chooses a future with either Katherine, Catherine, or simply himself.

The primary focus of gameplay lies in the nightmares, which typically follow a similar pattern. Vincent starts at the bottom of a large stack of blocks, which stretch up toward an eventual goal marked by ringing bells. The player must control Vincent to push, pull, and climb blocks in order to reach the top as quickly as possible, since the blocks begin to fall away from the bottom sequentially over time. Different blocks have different properties that the player must learn, and new blocks appear as the levels grow increasingly difficult; some levels even feature other men attempting to climb, often interfering with Vincent's progress unless he evades them or knocks them out of the way. After solving each puzzle, the player is graded for how quickly and effectively she guided Vincent to the top and is awarded a corresponding score. Should she lead Vincent to failure too many times, however, the game is over, and the player is greeted with his body splattered over a pile of rocks with the message "LOVE IS DEAD." An earlier save must be reloaded in order to try again and bring Vincent closer to the goal.

From these basic rules emerges a core image of sexual spatiality: namely, ascension toward a set point. While the player is repeatedly encouraged to consider the possible options available to Vincent, any amount of maneuvering boils down to figuring out how to climb higher and quicker toward the goal—revealed at the end of the game to be a giant cathedral. The tolling bells at the end of each level emanate from it, suggesting that the outcome of *Catherine* comes in one of two forms: marriage or death. As a fellow climber puts it, "We all have the same fate here. If you don't want to die, you've gotta climb." This compulsory fate, enforced during the levels by the ever-collapsing floor, demands the player either learn the proper logics of climbing or be doomed to watch love "die" repeatedly. The introduction of the other male climbers, all of whom appear as sheep within the dream, reinforces the fact that these logics do not apply merely to Vincent; it is a collective task and, more often than not, one built around competition rather than collaboration. Each man desperately attempts to climb toward the assigned destination of the church, only without much knowledge as to *why*: at small intervals between stages, the sheep can be found debating as to what this place is and how they ended up there and expressing their growing suspicion that a woman placed them there. When the sheep do choose to help Vincent, it is only through "techniques" for better climbing; as a group "herded" together, they bond by more efficiently reaching a destination outside of their own choosing.

The sheep imagery takes on an added resonance when considering the current cultural climate of Japan itself. As Chen (2012) notes in a study of masculinity and consumption in contemporary Japan, the term *soushokukei danshi* ("grass-eating type men" or "herbivore men") is used "to describe heterosexual Japanese men who lack ambition, engage in feminine consumption practices, and shirk relationships with the opposite sex. . . . Rather than pursue relationships with women, they prefer being alone playing video games and surfing the Internet" (285). As Chen further describes in evocative spatial phrasing, "Rather than pursuing upward social mobility through an intense work ethic, they prefer comfortable lifestyles, which allow time for hedonic pursuits. Aphorisms like 'life is short' and 'doing okay is okay' drive their life philosophies" (286). Marked visually in the game as literal grass-eaters, these sheep men—having shirked their "proper" heterosexual responsibilities, both romantically and societally—must climb a spatial representation of the economic and sexual paths they have failed to follow. Vincent's comments to Katherine at the beginning of the game echo the aphorisms Chen cites, claiming that "sometimes easy is best, isn't it?" when asked about his job and their relationship. His tone is, in multiple ways, "sheep"ish: conciliatory to her eventual demands but marked by his lack of desire in pursing them.

The description of Vincent's profession further amplifies his connection to the *soushokukei danshi*. According to the game, Vincent is a "poorly-paid systems engineer for a non-descript technology company. He doesn't need to wear a suit or a tie for his job, since he has no contact with his business's customers." This absence of "contact" places him at the periphery of importance, and the modifiers of both his job and his company—"poorly-paid" and "non-descript"—affirm his absence from the social promotion path. In fact, the only time Vincent is shown at work in the game is on trips to the bathroom, where he spends his time on the phone looking at text messages. His job is, apparently, shit: performed out of sight and producing nothing of value. The game's levels attempt to correct this pattern in part through the enticement of the score system; numerous piles of coins litter the various puzzles, and picking them up increases the player's score and the "prize" at the end of the level. These results go into an online database of high scores, letting the player compare her performance to others and earn rewards. While Vincent is lacking the drive for a better career on a narrative level, the player's role in making him "climb the ladder" can spatially supply a capitalist mentality *for* him; she provides an ambition he lacks.

If the game's levels attempt to put Vincent back in line in terms of producing material, they also try to guide him into *re*productive line. These two elements are deeply tied among the *soushokukei danshi*; as Chen notes, a growing retired population in Japan cannot be sustained by the working adult population at the current rate. Producing children would help offset this trend, "but *soushokukei danshi* lifestyle choices are stymieing this effort. The need for population inflation is so dire that the Japanese government is offering families 13,000 yen ($150) a month per child to stimulate growth" (288). *Catherine* is loaded with references to reproduction and its linkage to finances, particularly in how it affects both sexes; at one point, Katherine comes to believe she is pregnant—and uses it as a chance to both declare she will handle "all our banking accounts" and also warn Vincent to watch his spending due to the baby. A billboard in the background declares "How long are you gonna stay with him? Beyond matrimonial age?" as Vincent rides the train home, driving home how the collapsing nature of the game's levels echoes not only the masculine role pushing Vincent "upward" into adulthood but also the ticking social and reproductive clock governing Katherine. It is appropriate, then, that she is forced into one of the last levels of the game, climbing alongside Vincent as they both attempt to scale the tower. If she dies, the level ends for Vincent as well; the player must protect her while commanding Vincent, further tying their spatial fates together.

This is not the only appearance Katherine makes in the levels, however; her first appearance comes as "the Doom Bride," a gigantic, decaying monster in a bridal gown that chases Vincent while screaming, "You won't escape! I won't let you escape!" She is one of a series of bosses throughout the game, each marking the end of a puzzle section and posing a significant challenge in reaching the top. Each boss ends up representing a reproductive societal mandate that pursues Vincent spatially: a giant baby that screams "Daddy!" as it clamors after him, a shadow of Vincent himself showing the consequences of his infidelity and failure to marry, and a creature called the "Immoral Beast" that appears after Vincent cheats for the first time. The "Beast," which resembles a set of devouring female buttocks, suggests both the monstrousness of Vincent's cheating and the deviant, nonreproductive nature of what that cheating entailed; Catherine's claim the next day that "I've never done anything like *that* before" suggests Vincent may have directed his desire to both the wrong person and the "wrong" orifice.

Should Vincent manage to evade these bosses and reach the final level of the game, he finally gets to confront the entity that threw him into the nightmare in the first place. Demanding an answer as to why he suffers these nightmares, Vincent is hit with the most explicit explanation of the tower's role in "correcting" his path as an out-of-line *soushokukei danshi*:

> When there are people like you who spend a long amount of time with a partner without commitment, it impedes the population model . . . the growth of population is less than optimal. So I have these hesitant gentlemen climb that tower. Wasting a woman's time of greatest fertility is a hindrance to the future of the species. So we separate these non-fruitful couples and redistribute the women to men who follow the natural order, you see.

The language of men "follow[ing] the natural order" by being forced to learn how to scale the game's levels again reveals Ahmed's point about how the natural is shown to be decidedly *not* so due to "the necessity of the enforcement of that orientation" (85). The "natural" is shown in fact to be a formula, a code, an *algorithm*: Vincent's job as a systems engineer takes on an added resonance when considered in relation to how he is oriented within larger social systems built to run at maximum efficiency. He is set on a path to the future, and any wasting of time within that project sets it off-track—or specifically, "impedes" it. The concepts of blocks and impediments, so crucial to the player's ability to reach this point in the game, suddenly flips, as it is the player *as* Vincent who stands as a "block" in the path of proper reproduction.

Vincent's ultimate role in the reproductive system is largely determined by the game's moral system, which is decided in part by actions at a bar titled the Stray Sheep, where Vincent and other men suffering from the nightmares meet to drink and commiserate at night. The spatial resonance of its name suggests those "grass-eating" men who have gone astray from the reproductive path they should follow, since "to be 'in line' is to direct one's desires towards marriage and reproduction; to direct one's desires toward the reproduction of the family line" (74). Both Catherine and Katherine will attempt to contact Vincent at the bar, and the player chooses his responses to each. Responding positively to Katherine and negatively to Catherine moves the player closer to the "order" side of a moral scale, marked with blue coloration and a picture of an angel; doing the opposite skews the player toward the "freedom" side of the binary, which is colored red and has a devil overhead. Nothing the player does while actually solving the block puzzles shapes the moral construction of Vincent's character; it is only in moving him toward a *romantic* object choice that defines the eventual narrative path of the game.

One other location, however, has a particular impact on defining Vincent's path—and in a decidedly Foucauldian move, that space happens to be the confessional booth. Between puzzle levels, Vincent must enter a confessional and answer a series of questions about "himself" to the unseen power controlling the nightmare. With such questions as "Does life begin or end at marriage?" and "Do you consider yourself a pervert?" the confessional is meant to further define Vincent's orientation toward sexual ethics, and each question directly impacts his standing on the moral scale. A blurring line appears here, as the player must decide which "you" to answer for: her own moral feelings on the issue, or the way she wants to construct Vincent's morality within the game. This is further complicated by the fact that, should the player have an active internet connection available, the game uploads her answer to a server and displays a pie graph of how every other player with a copy of *Catherine* answered the question. A series of "private" spaces begin to collapse: the intimacy of the confessional booth within the game space, the union between Vincent and the player, and the larger relationship between player and game. Rather than a discrete, one-to-one relationship between avatar and player, choosing Vincent's path now enters a larger debate of how the player community in general chose to orient their Vincents; the player may feel guilty for choosing a particular option if it is shown to be widely avoided by other players or may even *deliberately* choose unpopular options for the sake of subverting the masses. Ahmed's suggestion that "we follow the line that is followed by others (15)" turns the confessional into a place of collective line creation and determination, as seemingly confidential answers transform into openly shared community discourse on pathmaking.

This blurred line between public and private in constructing Vincent's narrative also bleeds into another space: the Stray Sheep bathroom. Throughout the game, Catherine offers to send lewd pictures to Vincent's phone, asking if he wants to see more of her. While Vincent may be the explicit recipient of the images, the clear intended audience is the player; hilariously, Vincent must retire to the bar's bathroom to view the pictures in a "private" place. He is, of course, not alone, as the player sits "with" Vincent, and his occasionally muttered comments like "Oh man!" as the player scrolls through the various images suggests a voyeuristic union between them. The player must actively encourage Vincent to ask for more of these images via text message, further implicating her in "his" interest in Catherine's body. The eventual revelation in the game's plot that Catherine is, in fact, a demonic hallucination sent to stop Vincent from keeping Katherine in a nonreproductive relationship has an unexpected double meaning due to this shared desire. She is "not real," and Vincent sees it as proof that he is ultimately innocent of infidelity: "In the end, what am I guilty of? If the girl doesn't exist, it's not cheating!"

This claim leaves another idea hanging in the air: the nonexistent nature of Catherine as a digital entity to begin with, and what it would mean for the player to actually desire *her*. When Catherine notes in her "good" endings with Vincent that "the whole kid thing would have to be off the table" due to her nature as a succubus, it also invokes the nonreproductive future of the player's "union" with her. This is not to say that organic-digital relationships are at all progressive in their depiction of relationships, or that they destabilize gender dynamics in the process of complicating "natural" orientation. In many cases, they often echo and even exemplify the assumptions of masculine and feminine identity existing in society. While the prospect of falling in love with a digital object—or it falling in love with the player—may represent an intriguingly queer image of where sexual attraction can be directed, the mechanisms that establish and maintain that relationship may not be queer at all.

Such mechanisms define the game's ending, which is built around how the player has chosen to orient Vincent toward his object of choice. Upon reaching the final stage of the game, Vincent is asked to answer a series of questions that will set him up with either Catherine or Katherine after his climb. Both women are, in essence, rewards for completing the spatial gauntlet of the game, and what awaits Vincent at the top is that enormous cathedral mentioned earlier, meant to finally bind him to the woman of "his" choosing. There is a twist to this, however: the player *must* be sure to answer that Vincent wants the girl associated with where he stands on the moral scale, or his offer of a relationship will be rejected. A player who sits in the "order" side of the scale and pledges love for Catherine finds her telling Vincent that "our bodies just aren't compatible," and a "freedom"-oriented Vincent who chooses Katherine is told he lacks the necessary responsibility to be her partner. In addition, the most "positive" endings of the game (labeled as "true" endings) are only given to players who are *entirely* one side of the scale—and each of them ends with a wedding. Again, the logics of going "astray" emerge, as leaving the moral path assigned to a particular body leads to failure and a "bad" ending. The binary of "order" and "freedom" turns out to be patently false, as *all* of it is governed by order; in order to get the true endings, a player must habitually choose only one color or another to ensure they meet the necessary requirements.

All players of *Catherine*, regardless of whether or not they want a free or steady life, will find the game's systems decidedly reliable and consistent in the outcomes provided. The very binary itself captures the encoded nature of game narratives, which tend to provide, in essence, orderly freedom. Even more ironically, the most difficult ending to get in the game is the one where Vincent chooses *not* to marry, as the player must perfectly balance freedom and order answers across the game in order to keep him right in the middle of the scale. What provides the player in the end with limited agency is the adherence to a path, the accumulation of various actions that have oriented her Vincent one way or another. Ahmed, in discussing the spatial histories of bodies, notes that "in a way, the utterance 'I can' points to the future only insofar as it inherits the past, as the accumulation of what the body has already done, as well as what is 'behind' the body, the conditions of its arrival (159)"; *Catherine* renders that tethering to a bodily legacy as playable, where what can be done with its various bodies rests entirely in the moral inheritance from the levels and choices now "below" Vincent's climb.

This extends beyond simply the core triangle of Vincent, Catherine, and Katherine. One particular pair of bodies bears the mark of Vincent's climb: the couple Toby and Erica. Toby, a young man who hangs out with Vincent and his buddies, loses his virginity to the older waitress Erica during the game. He notes to his friends that "there was something weird about it. . . . You know, I can't really explain it." All of them look knowingly at one another, but the player is not let in on the full "weirdness" of the encounter unless she achieves Vincent's true ending with Katherine—where it is revealed at their wedding party that Erica was once assigned the male name *Eric* and underwent sex reassignment surgery after high school. By directing Vincent toward the highest level of "order" in the game, even bodies that are proximate to his path are labeled, defined, and exposed. Erica's identity is peeled back, and her "true" history is revealed, marking her as knowably queer and Toby as tainted by association. "The other guys knew you as 'Eric' back in school! I want my damned V-card back!" he cries out, but the action cannot be undone, as Erica's response—"Sorry, but once that hole is punched, there's no refund!"—deliberately evokes Toby's sudden mortification at the penetrative logistics of their encounter. For a game that, at times, openly calls into question the nature of heterosexual relationships, no such awareness is shown for Erica; she is a punchline, and as Toby's friends laugh at him while Vincent and Katherine sit in wedded bliss a few feet away, the game makes clear its utilization of the transgender body as a prop against which both "natural" sexuality and masculine and feminine performance are measured.

"Let's Meet Again at the Top": Conclusions

Ultimately, *Catherine* ends up using its allegorized depiction of digital space as a means of upholding the lines of desire that exist between bodies socially; it situates mastery as the most desirable subject position to hold and deploys its female and queer characters as barometers against which to measure the extent of Vincent's final "conquering" of his nightmares. Even the bonus levels uphold this ideology, where a character named Trisha, who has served as the "host" of the game's narrative so far, begins speaking directly to the player about the desire she has for *her*, spurred specifically by the player's spatial skills. Talking in a sultry whisper, Trisha notes how aroused she is by the player's performance, "like when you made that jump . . . and the . . . ooh, just thinking about it makes me excited. Don't you get it? I'm head over heels for you. You possess a power beyond anyone else. Why don't you let me in?" She offers a liaison for anyone who can reach the top of the last level—and in case the player has any confusion about the "you" being referenced, Trisha makes it clear: "Don't misunderstand. I don't mean 'Vincent.' I'm talking about you, the one who borrowed his form to make it here."

By explicitly making Vincent a "borrowed" body for the use of the player's own interests, *Catherine* again twists the divide between what Vincent does and what "I" do into a far more complicit relationship. It is not just Vincent viewing the pictures in the bathroom but the player sending him there to watch alongside him; as Vincent climbs the puzzles to reach his inevitable goal, it is the player who forces him there, trying to follow a line of her own. His body becomes a possible means of fulfilling the player's own interest in being acknowledged and desired. Yet this experience is only offered to the *best* players who can only imagine this union in the shape of a buxom female to be "won"; the game must be dominated, so to speak, and Trisha's reactions to the player are decidedly reminiscent of Katherine's fawning over Vincent upon their wedding day. There is no possibility for a "weak" player to be desired, nor for Trisha to respond in any other way than with slavish praise. "Let's meet again at the top," she tells the player, and in this moment of being directed to a digital liaison—but only for the "top" players to claim their due victory in the form of a suppliant woman—*Catherine* all too clearly points to the way that climb of desire refuses so many bodies from ascending: both digitally and socially.

References

Aarseth, Espen. 2007. "Allegories of Space: The Question of Spatiality in Computer Games." In *Space Time Play: Computer Games, Architecture, and Urbanism: The Next Level*, edited by Friedrich von Borries, Steffen P. Walz, and Matthias Böttger, 44–55. Basel: Birkhäuser Press.

Ahmed, Sara. 2006. *Queer Phenomenology: Orientations, Objects, Others.* Durham: Duke University Press.

Ash, James. 2010. "Teleplastic Technologies: Charting Practices of Orientation and Navigation in Videogaming." *Transactions of the Institute of British Geographers* 35 (3): 414–30.

Butler, Judith. 1993. *Bodies That Matter: On the Discursive Limits of "Sex."* New York: Psychology Press.

Caillois, Roger. 2003. *The Edge of Surrealism: A Roger Caillois Reader.* Durham: Duke University Press.

Chen, Steven. 2012. "The Rise of Soushokukei Danshi Masculinity and Consumption in Contemporary Japan." In *Gender, Culture, and Consumer Behavior*, edited by Cele C. Otnes and Linda Tuncay Zayer, 285–310. New York: Taylor & Francis.

Diprose, Rosalyn. 2002. *Corporeal Generosity: On Giving with Nietzsche, Merleau-Ponty, and Levinas.* Albany: State University of New York Press.

Gallagher, Rob. 2012. "No Sex Please, We Are Finite State Machines: On the Melancholy Sexlessness of the Video Game." *Games and Culture* 7 (6): 399–418.

Walz, Steffan P. 2010. *Toward a Ludic Architecture: The Space of Play and Games.* Pittsburgh: ETC Press.

Zimmerman, Eric and Katie Salen. 2003. *Rules of Play: Game Design Fundamentals.* Cambridge, MA: MIT Press.

Game cited

Atlus Games. 2011. *Catherine.* Atlus.

16

Assessing player-connected versus player-disconnected sex acts in video games

Brent Kice (University of Houston-Clear Lake, USA)

Are simulations of sex in video games worthwhile? Some games receiving ESRB (Entertainment Software Rating Board) ratings of "M Mature 17+" or "AO Adults Only" or PEGI (Pan European Game Information) ratings of "18" may have the designation of containing sexually explicit material, such as allowing players to engage in sex acts. Depending on the design of the game, these sex acts might involve passive participation by observing a cutscene or active participation by pushing a button to prompt action by a game's character. The inclusion of sex in video games raises concern due to the label of immaturity placed upon the medium and the gaming community. Players should question if a sex act in a game is being used as a "money shot" to sell a game or if the act truly is being used to simulate a sexual experience. So, the gaming community should consider the value of including sex acts in games, especially in an effort to dispel labels of immaturity.

Since the act of sex typically is seen as a mature act, we then have to ask ourselves if sex acts are being included in video games to make the medium appear mature. Although sex itself might be viewed as a mature act, video game simulations of sex do not accurately reflect the experience, just as killing a player in a game, stealing a car in a game, or playing a soccer game do not accurately reflect those "real life" experiences.

I view purposeless sex acts in video games as tarnishing the reputation of the medium. Sure, sex sells. And meaningful sex can add to the success of a game's narrative. However, sex acts in games that do not extend the game's experiential narrative or establish identification between a game's character and a player are detrimental to the industry. Gamer culture has often been viewed as immature, and the inclusion of purposeless sex acts perpetuates that immature perception. The overused line of a grown man or woman living in her or his parents' basement playing video games comes to mind here. Gary Cross, in his 2008 book, *Men to Boys: The Making of Modern Immaturity*, acknowledges the role that video games play in the lives of modern men, who he labels as "boy-men" when compared to previous generations. In light of possible immature stigmas on the medium, I propose that game developers reconsider the purpose of sex acts, if any, that they include in their games. I do not envision myself as an Anthony Comstock attempting to censor sex; rather, I see myself as adding to a conversation that shapes the use of sex in a participative medium. The games industry already has the ESRB in the United States, the PEGI in Europe, and numerous other ratings bodies in various countries to assess the appropriateness of games for players.

This chapter will not focus on the appropriateness of sex and the age level of players; rather, it will advise critics in questioning the purpose of developers including sex in their games, regardless if a game were to receive a M for Mature (or 17+) rating or not. This chapter is not promoting censorship; it is promoting consideration. To accomplish this, I develop an assessment tool of game developers' usage of sex within games to determine if developers use the act of sex as a cheap tool to perpetuate a commoditization of sex that I will label as a player-disconnected sex act or as a tool to enhance emotional attachments in games that I will label as a player-connected sex act. With this perspective in mind, I argue that games attempting to develop the act of sex as an emotional player-connected human action contribute to the positive progression of game development, whereas insignificant player-disconnected sex acts within games contribute to a stagnant commoditized viewpoint. To achieve this, I will apply Foucault's concept of bio-power to the gaming industry to reveal the disciplinary tool of nonplayable character (NPC) sex; then, I will offer a Gameplay Sex Act Test as an assessment tool to judge the merits of sex in games. As a basis for the Gameplay Sex Act Test, I reference the SLAPS (serious literary, artistic, political, or scientific value) portion of the Miller test from the 1973 US Supreme Court case *Miller v. California* as an aid in formulating components to identify player-disconnected sex acts and player-connected sex acts for the purpose of game criticism. To reach conclusions of player-disconnected or player-connected sex acts, the Gameplay Sex Act Test comprises three components: a participative element, an emotional connection, and an objective. This method will guide critics and developers in considering the use of sex acts to create positive progressions in gaming experiences. Although personal and social values of sexual material are debatable, I argue that player-disconnected sex acts, as they stand in the current generation of gaming, do not contribute to meaningful development in gaming. Essentially, this chapter will clarify the value of player-connected versus player-disconnected sex acts in video games.

Bio-power

Foucault's (1978) notion of bio-power offers insight to the gaming industry regarding the design of games. Although Foucault's concepts of "anatomo-politics," or a disciplining of individual bodies, and "bio-politics," or broader strategic control of a population, were conceptualized to refer to the alteration of power over populations (139), application of Foucault's concepts to the evolution of game design reveals strategic control over players. When the concepts are applied to the realm of video games, critics can recognize game developers' attempts to control game players through bio-power as well.

The realm of video games presents a microcosm of bio-politics. When the video game medium was in its early stages, such as the golden age of arcade games in the early 1980s, many games were designed to make players lose, such as the challenge of jumping over barrels in *Donkey Kong* or avoiding the ghosts in *Pac-Man*. Players played until their characters lost all their lives, thus depicting the challenge of the high score or the furthest level attained. The design of these games was to stop the player from proceeding further in the game. This relied on a strategy of challenging the player through death upon failure or, as Foucault might explain it, the designers' "'power over life and death' . . . the right to *take* life or *let* live" (136). Developers' reliance on killing a player's character begot the churning out of more quarters, assuming that the player accepted the challenge. Console games, however, required more than a $0.25 commitment from the player; these games needed players to invest larger amounts of money on consoles and console games.

Fast-forward almost three decades, and video game developers have changed the strategy of player engagement to one that "invest[s] life through and through" (Foucault 1978, 139). In contrast to a challenging design to kill a player's character, many games now come with save files and checkpoints to aid the player in winning a game. For example, imagine playing through *Fable* (Lionhead Studios 2004) without the mental safety net of knowing that if a player's character dies, the character will be resurrected. As Foucault states, "The old power of death that symbolized sovereign power was now carefully supplanted by the administration of bodies and the calculated management of life" (139–40). In addition, the inclusion of online play and downloadable game content has altered game design with the removal of games' end points.

Now, many games might be designed to be played more for the experience than for the completion of the game. So, it is in the developers' and publishers' financial interests to extend players' in-game time. This evolution of the bio-politics of the gaming industry precipitated numerous disciplinary strategies to encourage prolonged player interaction within a game.

With the bio-political evolution of games at play, developers instigated various strategies to discipline players to keep playing. Foucault states:

> During the classical period, there was a rapid development of various disciplines—universities, secondary schools, barracks, workshops; there was also the emergence, in the field of political practices and economic observation, of the problems of birthrate, longevity, public health, housing, and migration. Hence, there was an explosion of numerous and diverse techniques for achieving the subjugation of bodies and the control of populations, marking the beginning of an era of "bio-power." (140)

Past reliance on a strategy of using character death as a means to challenge players to keep playing was placed aside for a more inclusive approach to drawing in players. Comparable to Foucault's mention of "political practices and economic observation" (140), the gaming industry also saw the need to manage the in-game time spent by players, the discouragement brought on by character deaths, and the need to expand the field of play. So, the gaming industry also developed techniques to alleviate these problems, such as the inclusion of saved-game files and side quests to direct players to various areas of a game map. Replace Foucault's "birthrate" with the acquisition of new players, "longevity" with in-game options to extend game time, "public health" with the elimination of permanent death, or "migration" with enticing players to travel throughout game worlds. These inclusive strategies were focused on the acquisition of profit. Dyer-Witheford and de Peuter (2009) offer an extended analysis of Blizzard's application of bio-power to manipulate the in-game world in *World of Warcraft* to increase profit for the company. For example, offering expansion packs and new character level caps are strategic forms of bio-power to manage a population of players and increase capital (130). Dyer-Witheford and de Peuter state, "It is therefore no surprise that Blizzard's most energetic exercise of bio-power in [*World of Warcraft*] is directed at preserving this profitability and that the fiercest struggles about control of the virtual world hinge on issues of accumulation" (132). Player reproduction, or the need for a player to keep coming back—to keep playing, became the capitalist driving force of the games industry.

In particular, many in-game disciplinary strategies have transformed the purpose of NPCs. Rather than being used as signposts to point the way or merely provide information, NPCs have evolved as tools to engage the player in staying invested in the game. NPCs strategically enhance player reproduction. So, NPCs received extended purpose in the evolution of games. Utilization of NPCs was one of numerous techniques to establish bio-power over players by keeping them engaged. Foucault asks, "How could power exercise its highest prerogatives by putting people to death, when its main role was to ensure, sustain, and multiply life, to put this life in order?" (138). NPCs provide the answer by having their purpose in the prevention of death and the extension of life. In this case, the "prevention of death" refers to the NPCs' enhancement of a player's experience, giving a player reasons to keep playing. NPCs extend the hand of game developers to keep a player's experience "in order." Critics should be conscious of how game developers employ NPCs to enact bio-power. An NPC might be used to create a meaningful bond, explore relational emotions, or prompt players to engage a game with more commitment. For instance, the inclusion of NPCs in the *Assassin's Creed* series provides the catalyst for the game's entire purpose of weaving in and out of populations unseen. Although the NPCs in the *Assassin's Creed* series are numerous, each one potentially could spark a jumping-off point of player engagement, such as an innocent assassination or a subtle pickpocket.

While Foucault discusses several techniques to enact control through bio-power, this chapter will focus on the technique of sexuality, specifically the use of sex acts between a player and an NPC. Foucault designated "the deployment of sexuality" as an important technique of power (140). Likewise, players must be vigilant of the techniques at play in video games. Game developers intertwine sexuality between player and NPC as a disciplinary tool to engage players. The category of games utilizing the act of sex between players and NPCs in passionless ways with no connection between the players and the NPCs—or game narrative as player-disconnected sex acts—will be clarified and distinguished from player-connected sex acts. Sex acts fall in line with Foucault's notion of bio-power in that game developers create massive worlds in order to intrigue players into prolonging play within the game. Game developers use NPCs as a form of digital bio-power within the fabricated world and manipulate NPCs as tools to control the player. NPCs provide the guise of people to justify players' engagement in digital acts of sexual gratification within the fabricated world, even though these sexual acts often contain no true sexual act other than possibly sounds or some images. Insignificant player-disconnected sex acts are not sex acts at all; they contribute to an objectification of the act of sex. In turn, this objectification of sex specifically is employed as a disciplinary management tool to create capital. Thus, video games utilizing NPCs to allow sex acts between player and NPC demand a critical assessment tool to dissect the worthiness of the sex act in question for the purpose of improving player experiences.

Gameplay Sex Act Test

It is not without a sense of irony that the games industry utilizes the disciplinary tool of NPC sex to instill player reproduction. The interactivity of the games medium allows for a player to perform certain actions. We must acknowledge that these actions are simulations of the physical world but also gauge how close the actions are to their physical world counterparts. When game developers include sex acts in games, critics should question if the developers truly are attempting to provide a close simulation of the physical act of sex. If this is the case, current technology does not allow for an accurate virtual representation. So, developers must decide if they wish players to take an active or passive role in sex gameplay. If developers are attempting to recreate human emotions surrounding sex acts, then the particular emotion should be considered strategically. For instance, a developer might try to illicit feelings of sexual arousal or flirtation or forge a personal bond in the player. So, developers face the challenge of adequately matching in-game actions with the emotional objective. For instance, a cutscene where a player passively watches a sex scene can elicit feelings in a player; however, the passivity means the player is not physically performing the action on screen. On the other hand, a player could actively push buttons to prompt a character to perform an action, but the button pushing itself might not instill sexual feelings in the player adequately.

Given these challenges in game design and play experiences related to sex, game critics need a standardized "test" to assess sex acts in games for the purpose of determining to what end developers are manipulating players. Such a test should determine if a sex act enhances gameplay or if it is merely a means to prolong gameplay. Based on the evolution of bio-power within the gaming industry, critics can accept that developers will control players; however, developers must be scrutinized for their manners of manipulation. Developers' presentations of worthwhile experiences in the form of player-connected actions are akin to symbiotic relationships where both parties benefit. On the other hand, when developers rely on player-disconnected actions, the developers fail to provide a fully developed experience for the player while the developer reaps profits, similar to a parasitic relationship. While the disciplinary strategies of bio-power by game developers will continue, players should at least benefit from worthwhile experiences in developers' and publishers' quests to increase profit, especially when those strategies rely on the commoditization of sex.

It should be noted that this argument places higher value on emotional connections between a player and an NPC than on emotionless interactions. Although some might respond that lack of emotional connection between individuals engaging in sex can be rewarding, we must look back on the difference between the physical act and the simulation. As stated earlier, the simulation does not accurately reflect the physical experience; therefore, player-disconnected sex acts cannot be compared to emotionless physical sex. It is not the intent of this chapter to offer any perspective on manners of sex engagement by individuals in the physical "real" world.

In order to assess the value of sex acts in video games, we can look toward court precedent as a means of practical guidance. On numerous occasions, the US court system faced the need to clarify acceptable forms of sexual content and what crossed the line to be labeled obscene, thereby lacking protection under the First Amendment (free speech) to the Constitution. In particular, the Supreme Court in *Miller v. California* (1973) developed the "Miller test" to replace the previous "Roth test" when determining if a form of media is obscene or not. In particular, a component of the Miller test, known as SLAPS, was an attempt to add clarification between worthwhile speech and worthless speech. Again, this chapter is not proposing censorship, but the court's identification of the obscene category provides the gaming industry with a starting point for developing its own tool to identify player-connected or player-disconnected sex acts. Chief Justice Berger defines the SLAPS component of the Miller test in the opinion of the Supreme Court regarding the 1973 *Miller v. California* ruling as, "whether the work, taken as a whole, lacks serious literary, artistic, political, or scientific value." The gaming community should be concerned most with what serious literary, artistic, political, or scientific value a sex act in question adds to a game. As previously noted, various ratings boards and governments already assess the appropriateness of sexual content regarding age level or censorship concerning cases of obscenity; however, the SLAPS portion of the Miller test provides guidance in determining the value of a sex act in a game. Critics merely are left trying to determine what makes a particular game's sex act worthwhile or not.

I propose a Gameplay Sex Act Test to evaluate the meritorious contributions of individual sex acts in games. The purpose of this test is not to censor speech; rather, the test is intended to push self-reflection in game design in an effort to discern the manner of developers' bio-political control and to dispel the stigma of immature labels of the gaming community. Hopefully, such a test will offer more clarity than Justice Potter Stewart's famous candid statement, "I know it when I see it," when assessing sex versus potentially pornographic material in ruling on an obscenity label charge against the film *The Lovers* in *Jacobellis v. Ohio* (1964). In addition, this test could also force developers to produce the best experiences available, given the unique performance components of the medium. A final sex act designation of either player-connected or player-disconnected would be based on the three components of the Gameplay Sex Act Test: (a) participative element, (b) emotional connection, and (c) objective. A test of this type addresses the concern of Voorhees (2013) for scholars "to discern the creative act of play and see through play practices to trace the affordances and constraints of the game" (19). The *Fable* and *Mass Effect* series will be used to illustrate the three components of the test.

Participative element

Does the sex act actively engage the player in performance? Voorhees states, "Gameplay is more than simply an intersection between an agentic player and the structure of the game; gameplay is the agonistic struggle—playful but consequential—out of which meaningful human action emerges" (16). Performance through games makes the medium unique. This uniqueness is displayed when the player actively participates, as opposed to being a passive observer. Since the pushing of a button translates to the symbol that the button pushing represents (McDonald 2013), the physical action required of the player should best translate to the desired on-screen symbol. Although a developer might desire that pushing a certain button will be translated by a player in a certain way, individuals do not always agree on translations. Performance anxiety could result when a player does not care for the physical action associated with the symbol. For example, a player could be turned off by having to push a button in succession rapidly or wiggle a controller. In turn, this performance anxiety might not produce the desired result for which the developer was aiming. In addition, the length of time required for the sex act to unfold should be considered. A sex act could be a short tangent with little intertwining to the player's experiential journey, or it could be a drawn-out experience, such as flirtatious behavior throughout a player's experience, culminating in a final sex act. In this manner, the player might fulfill a story, and critics should question the complexity of the player's performance regarding the plot resolution.

Both the *Fable* series and the *Mass Effect* series rely on a player's pushing of buttons to initiate a sex act. However, button pushing in *Fable* is predetermined with little sense of player control. For example, the player buys a house, selects available "flirtatious actions," and then offers an NPC increasingly more valuable gifts, from chocolate to an engagement ring. These linear steps result in an initial sex act with an NPC, with flirtatious actions and gifts required for repeated sex acts with an NPC spouse. Although *Mass*

Effect has preset dialogue choices that culminate in a sex act, the player is unaware of the "winning" formula and must select precise dialogue choices with a particular NPC throughout the game, leading to a greater perception of control in the player. In addition, the culminating dialogue with choices corresponds with engagement in flirtation, resulting in the sex act. Whereas both games position the player to passively watch, or listen to, a cutscene, players in *Mass Effect* actively engage in simulated flirtatious foreplay through the translation of pushing buttons.

Emotional connection

Does the sex act lead to an emotional bond between player and character/s? Essentially, game developers attempt to "elicit conditions" that make the result of player emotions possible (Jarvinen 2008, 220). Developers cannot force emotions onto a player, but the establishment of game rules provides the opportunity for a player to feel. Sexuality plays a significant role in establishing a bond between a player and a player's character, with a possible erotic attachment for some players (Consalvo 2003). The previously mentioned simulation of flirtatious foreplay in the *Mass Effect* series relies on emotional suspense to connect a player to a character and/or an NPC. Jarvinen points out suspense as an integral emotion for a player's experience due to the intertwining of "the emotions of hope, fear, and uncertainty" (356). In the *Mass Effect* series the player experiences lean toward a developed connection with the characters. The narrative element of saving the galaxy in which the player engages over the course of three games creates a perception of high stakes and an in-depth experience. For instance, a possible sex act between a player's male Commander Shepard and a female Ashley NPC in *Mass Effect 3* relies on a player's memories of shared experiences with the NPC over the course of the entire series as an additional element to elicit conditions of suspense, flirtation, and emotional attachment.

Conversely, a player's relationship with NPCs in the *Fable* series lacks an emotional connection between a player and NPCs. Many of the NPCs available for sex acts lack names and fall within plain, good-looking, or beautiful visual categories. This visual scale of beauty also correlates with the effort required of the player to initiate a sex act. And if an NPC divorces a player's character, there are numerous NPCs to fill the void, decreasing a player's emotions of fear and uncertainty in the maintenance of NPC relationships in the *Fable* series. Although *Fable* elicits emotions, the emotions are often aligned with humor, in particular, potty humor. This type of humor with nameless NPCs lacks the requisite for establishing an emotional bond.

Objective

What is the objective of a game's sex act, and how is it achieved? Simulation duplicates the "behaviors" of an original action (Frasca 2003, 223). So, a game's developer should have a particular behavior in mind when including a sex act in a game. As previously mentioned, emotions stimulate a player, so developers should link a behavior to a desired emotional experience. If a developer has a desired emotional experience in mind, the manner of how the conditions will be elicited (Jarvinen) is a prime objective for a developer wishing to steer the emotional state through game rules. For instance, if a developer desires to simulate the experience of flirtatious banter, the developer must consider the most effective means of simulating the emotional behavior. Rather than attempt to simulate the overall act of sex itself, developers need to focus on specific aspects of a sexual experience that can be attainable through simulation.

The black-screen sex scene in the *Fable* series would appear to have laughter as a goal. The "ohs and ahs," and sometimes revelation of a baby, harness the behavior of laughter on behalf of the player. It would seem that the developers had the objective of making the player laugh as the culminating moment of the player wooing an NPC in order to bed his or her character. This objective of laughter, while meaningful, is misaligned with the simulation of a sex act. The *Mass Effect* series, on the other hand, appears to have the objective of mimicking, through sex acts, a developed emotional attachment. Although several options for sex acts exist, the vast majority of these acts require player engagement with an NPC through the relational act of listening. Typically, an NPC will reveal "personal" information over a prolonged period of time and require the player to select dialogue options that are appropriate relational responses. Here, sex acts, with each game in the series usually allowing only one sex act, are the result of establishing simulated emotional intimacy.

Conclusion

An application of the Gameplay Sex Act Test reveals player-connected sex acts in the *Mass Effect* series. Sex acts in the *Mass Effect* series rely on active engagement in flirtatious foreplay (although passive viewing of a sex cutscene), create emotional bonds between player and NPCs while eliciting feelings of suspense, and establish an objective of simulating emotional intimacy and foreplay to provide player-connected sex acts. On the contrary, sex acts in the *Fable* series rely on preset actions leading up to a passive cutscene, lack emotional bonds between player and NPCs while eliciting emotions of humor, and misalign an objective of laughter with a sex act. *Fable* fails the three elements of Gameplay Sex Act Test and therefore does not result in player-connected sex acts.

Character sex in the *Fable* series is passionless and player-disconnected, taking a different route regarding the act of sex than games like the *Mass Effect* series that attempt to use sex as an emotional player-connected bond between players and characters to add emotional depth to stories. However, the designers of both the *Fable* and *Mass Effect* series appear to use sex as a means to instill further control over the player in the game. For example, character sex is not required by the player; sex gives purpose to the NPCs as a means of the developer's bio-power to control the fabricated world. Although character sex in the *Mass Effect* series is not required by the player, the developers use it as a player-connected sex act to strengthen emotional bonds between players and the NPCs. Naturally, the NPCs in *Mass Effect* available for sex acts have actual names and contribute to players' narrative experiences within the game. The *Fable* series follows a patriarchal monetization of sex as a real-world tool to reproduce capital while simultaneously stripping the act of sex of any human element and reducing in-game sex to a form of paid transaction—just chocolates and a ring in lieu of actual currency.

The Gameplay Sex Act Test is not intended as a means of censorship; rather, it is an attempt to encourage critics to increase awareness of the merit of the use of sex in games and how the inclusion of sex acts either enhances a player's experience or perpetuates a label of immaturity in the gaming community. The application of the test to discern player-connected versus player-disconnected sex acts in games positively will steer game development toward enhanced experiences for players. It is no coincidence that potty humor is associated with a player-disconnected sex act in *Fable*, perpetuating notions of immaturity in gaming. Applying Foucault's treatment of bio-power to the evolution of bio-political and disciplinary strategies employed by game developers reveals the role that nonplayable characters have in extending players' in-game time, especially by the means of game sex. Developers' enhanced strategies of bio-power are symptomatic of an expanding medium—an expansion of which the gaming community should be proud. Rather than taking NPCs for granted, players should be ever vigilant in questioning how each NPC in a game is designed to prolong gameplay and manipulate players' experiences. Accepting that developers design games as a means to control players of the gaming population in order to maximize profit, it should be safe to assume that players will pick the games that give the best experiences. If sex acts are included in games, wouldn't we all prefer player-connected experiences over player-disconnected experiences?

References

Consalvo, Mia. 2003. "Hot Dates and Fairy-Tale Romances: Studying Sexuality in Video Games." In *The Video Game Theory Reader*, edited by Mark Wolf and Bernard Perron, 171–94. New York: Routledge.

Cross, Gary. 2008. *Men to Boys: The Making of Modern Immaturity*. New York: Columbia University Press.

Dyer-Witheford, Nick, and Greig de Peuter. 2009. *Games of Empire: Global Capitalism and Video Games*. Minneapolis: University of Minnesota Press.

Foucault, Michel. 1978. *The History of Sexuality*. Vol. 1. Translated by Robert Hurley. New York: Vintage.

Frasca, Gonzalo. 2003. "Simulation versus Narrative: Introduction to Ludology." In *The Video Game Theory Reader*, edited by Mark Wolf and Bernard Perron, 221–35. New York: Routledge.

Jacobellis v. Ohio. 1964. 378 US. 184.

Jarvinen, Aki. 2008. "Games without Frontiers: Theories and Methods for Game Studies and Design." Doctoral dissertation, University of Tampere.

McDonald, Peter. 2013. "On Couches and Controllers: Identification in the Video Game Apparatus." In *CTRL-ALT-PLAY: Essays on Control in Video Gaming*, edited by Matthew Wysocki, 108–20. Jefferson: McFarland.

Miller v. California. 1973. 413 US. 15.

Voorhees, Gerald. 2013. "Criticism and Control: Gameplay in the Space of Possibility." In *CTRL-ALT-PLAY: Essays on Control in Video Gaming*, edited by Matthew Wysocki, 9–20. Jefferson: McFarland.

Games cited

Big Blue Box. 2004. *Fable*. Microsoft.
Bioware. 2007. *Mass Effect*. Microsoft.
Bioware. 2010. *Mass Effect 2*. Electronic Arts.
Bioware. 2012. *Mass Effect 3*. Electronic Arts.
Blizzard. 2004. *World of Warcraft*. Blizzard.
Lionhead Studios. 2008. *Fable II*. Microsoft.
Lionhead Studios. 2010. *Fable III*. Microsoft.
Namco. 1980. *Pac-Man*. Midway.
Nintendo. 1981. *Donkey Kong*. Nintendo.
Ubisoft. 2007. *Assassin's Creed*. Ubisoft.

Index